INTERACTIVE MEDIA AND SOCIETY

INTERACTIVE MEDIA AND SOCIETY

Editor
Dr. Neeraj Khattri

KALPAZ

ISBN: 978-93-5128-014-9

Price : ₹ 950

First Published 2014

Published by

Kalpaz Publications
C-30, Satyawati Nagar,
Delhi - 110052
E-mail: kalpaz@hotmail.com Ph.: 9212142040

Laser Typesetting : Rajender Vashist, Delhi
Printed at : G. Print Process, Delhi

Cataloging in Publication Data—-DK
Courtesy: D.K. Agencies (P) Ltd. <docinfo@dkagencies.com>

Interactive media and society / editor, Neeraj Khattri.
p. cm.
Contributed articles.
Includes index.
ISBN 9789351280149

1. Mass media—Social aspects. I. Khattri, Neeraj.

DDC 302.23 23

Dedicated to my grandfather
Late Madhav Prasad Khattri
and
my grandmother Late Laxmi Khattri

Contents

Patrons 9

Foreword 11

Acknowledgements 13

List of Contributors 15

1. **New Media and Youth** 17
Introduction • New Communication Technologies • Aims and Objectives • Objectives: • Methodology: • Analysis of the Data: • Major Findings • Bibilography. *B. Shailashree.*

2. **Use of ICTS for Providing Quality Extension Services to Farmers** 27
• Introduction • Methodology • Findings. *M.A. Kashem*

3. **Technological Convergence : A Study on Awareness of New Media Devices among People of different Age Groups of Haryana** 37
Keerty Goyal, Anuradha Vashisth

4. **Across The World in 80 Seconds Exploring the Role of Narrative Styles in Building Communities: A Transition from Traditional Media to New Media** 49
The Premise • Methodology • Spatiality: • Understanding Social space: • Virtual Community: • Narrative Styles.
Gaman Palem, Uma Balu

5. **Family Vs Friends: Who take the Top Spot?** 61
Introduction • Review of Literature • Methodology • Analysis and Findings • Subjects of Status Updates • Specialties of the Updates.
Titto Varghese

6. **The Relationship between Culture and Communication in the Context of Social Change and its Conflicts** 73
Aspects of Cross Cultural Communication: • Forms of Conflict: • What can go wrong? • Rights, Values, and Needs • Improving Intercultural Communication • Social Issues: • Over Population • Poverty • Corruption: Causes, Consequences and Cures • Terrorism • Impact of Terrorism on Society and Economy • Caste based Discrimination • Sanitation • The Critical Analysis. *Anjali Pundhir, Mridula Singh*

7. **POKE ME: Social Networking Sites; a Weapon, a Threat and a Target** 87
Weapon: • Threat: • Target *Yashaswee Bahradwaj*

8. **Social Concern's and Role of Media: With Reference to Conversion Disorder** 91
Introduction • Symptoms • Causes • Statics Related to Conversion Disorder • Conversion Disorder at Different Stages of Life • Conversion Disorder and Workplace • Role of Mass Media and Health Promotion.
Sonali Senger, Neha Gupta, Abid Rizvi and *Prashanta Kumar Pal*

9. **Face Book or Book Face** 99
Introduction • Social Sites May Convert into Social Parasites • Social Sites are Backed by Killer Technologies • Face Books or Book Face: What is the Truth.
Sandeep Shandilya

10. **New Media and Soceity** 105
Introduction • Facebook: World Scenario • Facebook Addiction or Facebook Addiction Disorder (FAD) • Facebook Addiction: Effect on Kid's • Facebook Addiction: Effect on Youths • Facebook Addiction: Impact on Relationships • Facebook Addiction: Impact on Moral Values • Facebook Addiction: Impact on Physical Health • Ways to Cure Facebook Addcition Disorder (FAD).
Aditya Kumar Shukla, Sharddha Tripathi

11. **Reflection on New Media** 123
Introduction • History • Definition • Globalisation and New Media • As Tool For Social Change • National Security • Interactivity and New Media • Industry.
Minal

12. **Obsessive Compulsive Disorder, Relevant Social Conditions and Role of Media** 135
Introduction: • Treatment: • Literature Review: • OCD Famous People. • Gary Schwitzer • Ganapati Mudur: The Media May be the Most Important Source of Health Information for the General Public • David Henry and Amanda Wilson: Health Journalists Should Discuss Benefits and Harms of New Treatments and Use Independent Expert Sources • Merrill Goozner: Medical Reporters Must Get Beyond the Hype and Hope When Reporting on the Latest "Breakthrough" • Maria Simbra: Whatever News Managers Want, Viewers Get—As Medical Reporters Are Pressed to Feed the Media Beast Top • TV Reporters Rarely Cover Medicine Exclusively—One day it's Finance, the Next it's Health • Melissa Sweet: Remember the Commercial Imperative When Examining Media Coverage of Health Top • Katherine A. Baverstock: The Media Can Play a Special Role in Providing a Voice for People to Express Their Experiences of Illness Top • Role of Media Conclusion.
Dinesh Chaudhary, Zainul Abdeen, Abid Rizvi and *Prashanta Kumar Pal*

13. **Power of Social Media in india** 155
• Introduction • Background of the study • Objectives • Hypothesis • Classifications • Power of Social Media in Indian Political, Social, Economical and Cultural aspects • Power of Social Media in Indian Politics • Social Media and Social Changes in India • Impact of Social Media on Indian Business • Social Media for Recruitment • Why Social Media Recruitment Required? • Advertisements in Social Media.
S.D. Livingston, P. Rajendran

14. **Acceptability of Women-Can Media Play a Constructive Role ?** 169
Introduction • Participation and Expression • Women's Portrayal in the Media • Electronic Media • Print Media • Newspapers • Magazines and Journals. *Dewan Anjali*

15. **Innovation in Media Management** 179
What Is Innovation? • Power of the Innovation • Reacting to Challenge • The Innovation Continuum • Why Innovate? • Why Innovations are stopped? • How to Achieve Success • Motivation for Innovation • Perception • Motivation • Organization • Doing The Impossible • 8 Characteristics of Creative People and Team • The New Product Process • An Eight-step Plan • Managing the Process.
Masoumeh Shiri Aminlou, Maryam Taherian

16. **Socio–cultural Impact of Television on Children Against Regulations and Compliance of the Global Discourse** 203
Children's Television Act • Censorship, Violence and the First Amendment • Proposed Solutions to Violence on Television.
Maumita Chaudhari

17. **The Perennial Effect of Corruption on Communication on the Social and Professional Well-being: A Critical Analysis of the Role of Media in Moulding the Issues** 229
Importance of Communication in today's world • Objectives of Communication • What is Corruption? • Role of Media on Corruption and its Impact on Communication • Who is Responsible? • Effects of Corruption • Suggestions.
Garmia Sharma, Preeti Sharma, Dauji Agarwal

18. **Social Change Communication: A Study of Media framing on HIV/AIDS News Stories** 235
Introduction • Objectives and Methodology • Literature Review • Media coverage of HIV/AIDS: A Theoretical Perspective • Concerns and Challenges of the Media Sector. *Uttam Kr Pegu*

19. **Ten Years of Private FM in India: Analysing Policy Perspective and Prospects** 245
Initial Steps Towards City Centric FM Broadcasting • First Phase of Private FM Broadcasting • Policy on Private FM Radio in Phase II •Fresh Efforts For Revamping Private FM Radio • Phase III Policy on Expansion of Private FM Radio. *Ambrish Saxena and Susmita Bala*

20. **Mass Communication Paradigm in Conflicted Society** 257
Introduction • Mass Media in Manipur • Mass Media and Conflict Resolution Initiatives • Conclusion. *Nawaz Khan*

21. **Creative Use of Media (Print Media) For Development: Some Less Known Stories** 263
Introduction • Media Potentialitys • The Udayavani • The Adike Pathrike • The Gramyavani • The Approach. *Pramoda Kumar Jena*

22. **Film Studies and Society** 271
Introduction • Titling of Films • Impact of Films on the Society: • Conclusion *Saloni Saxena*

23. **Schizophrenia: Health Issues, Social Changes and Responsibilities of Media** 279
Introduction • Causes of Schizophrenia • Schizophrenic Symptoms and Signs • Diagnosis of Schizophrenia • The Risks of Getting Schizophrenia • Prognosis for Schizophrenia • Occurrence of Schizophrenia compared to other well-known diseases • Suicide Risk in Schizophrenia • Schizophrenia and Violence • Schizophrenia and Jail • Management aspect Regarding Schizophrenia • Awareness Activities • Myths regarding Schizophrenia • Possible Media Responsibilities Relevant to Schizophrenia • Net Sources.
Chhavi Bartaria, Shashank Bharadwaj and *Prashanta Kumar Pal*

24. **Coverage of MGNREGA in Two National Dailies: Comparative Study of The Hindu and the Times of India** 287
Introduction: • Findings: • News: • Editorial/ Oped: • Comparison and Conclusion: • Inference. *Shah Alam*

25. **Green Growth – Environmentally Sustainable -Economic Growth** 293
Introduction: • The Need for Sustainable Consumption and Production • Material vs. Spiritual Wealth • The Economic and Social Cost of "Business as Usual" Growth in Asia and the Pacific • Global Initiatives on SCP • The need for Greening Business in Asia and the Pacific • Reinvestment into Human and Natural Capital • Social Capital • The Whole Systems Approach towards Greening Business • Eco-industrial Development and Circular Economy Systems • Sustainable Master Planning • Introduction to Green Tax and Budget Reform • Policy Strategies • The Co-benefits Approach to Climate Change and Development. *Ahshanuddin Haider*

Index 311

Patrons

Shri Pawan Jain,
Chairman, Board of Governors
Mangalayatan University

Shri Mohan Lakhamraju
Vice-Chairman, Board of Governors
Mangalayatan University

Prof. S.C. Jain
Vice Chancellor
Mangalayatan University

Shri Mohan Lakhamraju
Vice-President, Operations
Mangalayatan University

Foreword

Understanding media in today's world is more than a scholarly exercise, it is a necessary survival skill in a world that has been utterly changed by mass communication. All students, whether they will be practitioners, critics, or consumers, have to be able to analyze the ways in which mass media are being used to change the world. Here is the book edited by Mr. Neeraj Khattri which is very useful for the research scholars, academicians, professionals, thought leaders and students related to social science and media discipline. This book provides the tools they need to accomplish in the media.

The Interactive Media and Society book is very contemporary and hopefully, it will be very fruitful for young media workers and the students. The book contains the present status of Social Media and the changing face of democratic system in modern technological society. All research papers are beautifully written with inclusion of real life examples and future prospects of media. The language of the research papers in simple and the students will be able to understand the difficult concepts and research methods very easily. In my whole academic careers, I have seen a few good edited books in communication and media work of all contributors of this book. I convey my whole hearted good wishes to Mr. Khattri for his outstanding efforts and contribution of this publication.

With best wishes

Prof. Virbala Aggarwal
Chairperson
Department of Journalism and Mass Communication
Himachal Pradesh University
Summer Hill, Shimla
Email : virbala.aggarwal@rediffmail.com
Mobile : 09418168234

Foreword

Acknowledgements

I feel extremly delighted and honoured to present this book entitled "Interactive Media and Society". The book includes the papers written on the various sub themes under Social Media its several dimensions and impact on society. Papers are contributions of eminent scholars in the field of Communication and Journalism and other fields with an interdisciplinary approach.

The concept of this edited book is given by Prof. Girija Shankar Sharma and we are thankful for his valuable inspiration and suggestions received by us from time to time. I would like to convey my sincere thanks to all students, teachers, research scholars and other writers for their contributions in providing a valuable knowledge platform. I would also like to convey my deep sense of gratitude to Prof. Satish Chandra Jain, Hon'ble Vice Chancellor, Mangalayatan University, for his blessings.

I will always be thankful to Prof. Virbala Aggarwal from the care of my heart for her Inspiration, support and blessings. Further, I am also thankful to Prof. Devesh Kishore and Prof. Pradeep Mathur for their valuable suggestions. I convey my sincere thanks to all the members of the editorial Board for their continuous support during the course of editing of the book. I must thank to Pt. Amandeep and Shri Jai Prakash Rai for designing the book in a beautiful manner.

I would like to thank to my father, Shri Rajkumar Khattri and Mother, Smt. Shashi Khattri for being sources of motivation necessary for the making of this book. At the end, I express my deep sense of gratitude for my younger brother Shri Pankaj Khattri & my wife Smt Priya Khattri for their constant support.

February 25, 2012

Dr. Neeraj Khattri
Editor

List of Contributors

B. Shailashree, Assistant Professor, Central Campus, Bangalore University, Bangalore.

M.A. Kashem, Professor, Department of Agriculture Extension Education Bangladesh Agricultural University, Bangladesh.

Keerty Goyal, Department of Communication and Management, Guru Jambhashwar University of Science and Technology Hisar, Haryana.

Anuradha Vashisth, Department of Communication and Management, Guru Jambhashwar University of Science and Technology Hisar, Haryana.

Gaman Palem, Language and Culture Professional Titto Varghese, Research Scholar, Department of Mass Communication, Pondicherry University, Kalapet, Pondicherry.

Uma Balu, Language and Culture Professional Titto Varghese, Research Scholar, Department of Mass Communication, Pondicherry University, Kalapet, Pondicherry.

Titto Varghese, Research Scholar, Department of Mass Communication, Pondicherry University, Kalapet, Pondicherry.

Ms. Anjali Pundhir, Department of Communication Skills, Mangalayatan University, Aligarh.

Ms. Mridula Singh, Lecturers, Department of Communication Skills, Mangalayatan University, Aligarh.

Yashaswee Bahradwaj, Scholar, IBM, Mangalayatan University, Aligarh.

Sonali Senger, IBMER, Mangalayatan University, Aligarh.

Neha Gupta, IBMER, Mangalayatan University, Aligarh.

Abid Rizvi, IBMER, Mangalayatan University, Aligarh.

Prashanta Kumar Pal, IBMER, Mangalayatan University, Aligarh.

Sandeep Shandilya, Reader, IBM, Mangalayatan University, Aligarh.

Aditya Kumar Shukla, Lecturer, Department of Journalism and Mass Communication Dev, Sanskriti Vishwavidhayalaya, Shantikunj, Haridwar.

Shraddha Tripathi, JRF, Department of Clinical Psyclology, School of Yoga and Mental Health, Dev, Sanskriti Vishwavidhayalaya, Shantikunj, Haridwar.

Minal, Faculty Member, IBM, Mangalayatan University, Aligarh.

Dinesh Chaudhary, Aligarh.

Zainul Abdeen, Aligarh.

S.D. Livingston, Dr. P. Rajendran, Department of Journalism, D.D.E., Madurai Kamaraj University, Madurai.

Dr. P. Rajendran, Department of Journalism, D.D.E., Madurai Kamaraj University, Madurai.

Dewan Anjali, Department of Home Science, St. Bede's College Shimla.

Masoumeh Shiri Aminlou, Maryan Taherian, Department of Communication, Damavand Branch, Islamic Azad University-Taherian, Iran.

Maumita Chaudhari, Assistant Professor, Department of Journalism and Mass Communication, Barrackpore Rastraguru Surendranath College, North 24 Parganas, West Bengal.

Garmia Sharma, Lecturer, Department of Communication Skills, Dr. Preeti Sharma, Ph.D Dubai.

Mr. Dauji Agrawal, Lecturer, Department of Communication Skills, Mangalayatan University, Aligarh.

Uttam Kr Pegu, Assistant Professor, Department of Mass Communication and Journalism, Tezpur University, Assam.

Ambrish Saxena, GGSIP University (former) New Delhi.

Susmita Bala, VIPS GGSIP University(former) New Delhi.

Md. Nawaz Khan, Faculty Member, Department of Mass Communication, Manipur University, Imphal, Manipur.

Pramoda Kumar Jena, Associate Professor, Department of Communication Management and Technology, Guru Jambheswar University of Science and Technology, Hisar.

Saloni Saxena, Dev Sanskriti Vishwavidyalaya, Haridwar, Uttarakhand.

Chhavi Bartaria, IBMER, Mangalayatan University, Aligarh.

Shashank Bharadwaj, IBMER, Mangalayatan University, Aligarh.

Prashanta Kumar Pal, IBMER, Mangalayatan University, Aligarh.

Shah Alam, Research Scholar, Centre for Women's Studies AMU, Aligarh.

Ahshanuddin Haider, Director R.V Northland Institute of Management, Greater Noida.

1

New Media and Youth

Dr. B. Shailashree

Introduction

New Information and Communication Technologies have revolutionized the nature and pace of human interaction across the world, which is increasingly assuring the concept of a "GLOBAL VILLAGE". India is still far from becoming an "Information Society". But with a significant number of its workers employed in the information sector, it provides fertile ground for analysing the impact of New Communication Technologies on its society including their crucial role in Development.

New Communication Technology such as Internet, Computers, Mobile and others are bringing noticeable changes in the society. Communication Technologies include the hardware equipment, organizational structures and social values by which individuals collect, process and exchange information.

The New Media have certain characteristics that are similar-in certain respects for both of both interpersonal and mass media communication. Interpersonal communication consists of face to face exchange of ideas between two or more individuals. The message flow is from one. to few individuals, and the feed back is immediate. In contrast, mass media communication includes all those means of transmitting message such as Radio, Television, News Papers, Films that enable the information to reach the large audience. Some type of hardware equipment is always involved is mass communication. But interactive communication via new media like e-mail on the internet is some what like mass media.

The computer and its various application software, mobile phones, CD's are driving the social changes in India. These technologies, once distinctive are converging today to deliver data, voice and video in ways not dreamt of before.

New Communication Technologies

A Variety of communication tools from Analog to Digital, are classified under New Communication Technologies. Automation, high speed, interaction, Access and reach, connectivity, interactions, intensive and extensive services are some of the hallmark of New Media, Technologies.

Computer: Computer is one of the technical foundations of Information society. By changing the way we live, work and play, the computer has irrevocably altered the fabric of society. The computer has become both, a metaphor and a direct representation of thinking to the processing of information.

All modes of communication that we have devised since the beginning of humanity are getting combined into a single electronic system, driven by Computer.

Internet: The Internet has become a-household word as information wonder of the 93's. Internet is 'Network of Networks' that is an electronic interconnection of thousands of smaller networks which has the capacity to link millions of computers located throughout the world.

The Internet is a widespread 'information infrastructure'. Its influence reaches not only to the technical fields of computer but throughout society.

World Wide Web: World Wide Web is a vast electronic -library that spans the globe, comprised of millions of pages of information that can be viewed with a software program called 'web browser'. Many of these pages are "Hyperlinked" to one another with a simple click of mouse. There are millions of websites and billions of web pages accessible to anyone with an internet connection and web browsing centre.

It has become a communication medium for much wider, global audience. It is one of the important developments in the history of human communication. World wide web made the internet a household word, and brought the dream of Mc. Luhan's "global village" into reality.

HTML: HTML is the language of world wide web. It stands for Hyper Text Markup Language, which is a set of commands that tell the web browser to display and how to display.

Web Page: A Web page can include text, fonts, colors, graphic images, such as clip art or even photographs, sound bytes, video clips and hyper link- to other web pages or any combination of the above. These web pages are stored in the hard drive of a computer that is connected with it 24 hours a day.

Web Server: Web pages are stored on a web server which is nothing more than a computer running a software program that allows it to receive and process requests from users web browsers.

E-mail: In its simplest form, e-mail is an Electronic Message sent from one computer to another. One can send or receive personal and business related messages with attachment such as picture or formatted documents. Even computer programs can be sent through e-mail.

With the internet, sending e-mail takes seconds, allowing people to quickly communicate with people around the world at any time of the day or night.

Mobile Communication: The growth of mobile communication is fast. More and more people use mobile phones, wireless technology. Wireless data services are available in many regions, and wireless local area networks are used in many places.

Compact Discs: More than any other medium, recording is the history of new technological developments that seem to save the medium. A compact disc consists of music converted to a digital code that is ready for laser beam.

CD- ROM: Compact Disc-Read Only Memory CD-ROM) refers to an optical storage medium that can be read only once and data are initially recorded. The same technology as audio CD's used for music recording, CD-ROM is used to store computer data of all types.

Video Conferencing: Video conferencing is the interactive two way visual and audio communication over a distance. It is often referred to as "Video Conferencing" or "Video Tele Conferencing" both of which means the same thing. It is one of many technologies under the domain of "Video Communications" including broadcast television, video streaming, video assessment and video collaboration.

Aims and Objectives:

Volumes of literature is available on new media in India. Very few studies have empirically tested the growth, utility, adoption and the overall impact of new media on students. Therefore, this study attempts to collect data on the usage and responses of the students in Bangalore University.

The study was conducted to explore the impact of ICT on the youth of Bangalore especially the students

New Communication Technologies play a very important role in providing new information to the people and in that process shapes their career and helps in enrichment and broadening their outlook. Students have greater degree of exposure to all kinds of new media technologies. It is in this context that this tries to explore the awareness of new communication technologies and their usefulness among the youth of Bangalore especially the college students.

The study was conceived to explore the impact of ICT on youths of Bangalore.

New Communication Technologies play a very important role in providing new information to the youth and in that process shapes their career and helps in enrichment and broadening their outlook.

Objectives

1. To study the awareness of the ICT among the youth.
2. To study the use of ICT among the youth.
3. To evaluate the influence of ICT on their life style.
4. To know the kind of information accessed by youths.
5. To study the impact of new communication technologies on their education.

Methodology

The method used in carrying out the study is the survey method as it is concerned with describing, recording, analysing and interpreting the relationships between the variables.

The sample for the present study was selected from Bangalore City. Various colleges in Bangalore were surveyed out of 150 respondents only 110 furnished all the information required for the analysis.

Analysis of the Data

Table - 1 Showing the Income Category of the Respondents

Income Category	*No. of Students*	*Percentage*
5,000 – 8,000	36	32.72
8,000 – 12,000	29	26.36
12,000 – 15,000	11	10
15,000 – 20,000	09	8.18
20,000 above	25	22.72

Above table indicates that 32.72% of the youth come under the income category of Rs. 500 to Rs. 8000. it reveals that most of the youths (students) belong to the middle class family.

Table - 2 Awareness of New Communication Technologies by Respondents

New Communication Technologies	*Percentage of Respondents*
Computer	100
Internet	100
E-Mail	80
Cell Phones	100
CD	74.55
Website	75.45
Fax	56.36
Video Conferencing	51.82

The above table shows that computer, internet, cell phones witnessed 100% awareness among the youth. While only 80% of them were aware of e-mail, 74.55 were aware of compact discs. Only 56.36% were familiar with fax and 51.82% were familiar with video - conferencing.

Youths (students) were aware of computer, internet and cell phones while fax and video conferencing were familiar to 50% of the sample.

Table - 3 - Showing Place of Accessing ICT by Respondents

Place of Accession	*Respondents Percentage*
Cyber Cafe	71
College	65
Home	53
Library	35
Friends House	18

The above table shows that 71% of the respondents access to ICT at Cyber Cafe while 65% access to these technologies at colleges, 53% at home. The result indicates that majority of the respondents access to these new communication technologies at cyber cafe.

Table - 4 Showing Average Time Spent Browsing the Internet

Browsing Hours	*Percentage*
0–15	7.27
15–30	15.45
30–60	38.18
1–2 hrs	24.55
More than 2 hrs	14.44

The above table indicates that out of 110 students 7.27% browse internet for (10 – 15 min), 15.45% browse for (15 – 30) minutes, 38.18% browse for (30 – 60) minutes on the other hand 24.55% browse for (1-2 hours and 14.55% more than 2 hours majority of the respondents browse internet for 30 – 60 minutes per day.

Table – 5: Showing the Reasons for Using ICT

Statement or Reasons	*Percentage of Responses*
To improve Gen. Knowledge	75
Career opportunity	58
To transmit message quickly	47
To keep in touch with friends	43
To maintain contacts	2
To know about current events	38
Latest service and products	29
For E-Mail	29
To save time	2
For SMS	11
For quicker medical attention	08

The above table indicates that 75% of the respondents use ICT for improving their General knowledge, while 58% for getting information on career opportunity. On the other hand 47% use it to transmit message quickly, 43% to keep in touch with friends, 42% to maintain contacts, 38% to know about current events etc. Therefore, most of them use ICT to improve general knowledge.

Table - 6: Showing Contents Utilize Through ICT

Contents	*Percentage in favour of it*
Syllabus and education	60.00
News and Current Affairs	55.45
Product related information	22.73
Political happenings	15.45
Health Information	12.73
Pornographic material	3.64
Others	2.73

Majority of the youth (students) (60%) use ICT for syllabus and education related contents. On the other hand, 55% utilize news and current affairs contents and 22% witnessed the usage of product related information contents. The result indicates that syllabus and education related contents were mostly preferred followed by news and current affairs.

Table - 7: Showing the Response of ICT in Educational Career

Technology useful extent	*Highly of some*	*Useful opinion*	*No useful at all*	*Not so useful*	*Not*
Computer	75.45	21.82	2.73	0.00	0.00
Internet	61.82	26.36	7.27	4.55	0.00
E-Mail	29.09	40.00	20.00	8.10	2.73
Cell Phone	24.55	22.73	29.09	16.36	7.27
CD	25.45	37.27	20.91	13.64	2.73
Website	51.82	22.73	19.09	4.55	1.82
Fax	10.91	21.82	38.18	14.55	14.55
Video Conference	19.09	16.36	37.27	12.73	14.55

The above table shows that 75.45% youth opine that computer is highly useful, 21.82% say it is useful to some extent, 2.73% were of no opinion, 61.82 opine that internet is highly useful in their educational career followed by E-mail, cell phones, CD's, websites, fax and video conferencing. Students considered computer, internet and website as highly useful in their educational career.

Table - 8: Showing How New Communication Technologies Affected Life of Students

Statement	*Percentage of Responses*
Decrease out door activities	63
Increased visit chat rooms instead of meeting friend	60
Reduced personal relationship	56
Reduced interaction among family	55
Anxiety and stress	46

The above table depicts that majority of the youth (63%) experience decreased outdoor activities by virtue of these new communication technologies. On the other hand 56% felt that ICT have reduced personal relation and 55% feel that their interaction with family members is getting reduced.

The net result is that new communication technologies have led to the decreased outdoor activities among students followed by personal relationship.

Table - 9: Table Showing Response of Youth about whether ICT have Increased their Interest in Education

Response	*Percentage*
To great extent	54
To some extent	40
No opinion	6
Not so much	0
Not at all	0

The above table reveals that 54% of youth see ICT of a cause behind ICT increased interest in education their increased while 40% indicate some extent, 6% of them are of no opinion.

Youth especially students felt that ICT have increased their interest in education.

Major Findings

1. Majority of the students belong to the income category of 5000 to 8000 (32.72)
2. Most of the youths access to internet either at home (48.18%) or hostel (47.27%).
3. Computer, internet and cell phones witnessed maximum awareness among youth.
4. 4. 38.18% of youth browse internet for 30 - 60 minutes.
5. Most of the students (75%) use ICT to improve General Knowledge.
6. Syllabus and education related information is the content utilized through ICT (60%)
7. Computer is highly useful (75.45%) among the youth.
8. Majority of the youths feel that ICT has decreased out door activities (63%) and has reduced personal relationships.
9. 92% of the youth feel that ICT have increased their interest in education

Conclusion

Information and communication technologies have played a major role in the lines of the youth in Bangalore City. Information and Communication Technology has increased their interest in education and has saved time in searching information regarding their course. ICT have decreased the outdoor activities of youth and there is also reduction in personal relationships.

Bibilography

1. Baran Stanley, J. and Davis Dennis, K. 'Mass Communication Theory' Thomas Wadsworth, 2005.
2. Chakravarthy Jagdlsh, 'Net, Media and Mass Communication', Authors Press 2000.
3. Gordon, W. Terrence, 'Everyman's MC Luhan', DTG Magazine, 1980.
4. Jones Steve, 'Encyclopedia of New Media' 1998.
5. Panna Kishwar, 'Mass Media Research', Himalaya Publishing House, 1994.

2

Use of ICTs for Providing Quality Extension Services to Farmers

M.A. Kashem

1. Introduction

With a population of about 165 million in an area of 147,570 sq km, Bangladesh is one of the most populous developing countries. Over the last 15 years, Bangladesh has made important economic progress with a GDP growth rate averaging 5 per cent per year. The incidence of poverty has steadily declined, and considerable progress has been made toward achieving the Millennium Development Goals (MDG). D-Net, Katalyst and BIID (Bangladesh Institute of ICT in Development) are also performing commendable job in disseminating need-based information to rural people. Katalyst is a development project in Bangladesh with the aim to contribute to alleviate poverty through creation of jobs and income by facilitating measures to enhance the effectiveness of small and medium enterprises (SME) and farmers. The role of Katalyst as a facilitator is as follows (Katalyst, 2011):

- *Understanding the market*: Supporting the franchisers to understand the needs of the target groups and the corresponding services and modes of delivery.
- *Content/Service Development*: Promoting commercial content providers, who collect, validate and compile relevant information on demand to be disseminated through the fast proliferating telecenters around Bangladesh, and linking them with the franchisers.
- *Promotion:* Supporting franchisers to formulate and roll out promotional campaigns through commercial service providers to attract rural entrepreneurs, farmers and the general populace into the centers.
- *Capacity Development:* Building capacity of center operators and franchisers through professional trainers and consultants.

The BIID is a distinct initiative to support development and promotion on Information and Communication Technology (ICT) based services in Bangladesh. The overall mission of the BIID is to: (i) harness ICT as a tool for development, (ii) enhance strategic partnership, (iii) create opportunities for improving rural livelihoods, (iv) understand the market dynamics, (v) initiate market driven approach, and (vi) serve the poor through profit (BIID, 2011). BIID is now on the verge of forging a multi-stakeholder collaboration involving relevant stakeholders including private sector, non-profit, research organization and market development projects with a view to scale-up the e-Krishok (empowering farmers and advancing towards e-agriculture in Bangladesh) pilot experiences nationwide by expanding the network of service delivery points, creating sustainable provision for content creation and delivery and promoting the services and access points using both local and mass outlets. The e-Krishok initiative is an integrated approach to address three major areas namely, awareness building of the farmers about the services through direct communication, capacity building of the service delivery points (HR capacity) and service provisions.

The total number of Mobile Phone Active Subscribers has reached to 74.188 million at the end of April 2011 (Anonymous, 2011). The mobile phone subscribers of different mobile companies are shown in Table 1.

Table 1: The Mobile Phone Subscribers in Bangladesh up to October 2011

Operators	*Active Subscribers*
Grameen Phone Ltd. (GP)	35.691
Orascom Telecom Bangladesh Limited (Banglalink)	22.681
Robi Axiata Limited (Robi)	15.555
Airtel Bangladesh Limited (Airtel)	5.570
Pacific Bangladesh Telecom Limited (Citycell)	1.736
Teletalk Bangladesh Ltd. (Teletalk)	1.207
Total	**82.442**

*Subscribers in Millions.

**The above subscribers' numbers are declared by the mobile operators.

A recent study conducted by Kashem (2009) shows that among 12 communication media used by farmers in receiving technological information, mobile phone ranked 5th in position (cf. Figure 1).

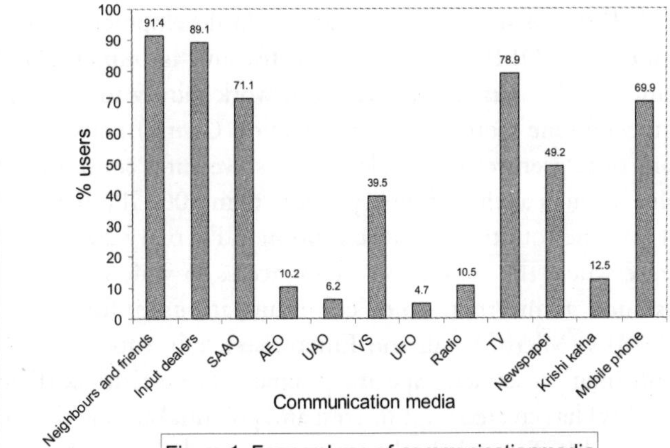

Figure 1. Farmers' use of communicationmedia

1.1 Agriculture Information and Communication Centre (AICC)

Information and communications technology (ICT) has become a very important feature in Bangladesh agriculture sector in contemporary times. Use of ICT provides opportunities for both the innovator and practitioner to disseminate innovations in the agricultural sector and gain knowledge and skill to practice the innovations. The AIS (Agriculture Information Service), a government organization of the Ministry of Agriculture, is playing a vital role for quick and timely transfer of technology through ***e*-Krishi** by establishing Agriculture Information and Communication Centre (AICC) at the village level. The purpose of AICC is to increase farmers' access to information on agri-business (production, processing, marketing etc.), to increase farmer to farmer information dissemination, and to empower farmers for institutional development at community level. There are about 20,000 farmers' clubs around the country, working with the welfare of the farmers in mind. Appropriate information and communication tools to these information centres and/or clubs play important roles to enhance and improve the efficiency and effectiveness of service and information delivery to a great extent. These centres provide livelihood-based information on agriculture, fisheries, poultry and livestock, education, non-farm initiatives, appropriate technology, human rights, employment, disaster management etc. A few private sector organizations have also come forward in the name of 'Call Centre', 'Community Information Centre' 'Palli Tathya Kendra' (Rural Information Centre) and so on.

1.2 Grameenphone's Activity in Rural People's Live-lihoods Improvement

Grameenphone in collaboration with Bangladesh Institute of ICT in Development (BIID) and support from Katalyst (a development project in Bangladesh funded by DFID, SDC, and SIDA, and is implemented by Swisscontact and GTZ International Services), work jointly to develop the GP CIC (Grameenphone Community Information Centre) network as the leading network of telecentres in Bangladesh to serve rural communities to avail ICT enable services at their doorstep. More than 500 GPCICs are now operational all over the country since its inception in February 2006. GPCIC is shared premise where the rural people have access to wide range of ICT based services such as internet, voice communications, information on agriculture, MSMEs (Micro, Small and Enterprises), job, education related and all other information services. Specific programs like e-Krishak (Farmers availing ICT facility) has created huge interest and potential among the farmer communities to avail ICT enabled solution to increase their income through access to new technology and required information. GPCIC opened a new horizon of connectivity and access for the underprivileged communities in rural Bangladesh.

Services of GPCIC

Communication: E-mail, Chat, Mobile, Video conference.

Information: Agriculture, SME, Govt. forms (Passport, Tax identification, Birth registration, Bills for electricity, gas, water etc.), Public examinations, Results, Employment opportunities, DV lottery, Immigration, Health advice etc.

Business Advisory: Advisory services for micro, small and medium enterprises, online marketplace (Cellbazar, SME Portal), market linkage and input information.

Education and Training: Computer training, Educational tips.

Chronological Dev. of D-Net Activities

2003: Establishment of 13 Information Centre (IC) (through these centres information were collected for the types of information needed by the women, handicapped people and older people).

2004: Lady in IC was popularly known as "Mobile Lady."

(ML helped women, disadvantaged people to contact with experts in agric., livestock, fisheries, health and FP and law in the capital).

2005: D-Net received Gender and ICT Award.

2008: MLs were given 5 days training and their designation were changed to "Welfare Information Lady" (WIL).

D-Net has its own information centers and doing excellent jobs in providing need-based information especially to women and disadvantaged groups of people.

Facilities Available to WIL

1. Laptop having longer charge facilities
2. Modem for connecting internet for e-mail, skype and browsing for other purposes
3. Mobile Phone
4. Small printer
5. Digital Camera
6. Stethoscope for measuring blood pressure, and thermometer
7. Rain coat and an umbrella
8. Measuring device for pregnancy risk factors
9. Small photo printer
10. Television, scanner (optional).

(Initially a WIL has to invest BDT 70,000 – 80,000 on her own; 1US$ = BDT 75.00 approx.)

"JIGYASHA" (Queries) – Farmers' Call Centre

Banglalink – one of the major mobile phone operators in Bangladesh launched with the technological support of Agriculture Information Service (AIS), a new service 'Banglalink Jigyasa (Queries) 7676' which provides suggestions and answers to any query related to agriculture, vegetables and fruit farming, poultry, livestock, fisheries etc. The service gives people with easy access to advice and solutions to agriculture-related problems. To avail the service, a Banglalink customer needs to dial 7676, talk and get expert's advice on the problem. The promotional charge for the service is Tk 2 per minute. This call centre has recently become quite popular with over 5000 callers per day. Similarly, Banglalink customers can get advice related to health services if they dial 789. There are also other effective utilization of mobile phones in Bangladesh, such as Rural Information Centre (RIC) administered by D-Net, Telemedicine, paying electricity, gas and water bills in the bank, transferring money, students' submission of admission documents to universities by sending SMSs.

Through RIC farmers' get opportunities for solving practical problems, e.g. diagnosis, control pests, diseases of crops, animals and fishes. Through video conferencing doctors diagnose problems and then send SMS or advise through mobiles for treatment. A recent study contacted to ascertain the farmers' mobile contact with different information sources (cf. Figure 2). The findings reveal that farmers had the highest mobile contact with their relatives and friends followed by contact with businessman for market information, contact with sub-Assistant Agriculture Officer, contact with fertilizer dealer, contact with word member of union council, contact with insecticide dealer, contact with progressive farmers, contact for transportation of agricultural produce, and contact with seed dealers. However, no research study has been reported to determine the extent of effectiveness of the mobile phones as communication media. Hence, the present study was undertaken to ascertain the effectiveness of mobile phones as communication media to the poultry farm owners in Bangladesh.

In order to verify the extent of use of ICTs by the farmers for receiving agricultural information, a study was undertaken. The empirical data were collected from the poultry farmers in respect to their use of mobile phones for communicating with different communication sources for getting need-based information.

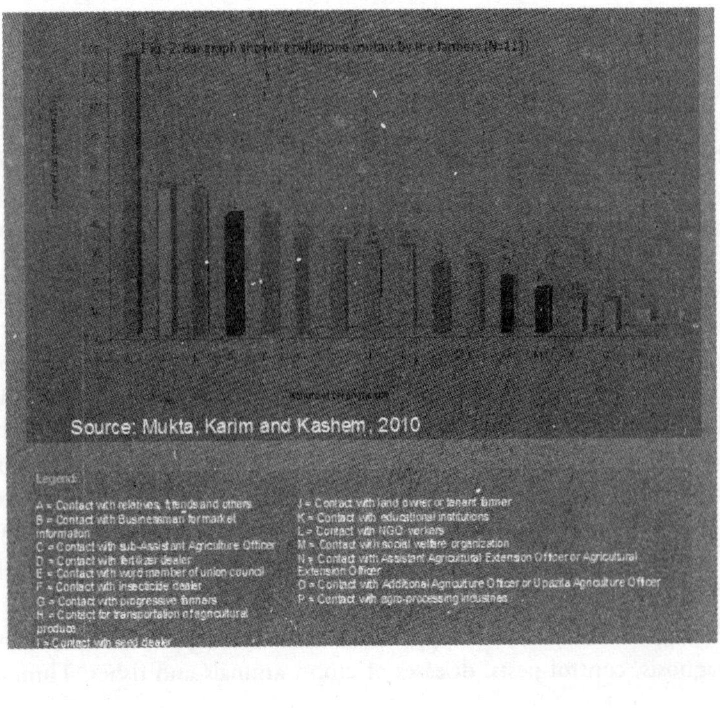

2. Methodology

The population for this study was the poultry farm owners of Sripur Upazila who frequently use the mobile phones, along with other available contact media, for collecting information from different communication sources. Data were collected during 10 April to 16 June 2011 from 103 poultry farm owners, out of 550. The sampled poultry farmers were asked to indicate the extent of effectiveness of 15 selected communication media in a five-point Likert scale. They were asked whether the effectiveness of the medium was *very high, high, moderately high, little*, or *very little*; the weights assigned to the responses were 5, 4, 3, 2, and 1 respectively. Communication media effective index (CMEI) was computed for each of the medium by multiplying by 5, 4, 3, 2, and 1 for very high, high, moderately high, little, or very little responses against each of the medium. The CMEI could thus vary from 103 to 515, 103 indicating the effectiveness of the medium as very little effective while 515 indicating the effectiveness of the medium as very high.

3. Findings

The findings indicate that the mobile contact by the poultry farm owners to poultry feed dealers ranked 1st (CMEI= 358) followed by mobile contact to Veterinary Surgeon (CMEI=330), mobile contact to Field Assistant (CMEI=324), mobile contact to dispensary for medicine (CMEI=312), and personal face to face contact of the poultry farm owners to the Field Assistants (CMEI=297). This clearly indicates that mobile phones are now very effective communication media compared to other conventional, print and electronic media. The CMEIs have been computed for all the 15 communication media. The findings have presented in Table 2. For clearer understanding the findings have been diagrammatically depicted in Figure 3.

4. Conclusion

The findings demonstrate that the effectiveness of communication media as perceived by the poultry farm owners of Sripur Upazila was the highest in respect of mobile contact to poultry feed dealers followed by mobile contact to Veterinary Surgeon, mobile contact to Field Assistants, mobile contact to dispensary for medicine, and personal face to face contact to Field Assistants. These findings clearly indicate the importance of mobile phones to the poultry farm owners for their effective contact with the available communication media. The policy makers and administrators may, therefore, give proper importance and attention the communication media where the effectiveness is relatively higher. In order to achieve higher output from the communication sources/ media it would be wise to render practical need-based training to them to increase their trustworthiness, credibility and reliability so that poultry farm owners can get more benefits and subsequently produce more quality poultry birds.

Table 2: Effectiveness of Communication Media as Perceived by the Poultry Farm Owners in Bangladesh

Sl. No.	*Communication Media*	*Extent of effectiveness*						
		Very high	*High*	*Moderate*	*Little*	*Very little*	*CMEI*	*Rank Order*
1.	Television	14	15	34	14	26	286	6
2.	Radio	14	3	21	29	36	239	10
3.	Newspaper	2	13	39	17	32	245	9
4.	Development magazine	1	2	21	35	44	190	11
5.	Leaflets and bulletins on poultry production published by BLRI	4	3	15	19	62	177	12
6.	Leaflets on poultry production published by DLS	3	3	11	23	63	169	14
7.	Bulletins on poultry production published by the DLS	0	6	9	31	57	170	13
8.	Personal face to face contact to Field Assistant	10	18	32	36	7	297	5
9.	Mobile contact to Field Assistant	9	29	38	22	5	324	3
10.	Mobile contact to ULO	2	19	34	31	17	267	7
11.	Mobile contact to VS	14	34	25	19	11	330	2
12.	Mobile contact to poultry feed dealers	27	28	24	15	9	358	1
13.	Mobile contact to BLRI for technical information	2	5	9	24	63	168	15
14.	Mobile contact to doctor for health problem	2	26	23	28	24	263	8
15.	Mobile contact to dispensary for medicine	10	27	36	16	14	312	4

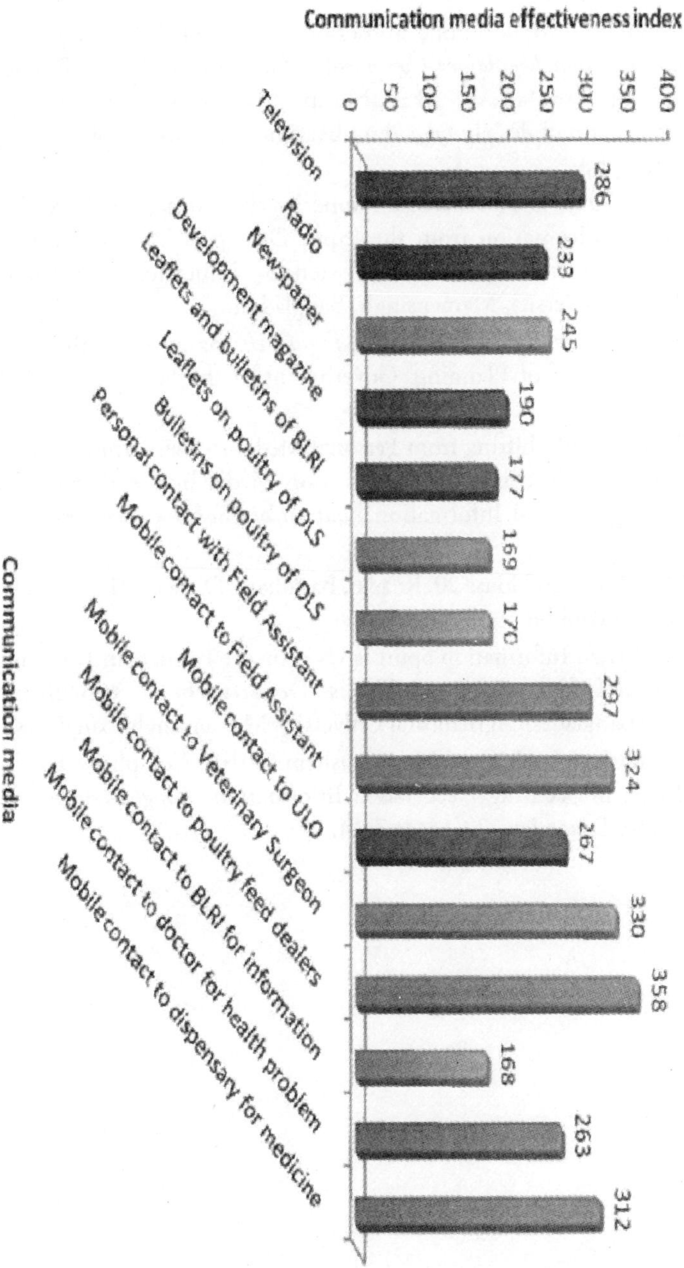

Figure 3. Effectiveness of different communication media for contacting with information sources by the poultry farm owners in Bangladesh (source: empirical data).

References

Anonymous (2011) Mobile Phone Subscribers in Bangladesh. *Bangladesh Telecommunication Regulatory Commission.* Government of the People's Republic of Bangladesh. Available at: http://www.btrc.gov.bd/newsandevents/mobile_phone_subscribers/mobile_phone_subscribers_April_2011.php

Barman, K.S. (2009). Use of Mobile Phone by the Farmers in Receiving Agricultural Information from the Input Dealers. M.S. (Ag.Ext.Ed.) Thesis. Department of Agricultural Extension Education, Bangladesh Agricultural University, Mymensingh, Bangladesh.

BBS (2010) *Statistical Pocket Book of Bangladesh.* Bangladesh Burea of Statistics. Ministry of Planning. Government of the People's Republic of Bangladesh.

Kashem, M. A. (2009) Shifting from Personal Media to Mass, Interpersonal and Interactive Electronic Communication Media by the Farmers for Receiving Agricultural Information. *Journal of Global Communication, 2(2).*

Katalyst (2011). Katalyst, House 20, Road 6, Baridhara, Dhaka-1212. Website: www.katalyst.com.bd

Mukta, J. N. (2010). Information Sources Used by the Farmers in Receiving Agricultural Information. MS Thesis. Department of Agricultural Extension. Bangladesh Agricultural University, Mymensingh, Bangladesh.

Mukta, J. N., Karim, A.S.M. and M. A. Kashem (2010). Cell-phone Use by the Farmers in Securing Need based Information. *Bangladesh Journal of Extension Education*, 22(1&2):7-14.

3

Technological Convergence

A Study on Awareness of New Media Devices among People of different Age Groups of Haryana

Dr. Keerty Goyal, Anuradha Vashisth

As new technologies make it possible to move more information faster than ever before, we are dazzled by millions of gigabytes that move across the world in nano seconds. We are infatuated by bandwidth, digital television, by gadgets and gizmos. Yet we hardly ask questions about the quality of information:

What is that we are communicating? Is it relevant? Does it make the world a better place? Does all this information add up to knowledge? Can this piece of monitor ever replace a warm hug or a pleasant smile? Today the challenge is to get information from where it is needed, through the most cost effective method possible. Only when information helps people communicate and participate it becomes knowledge. Technology is and has always been associated with innovation. Technology and innovation are complimentory to each other. Technology is definitely changing our lives and undoubtly for the better.

Technology accompanies with itself social changes and thus it's changing the way we work, relax, trade and communicate. The revolution in technology has given rise to chat rooms, discussion rooms, personalised web pages and online databases. The IT sector has completely changed the outlook of human communication with e-mails, video conferencing and instant messaging. With the advent of technology, people are building bridges to decrease the distances in their mind. The information technology is advancing at such a neck-break pace that it is difficult for even the most profound futurologist to say what will be the shape of the means of mass communications in the 21'st century.

However in the study, made in the Department of communication Management and Technology, Guru Jambheshwar University of Science and technology, an attempt has been made to understand the changes that the future has in store for us. The present study is under the broad banner of subject of technology convergence. Technology convergence is a new branch of information technology which deals with the latest technological devices combining sound, picture and data. Convergence can also be defined as a situation where both traditional and new communication services (be it voice, data, sound or picture) could be transmitted over many different networks

The theme of present study is "Study of new communication technology in media. Convergence - Access and Application. A study of Haryana". The present study seeks to identify qualitatively the upcoming technologies in media, as well as applications of new technologies in it. It aims to identify the convergence of new /emerging communication technologies in media; to find out the access of different categories of respondents to the new devices in communication technology; to find out the extent of use of new devices of communication technology by various categories of respondents. To know the level of knowledge of various types of respondents about rules and regulations with regard to emerging communication technologies; to find out the impact of communication technology on the lives of different group of respondents; to know the perception of various categories of respondents about the impact of new communication technology on employment.

The study basically an empirical one has been conducted in Haryana-one of the smallest but prosperous state of the Indian union. It has been selected for four of its cities—Karnal, Adampur, Hisar and Gurgaon. Further a sample of 300 respondents representing (75 from each city) which serves the purpose of study (choosing purposive sampling method) has been selected. However the actual responses received were 295 (Adampur 75, Gurgaon and Hisar 73 each and Karnal 74) and this constituted the universe of the study. Further, these respondents have been selected keeping in view their age, gender, profession and qualifications.

On the basis of age, respondents have been divided into three categories (a) below 20 years (b) between 20 to 30 years (c) above 30 years, while profession wise they were divided into two categories-a) IT oriented respondents and b) others. Likewise, on the basis of income, the respondents were divided into three parts: - 0-1 lakh, 0-1 lakh, above 3 lakh. The data so obtained from primary and secondary sources have been categorized, classified, tabulated and presented with the help of graphs/diagrams, analyzed and finally arrived at certain generalisations. Taking into consideration the exponential growth of the usage of convergent devices in the society, the present study seeks to evaluate impact of technology convergence in society. It is concern of each and every individual member of society to identify whether usage of technology convergent devices is creating social facility or social problems and to what extent and degree.

The universe of the study has been four districts of Haryana namely Karnal, Adampur, Hisar and Gurgaon. The sample size is 295 respondents representing all the four different districts. We resorted to purposive sampling but age and profession were kept in mind. Age of the respondent was further divided into parts as follows, (a) below 20 years (b) between 20 to 30 years (c) above 30 years. Income group of the respondent was divided into three parts: - 0-1 lac, 0-1 lac, above 3 lacs. Almost all the respondents were from middle and upper middle class family and with sound economic backing.

Age is one of the important factors of respondents' inclination towards technology oriented devices and thus has been given due place in the study. From the point of view of age the respondents have been divided into three broad categories viz. (i) Below 20 years; (ii) Between 20-30 years and (iii) Above 30 years. The category-wise data of these respondents is given in the following Table:

Age-wise number of respondents

Sl. No.	*Age Group*	*Frequency*	*Percentage*
1.	Below 20 years	73	24.7
2.	Between 20-30 years	85	28.8
	Above 30 years	137	46.4
	Total	295	100

Source: Interview Schedule.

The table shows that out of the total 295 respondents 137 (46.4%) fall in the age group of above 30 years while 85 (28.8%) belong to the age group of 20-30 years. The remaining 73 (24.7%) are in the below 20 years category. From this it can be inferred that the inclination towards technology oriented devices increases with the advancement of age.

The respondents were given schedule containing questions about their awareness and familiarity about convergent devices. The schedule was distributed to all the respondents and it was assured that their identity was kept anonymous. Further coding and then tabulation was done to get the results. Following were the major findings of the study:

This study reveals that the qualitative analysis of respondents having email-id shows that 32% respondents between the age group of below 20 years have e-mail id whereas 22% in the age group of 20-30 years and 75.6% in the age group of above 30 years have e-mail id. Hence the response regarding having an email ID does depend on age. Therefore the two variables i.e. age group and having an e-mail id are significantly associated. In case of gender 52.5% male and 23% females have their e-mail id. In the income group category of below 1lakh per annum 26% respondents answered yes on having e-mail id, whereas in income group of 1-3 lakh 30% agreed on having an e-mail id. Further 18% respondents having above 3lakh income per annum said they have e-mail id. In total 76% respondents agreed on having an e-mail id.

The above shows that almost all individuals are using convergent devices in their day to day life but only 68% respondents are familiar about the word convergence as the new trend. This is in spite of the fact when almost all of them are using convergent devices in some way or the other.

The study denotes that there isn't any significant response to the question that whether employment has increased or decreased because of technological convergence? However maximum respondents agreed that standard of living has increased but the problem of unemployment hasn't been solved. Furthermore the study underlines that up 87% respondents admitted to have cell phone as the most applicable convergent device in day to day life. Next comes on the list of the most applicable convergent device in their day to day life is computer, with a voting of 85% following T.V with 82% respondents in its favor. This study has revealed that cell phone has been found to be the most beneficial convergent device where as handy cam is the least preferred convergent device. The cell phone is found almost in all age groups, in all the income groups and also the same among man and women. The requirement of delivery system has totally changed the writing of journalist. It has become more of a visual and sensational story or in other words, there is more emphasis on visuals, i.e., more of camera work, bit of drama and a short script rather than a strong writing giving the news in its real form.

The graph below shows that almost 80% respondents are of the opinion that media technology can play rather is playing a very important role in bringing transparency in public administration. Of late this is even secured through hidden cameras along with other technological devices for the help of investigating journalist thus giving them the name, e-journalist.

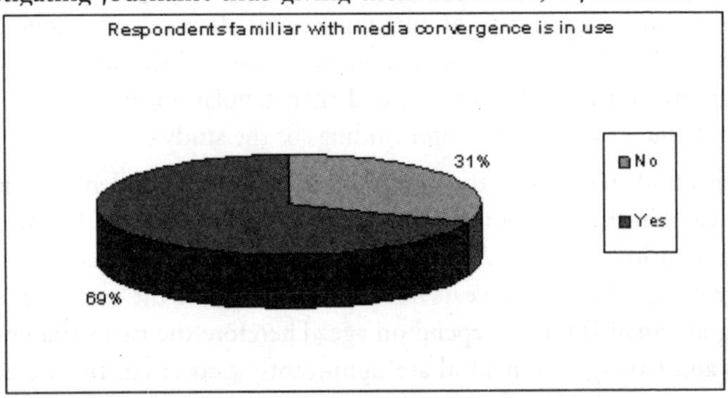

This study also reveals that even highly qualified professionals are also unaware about the rules and regulations regarding convergence. 77% respondents said that they are unfamiliar with any sort of law passed or any rule or regulation regarding information technology or convergence whereas 23% postgraduates showed familiarity with the rules having been passed, but they are unaware regarding the details. According to the study made 64% respondents disagreed on the role of tackling the adverse or emergency situation as journalist with the help of technology can only showcase or can give exact picture of the situation. This study also shows that in terms of news, live coverage from the place of happening does give more credibility to news and almost 91% respondents agreed to it. This study reveals that 95% respondents are of the opinion that the animated version of historical characters like hanuman, snow white etc. increases the temptation to view them. Cartoons along with sound effects and scripts keeping in mid target group does make a big difference in making such films a big hit.

This study shows that present journalist is rather called as e-journalist in the present scenario. Almost 76% respondents agreed to it. The reason being, today's journalist is equipped with technology oriented devices like cell phone, digital camera, internet etc.

Convergence in the common term refers to combination of sound, picture and data. When this technology is used in various facets of media it is called as media convergence. When asked about the familiarity of the term media convergence respondents of various age groups out of 25% only 12% in below 20 years age group, out of 29% only 22% in between age group of 20-30 years and finally 34% out of 47% in 30 above age group showed familiarity about media convergence in trend.

As shown in the table below when the respondents were asked about internet as the information provider about various convergent devices most of the respondents of various age groups agreed on Internet as a medium to the respondents for providing information about convergent devices. In the age group of below 20 years 18.3% responded yes, in the age group of 20-30 years 21.4%, in the age group of above 30 years 27.1% respondents responded yes, thus making a total of almost 67% people who believed internet as a medium for providing information about convergent devices. Only 33% respondents did not agree to it.

When the respondents were asked about effectiveness of media in bringing transparency in public administration 237 (80%) respondents out of 100% respondents said that media is effective in bringing transparency in public administration. In age group of below 20 years, 59 (20%) out of 73 (24.7%) respondents said that media is effective in bringing transparency in public administration. In the age group of 20-30 years 65(22%) out of 85(28.8%) respondents said that media is effective in bringing transparency in public administration. Finally in the age group of above 30 years 237(80.3%) out of 295(100%) said that media is effective in bringing transparency in public administration. Thus in total, majority of the respondents, i.e. 80.3% believed that media is effective in bringing transparency in public administration and only 19.7% did not agree to it.

Internet as a medium to the respondents for providing information about convergent devices			*No*	*Yes*	*Total*
Age group of respondents	Below 20 years	Count	19	54	73
		% of Total	6.4%	18.3%	24.7%
	20-30 Years	Count	22	63	85
		% of Total	7.5%	21.4%	28.8%
	Above 30 years	Count	57	80	137
		% of Total	19.3%	27.1%	46.4%
Total		Count	98	197	295
	% of Total	33.2%	66.8%	100.0%	

It was observed that almost 70% respondents responded that the concept of manual labor has not been affected by the introduction of media technology. In age group of below 20 years, 60 (20.3%) out of 73 (24.7%) respondents said that the concept of manual labor has not been affected by the introduction of media technology. In the age group of 20-30 years, 63(21.4%) out of 85(28.8%) respondents responded that the concept of manual labor has not been affected by the introduction of media technology. Further in age group of above 30 years 82(27.8%) out of 137(46.4%) respondents responded that the concept of manual labor has not been affected by the introduction of media technology. Thus to conclude almost 70% respondents in total, respondents responded that the concept of manual labor has not been affected by the introduction of media technology.

When the respondents were asked, that has the introduction of technology affected traditional ways of entertainment like theatre? Almost 74% respondents said 'yes'. Whereas 25.8% respondents said that folk art has a specific audience and therefore introduction of technology has not affected traditional ways of entertainment like theatre. In the age group of below 20 years 54(18.3%) respondents responded that introduction of technology has affected traditional ways of entertainment like theatre, whereas 19 (6.4%) respondents rejected this. Further in age group of 20-30 years, 71(24.1%) respondents confirm the impact, whereas 14 (4.7%) said 'no'. Finally in the age group of above 30 years 94(31.9%) respondents responded that introduction of technology has affected traditional ways of entertainment like theatre whereas 43(14.6%) respondents responded that introduction of technology has not affected traditional ways of entertainment like theatre.

The present study denotes that large number of respondents of various age groups responded that technology is not helpful in tackling adverse or emergency situation, though some respondents quoted that technology is helpful in creating awareness about adverse or emergency situation. Inage group of below 20 years 18.3%, in age group of 20-30 years 18.6% and in age group of above 30 years 27.1% respondents responded that technology is not helpful in tackling adverse or emergency situation. Thus in total 64.1% respondents responded that technology is not helpful in tackling adverse or emergency situation.

As shown in the table above it was seen that respondents of various age groups believe very strongly that live coverage from the place of happening gives more credibility to news. More than 90% respondents were in favor of this opinion. In the age group of below 20 years 68(1.7%) respondents said that that live coverage from the place of happening gives more credibility to news. In the age group of 20-30 years 79(26.8%) out of 28.8% respondents responded that live coverage from the place of happening gives more credibility to news, whereas only 3(1%) respondents said that live coverage from the place of happening does not give more credibility to news. Finally in age group of above 30 years 266(40.3%) respondents said that live coverage from the place of happening gives more credibility to news whereas only 13(4.4) did not agreed on this fact.

The study reveals that total 82% respondents of various age groups responded that different reporters from different places, reporting at the same time to the studio influence the viewership. In the age group of below 20 years 62(21%) respondents responded that different reporters from different places, reporting at the same time to the studio influence the viewership. Similarly in the age group of 20-30 years 68(23.1%) out of 85(28.8%) respondents responded that different reporters from different places, reporting at the same time to the studio influence the viewership. Again in the age group of above 30 years 112(38%) out of 137(46.4%) respondents responded that different reporters from different places, reporting at the same time to the studio influence the viewership, whereas only 19(6.4%) respondents responded that different reporters from different places, reporting at the same time to the studio does not influence the viewership.

The study reveals that, in the age group of 20-30 years, 74(25.1%) respondents said that casting votes through sms and choosing a winner on T.V certainly influence the TRP of the programme. In the age group of above 30 years, 110(37.3%) out of 46.4% said that casting votes through sms and choosing a winner on T.V certainly influences the TRP of the programme. Finally 83.1% in all responded that casting votes through sms and choosing a winner on T.V certainly influence the TRP of the programme, whereas only 7.5% respondents disagreed on this opinion.

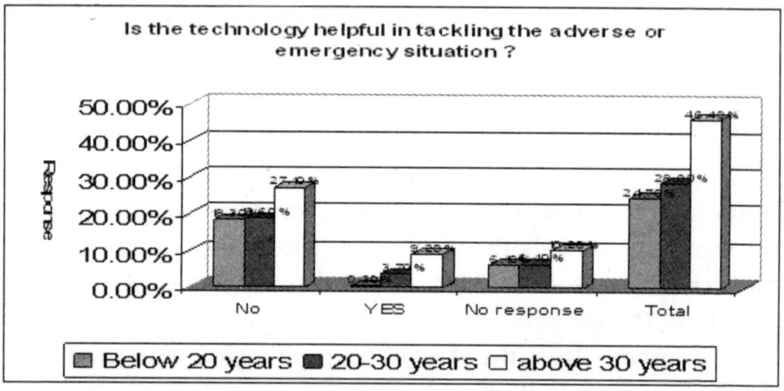

The present study reveals that communicating advice directly from the experts on T.V while sitting at home is a step ahead for the world to become a global village. Majority of respondents 246(83%) out of 295(100%) respondents were in favor of this statement. In the age group of below 20 years 55(18.6%) respondents said that communicating advice directly from the experts on T.V while sitting at home is a step ahead for becoming world a global village. In the age group of 20-30 years 78(26.4%) respondents agreed on this statement. Finally in the age group of above 30 years 113(38.3%) respondents responded that communicating advice directly from the experts on T.V while sitting at home is a step ahead for becoming world a global village.

The present study also reveals that the competition within the various companies has made cell phone accessible to every individual. Age group of below 20 years 51(17.3%) responded yes to it and 22(7.5%) respondents gave no response to this question. In the age group of 20-30 years 59(20%) respondents responded yes, whereas again 26(8.8%) gave no response. Finally in the age group of above 30 years 81(27.5%) said that the competition within the various companies have made cell phone accessible to every individual. Thus in total 191(64.7%) responded that the competition within the various companies have made cell phone accessible to every individual. Astonishingly 101(34.2%) respondents did not have any response to this question.

			Is the technology helpful in tackling the adverse or emergency situation?			
			No	*Yes*	*No response*	*Total*
Age group of respondents	Below 20 years	Count	54	1	18	73
		% of Total	18.3%	.3%	6.1%	24.7%
	20-30 years	Count	55	11	19	85
		% of Total	18.6%	3.7%	6.4%	28.8%
	Above 30 years	Count	80	27	30	137
		% of Total	27.1%	9.2%	10.2%	46.4%
Total		Count	189	39	67	295
		% of Total	64.1%	13.2%	22.7%	100.0%

			Are you aware of rule and regulation regarding convergence?		
			No	*Yes*	*Total*
Age group of respondents	Below 20 years	Count	65	8	73
		% of Total	22.0%	2.7%	24.7%
	20-30 Years	Count	63	22	85
		% of Total	21.4%	7.5%	28.8%
	Above 30 years	Count	98	39	137
		% of Total	33.2%	13.2%	46.4%
Total		Count	226	69	295
		% of Total	76.6%	23.4%	100.0%

The above table shows that majority of the respondents were unaware about rules and regulations regarding convergence. Almost 77% respondents were unaware about unaware about rules and regulation regarding convergence, whereas only 23% reflected their familiarity about rules and regulation regarding convergence. In the age group of below 20 years 65(22%) were unaware and only 8(2.7%) were aware about rules and regulation regarding convergence. In the age group of 20-30 years 63(21.4%) were unaware and only 22(7.5) were aware about rules and regulation regarding convergence. Similarly in the age group of above 30 years 98(33.2%) were unaware and (13.2%) aware about rules and regulation regarding convergence.

Convergence in the common term refers to combination of sound, picture and data. When this technology is used in various facets of media it is called as media convergence. When asked about the familiarity of the term media convergence, 130(44.1%) out of 130(44%) male respondents said that they are familiar with media convergence in trend, whereas 66(22.4%) male respondents said that they are not aware about media convergence. When asked about the familiarity of the term media convergence, 73(24.7%) out of (33.6%) female respondents responded that they are familiar with media convergence in trend, whereas 26(8.8%) female respondents said that they are not aware about media convergence. Thus to conclude male respondents were more familiar with media convergence in comparison to female respondents

This study shows that there are in all 295 respondents of various income groups. These respondents have been divided into three income groups: - 0-1 lakh, 1-3 lakh, above 3 lakh. Further 69 respondent of 0-1 lakh income group says that they spend weekly on computer, 39 use computer daily whereas 3(1%) do not use computer. Further 86 respondents of 1-3 lakh income group says that they spend weekly on computer, 27 use computer daily whereas 2(.7%)

do not use computer. In the income group of above 3 lakh 61(20.7%) use computer weekly and 5(1.7%) daily spend time on computer and only 3(1%) never spend time on computer.

The study reveals that the ratio of respondents of various income groups familiar with media convergence being in trend is 70:30.In the income group of 0-1 lakh 62(21%) respondents said that they are familiar with media convergence being in trend, whereas 49(16.6%) said that they are unaware about media convergence being in trend. In the income group of 1-3 lakhs 82(27.8%) respondents said that they are familiar with media convergence being in trend, whereas 33(11.2%) said that they are unaware about media convergence being in trend. In the income group of above 3lakh 59(20%) respondents said that they are familiar with media convergence being in trend, whereas 10(3.4%) said that they are unaware about media convergence being in trend.

Factors	0-1 lakh		1-3 lakhs		Above 3 lakhs	
	Yes	No	Yes	No	Yes	No
1. Through which channel you get the information about convergent device (Newspaper)	13	98	36	79	42	27
2. Through which channel you get the information about convergent device (Magazines)	24	87	32	83	30	39
3. Through which channel you get the information about convergent device T.V.	96	15	91	24	60	9
4. Through which channel you get the information about convergent device Internet	85	26	72	43	40	29

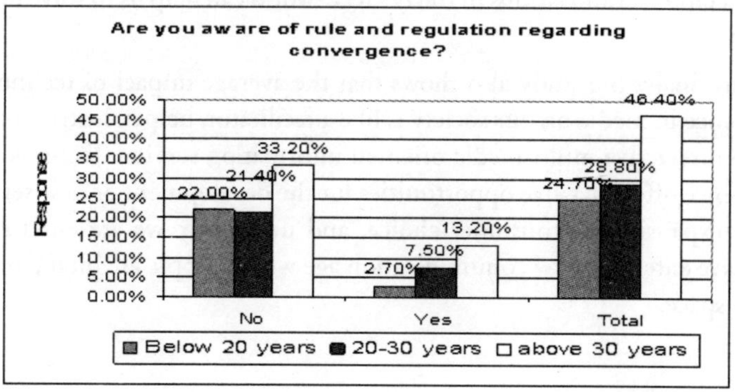

As shown in the above table, newspapers as a channel giving information about convergent devices, was not seen as a very effective means. In the income group of below 1 lakh, 13 respondents considered newspapers to be an effective means of giving information about convergent devices whereas, 98 respondents did not agree on this. In the income group of 1-3 lakh, 36 respondents considered newspapers to be an effective means of giving information about convergent devices whereas, 79 respondents did not agreed on newspaper as an effective information medium for communicating about convergent devices. In the income group of above 3 lakh, 42 respondents considered newspapers to be an effective means of giving information about convergent devices whereas, 27 respondents did not agreed on newspaper as an effective information medium for communicating about convergent devices.

It was very astonishing to note that majority of the respondents did not respond when they were asked that has degree of unemployment decreased or increased by the pro-gressive increase in technology? Respondents also quoted that they were not very clear about it. In the income group of below 1 lakh 36.9% respondents did not responded to it where as only 0.7% responded that unemployment has increased by the progressive increase in technology. Further in the income group of 1-3 lakh 32% respondents did not responded, whereas 2.4% responded that unemployment has increased by the progressive increase in technology and 4.4% said that unemployment has decreased by the progressive increase in technology.

It has been observed that with time, the use of internet is rising rapidly. The World Wide Web literally connects over 700 million people round the globe. The state-of-the-art technology has improved our means of communication as well as our educational standards. Due to the innovations in technology, an individual can gain knowledge about any topic at any place and at any point of time in his/her life. It has allowed the ease of availability of education. It has also improvised upon ways to fulfill our needs and to meet our expectations. Innovations in today's tech-world can help us to solve urgent problems.

Thus finally the study also shows that the average impact of technology convergence in media on our society is like a facilitator, helper, instructor and updated interactive multi-media oriented information service. Technological convergence offers massive opportunities for the development of new services and the expansion of consumer choice, and undoubtly we are entering or rather have entered a new communication age where people are interacting in timeless space.

4

Across The World in 80 Seconds

Exploring the Role of Narrative Styles in Building Communities:

A Transition from Traditional Media to New Media (With Special Reference to Phad Vachno, Bioscope, Youtube and Blogs)

Gaman Palem, Uma Balu

The Premise

This study explores the relationship between the three concepts -*Media Convergence*[1], **Participatory Culture** and **Collective Intelligence.**

Convergence means the flow of content across multiple media platforms and the migratory behaviour of media audiences who will go almost anywhere in search of learning and entertainment experiences. It involves technological, industrial, cultural and social changes depending on the speaker and thematic relevance. Convergence represents a cultural shift, where users are encouraged to search and share information from diversely dispersed media content.

Participatory Culture contrasts with the older perspectives of passive spectatorship. It leads to collective intelligence as an alternative source of media power. We are currently using this power for recreation; In the near future we will be deploying the very same skills for specific knowledge building and enhancement with a focused purpose.

Our observation and experience focus on the evolution of new media, where cultures converge, old and new media intersect and blend seamlessly.

1. Acoording to Henry Jenkins, in Convergence and Culture: Where Old and New Media Collide.

This paper focuses on ***reception studies***[1] the transition from passive spectatorship of olden times as found in Phad Vachno through the intermediate phase of the Bioscope, which introduced the concept of individual participation to the modern concept of community building through participatory culture using new media.

This research seeks to find:

- How effective is the role played by new media in promoting Participatory culture and Community building among specific learner groups.
- Does the new media bring up fresh concepts and ideas from around the globe to a common platform with a focus?
- What would be the specific outcome of this assimilated knowledge?
- How successfully can we blend in the creative contribution from sources that lack exposure to digital media to the mainstream group?
- What kinds of meaning a text can have, for whom is it meant, under what circumstances, with what changes over time and whether these meanings have any effects- Cognitive, Emotional or Social.

Methodology

The study utilizes a qualitative approach to study the usage of Youtube and blogs based on the following theoretical framework:

Reception studies - to study the impact of Youtube and blogs on a digital platform, to test individual perception and sensitivity and to enhance selective focus.

The Cultural studies approach will be applied whereby ***reader- response***[1] and mediated messages combine from Katz's Uses and Gratifications theory. On these lines, our focus would be on the need of audiences to utilize media for Participatory Culture and Collective Intelligence.

The researchers will use the ethnographic approach - based on principles of qualitative data collection and analysis. This method is to understand whether the existing level of comprehension and knowledge competency of Indian/ international audiences while reading blogs and viewing youtube content makes it easier for them to engage and channelize their time and situations better, thus leading to a broader understanding of the issues.

---

1. Jonathan Culler describes Reception Theory as "not a way of interpreting works, but an attempt to understand their changing intellegibility by identifying the codes and interpretative assumptions that give them meaning for different audiences at different periods."

Cultural and social anthropology has traditionally looked at a community through the lens of ethnographic fieldwork - which still continues to be an important methodology for the study of modern communities.

Individual attitudes and states of mind, what specific user groups could learn from blogs and youtube content,Temporal orderings, individual needs and expectations, preferred discourses and the social situations into which individuals enter are taken into account.

1. Spatiality

The ever dynamic "Space" may be considered "expandable" in the sense that certain scenes are "enlarged" and contextually made expandable where in others are "deflated." Not only content but also interior monologues of users are represented in either large or a small scale with accordance to their viewership and importance allocated per site.

The areas of kinesics, proxemics in terms of recreating spatiality and temporality while representing epic narratives depicting the nuances of immersive interaction are explored to kindle and create *chalana* (A Sanskrit synonym for motion, being disturbed and trembling) within oneself and to niche audiences.

We use ***periphery***[1] to name what we are attuned to without attending to explicitly. What is in the periphery at one moment may in the next moment come to be at the center of our attention and so be crucial. The same physical form may even have elements in both the center and periphery. The ink that communicates the central words of a text also peripherally clues us into the genre of the text though choice of font, layout, colour and framing of videos and pictures.

First, by placing things in the periphery we are able to attune to many things than we could if everything had to be at the center. Things in the periphery are attuned to by the large portion of our brains devoted to peripheral (sensory) processing. Thus the periphery is informing without overburdening.

Second, by re-centering something formerly in the periphery we take control of it. Peripherally we may become aware that something is not quite right, as when awkward sentences leave a reader tired and discomforted without knowing why. By moving sentence construction from periphery to center we

1. Jonathan Culler describes Reception Theory as "not a way of interpreting works, but an attempt to under-stand their changing intellegibility by identifying the codes and interpretative assumptions that give them meaning for different audiences at different periods."

are empowered to act, either by finding better literature or accepting the source of uneasiness and continuing. Without centering the periphery might be a source of frantic following of fashion; with centering the periphery is a fundamental enabler of calmness through increased awareness and power.

2. Understanding Social space

"We (the invisible divinity that works in us) have dreamed the world. We have dreamed it resistant, mysterious, visible, and ubiquitous in space and firm in time, but we allowed slight, and eternal, bits of the irrational to form part of its architecture so as to know that it is false."

-Jorge Luis Borges

The word "ubiquitous" can be defined as "existing or being everywhere at the same time," "constantly encountered," and "rampantly widespread." When applied to technology, the term implies that technology is omnipresent and we use it all the time. Because of the effective camouflage of these technologies, we tend to use them without thinking about the tool. Instead, we focus on the task at hand, making the technology effectively invisible to the user.

Ubiquitous technology is often wireless, mobile, and net-worked, making its users more connected to the world around them and the people in it. Ubiquitous computing can be seen as learning environments in which all learners have access to a variety of digital devices and services, including computers connected to the Internet and mobile computing devices, whenever and wherever they need them. Our focus of ubiquitous computing, then, is more converged on many-to-many than one-to-one or one-to-many, and includes the idea of technology being always available but not itself the focus of learning.

Moreover, our idea of ubiquitous centers the idea that both teachers, professionals and learners are active participants in the learning process, who critically analyse information, create new knowledge in a variety of ways (both collaboratively and individually), communicate what they have learned, and choose which tools are appropriate for a particular task.

Ubiquitous computing is changing our daily activities in a variety of ways. When it comes to using today's digital tools users tend to:

- communicate in different ways
- be more active
- conceive and use geographical and temporal spaces differently
- have more control

1. Acoording to Henry Brown, J.S. and Duguid, P. Keeping It Simple: Investigating Resources in the Periphery Solving the Software Puzzle. Ed. T. Winograd, Stanford University.

In addition, ubiquitous computing is:

- global and local
- social and personal
- public and private
- invisible and visible
- an aspect of both knowledge creation and information dissemination.

3. Virtual Community

Community means a group of people living together in some proximity (i.e., in space, time and relationship), or an area, who interact with each others. It usual consists of a larger social unit sharing common values and social cohesion. In human communities, intent, belief, resources, preferences, needs, risks and a number of other conditions determine communities.

Since the advent of the internet, the concept of community is not limited by topographical and demographical issues. People can now gather virtually in an online community and share a common platform with same interests. ***Sense of Community***[1] imbibes membership, influence, integration and fulfillment of needs and a shared emotional connection.

Active and passive net based learners build a successful community where they freely articulate their vision, experience and seek immediate gratification. People start talking by commenting, and they map the territory they have treaded. The environment in a holistic manner is conducive for zoned growth. The member database provides a profile thus creating a persona for the learner thus evolving a ***social identity***[1] and also at times an alternative social identity.

Social identity theory argues that there are two distinct aspects of the self-concept: personal identity and social identity. Although many self-esteem measures are available in the literature, they all focus on individual's evaluation of their personal identity, whether in private or interpersonal domains. No scale currently exists that assesses the positivity of one's social identity.

Virtual community[2] is a social network of individuals who interact through specific media, potentially crossing topographical and political boundaries n order to pursue mutual interests and goals. Computer mediated communication is mostly followed by chat rooms, electronic mailing, blogs and video casts encouraging interaction, focusing on a particular interest.

4. Narrative Styles

The narrative style offers a luminal experience to the viewer by illuminating the screen, offering them an out-of-the-world, out of the body experience. Computer viewing, thus becomes akin to a "religious" experience in a luminal zone where this-world of reality, the real world of temporal experience and the outer-world simulated by the "**pre-recorded" fantasy meet.**[3]

Phad Vachno, Bioscope, Blogs and Youtube are typical examples. The brain perceives the space and proxemics in an entirely disambiguous way, by assimilating awareness and understanding of the environment by organising and interpreting sensory information which in turn results from physical simulation of the sense organs, for example the light striking the retinas of the eyes.

(a) Phad Vachno

The three basic features associated with this art form are: the epic story of Pabuji, the Rathod chief of Rajasthan in the 14th century, who is extolled as an incarnation of Hindu God, and worshipped by the Rabari tribals of Rajasthan; the Phad or *Par*, which is a long scroll painting (or sewn) made on cloth; and the bard priests, known as the Bhopas (who belong to the cult of Pabhuji) of the nomadic tribe of Nayaks and specialists in narrating the story of the Pabuji in their sartorial best through the medium of the Phads used as a portable temple, all over the desert lands of the Thar in Rajasthan.

The Phads or Pars are painted by professionals called *citero*, known by the clan name 'Josi' of the Chipa caste. The Phad's epic narrations are attended primarily by the traditionally nomadic and camel-herding Rabari caste (for Pabuji is their principal deity)and also by the Rajputs of the village (Pabu's own warrior caste) as well as the royal class.

The musical and chanted narration is in colloquial Rajasthani dialect. Bhopa, the main narrator sings to the accompaniment of the *ravanhattho* (a desert zither or a spike fiddle with eighteen strings but without frets), which he crafts by himself. A dholak or drum is also part of the musical ensemble. During the entire narration, Bhopa's wife called the Bhopi, is present with him and joins him in singing. She also carries a lantern to shed light on the Phad as the Bhopa points out each scene with a stick and narrates the story. He sometimes dances and interjects his performance with jokes and banter with the audience. Collection of monetary contributions is part of the performance. Every time a donation is received, the Bhopa makes the announcement by blowing a conch-shell and mentioning the name of the donor.The present trend of narration has many intermissions for taking tea, singing devotional songs (bhajans), popular film music, thus making it partly an entertainment coupled with the "religious ritual of invoking Pabuji as a living deity".

1. In a seminal 1986 study, Mc Milllan and Chavis identified four elements of "Sense of community".

As Pabuji's devotees were semi-nomadic herders, his temple -the Phad visits the worshippers rather than the other way round.

(b) Bioscope

"Bioscopewallah……bioscopewallah ayah….

aao, dekho, nai purani filme sirf ek rupiya!"

(Here comes the Bioscopewallah, come and watch new and old films for just Re 1!).

The throw-back cry from the 1960s and 1970s, trying to lure children and adults to the magic of movies in a box still reverberates in the serpentine bylanes of Kolkata, mingled with the smell of moss and decay. Children would rush to his cart, clutching a rupee coin in their hands to experience the voyeuristic feeling of peek-a-boo cinema in the colourful wooden box under the shade of the ominously grave-looking black cloth.

Salim's journey on the Kolkata streets began more than 40 years ago. He recalls the golden days when his father's bioscope ruled the roost: "People used to come rushing out of their houses, especially children and women. They used to stand in the balcony for hours in order to catch the bioscopewallah."

Now in his late fifties, he laboriously pushes along his archaic projector on a hand driven cart. In this digital age, the wooden bioscope holds no attraction and Salim cuts a lone figure as he wanders from one street to another. The cry might not have the same verve, nor perhaps does it elicit the earlier enthusiasm. However, as he sets shop, a small crowd gathers around him - to lose itself in the garish, colorful, melodramatic and musical world of movies. The glamour, thrill, drama and dreams of Bollywood packed into three-four minutes of trailers transport the viewer into a makeshift world of movies — short lived, but an escape from the real world…

(c) Blogs

Ideas are infectious. They can spark from the remotest corner of the world…and spread like wildfire, thanks to technology which has shrunk the

---

1. Social identity theory is developed by Tajfel and Turner.
2. The term virtual community is attributed to the book of the same title by Howard Rheingold, published in 1993.
3. Pre recorded Fantasy refers to a pre-determined text and our immersive video content for the immersive experience will be a fantasy that is prerecorded.

globe to palm-size. Minds that think alike are brought to a common platform and all those ideas converge.. This ignites a process of transformation, elimination and evolution.. What emerges is a beautiful concept, combining all the essential elements with a clear focus.

The term "weblog" was coined by Jorn Barger on 17 December 1997. The short form, "blog," was coined by Peter Merholz, who jokingly broke the word *weblog* into the phrase *we blog* in the sidebar of his blog Peterme.com in April or May 1999. Shortly thereafter, Evan Williams at Pyra Labs devised the term "blogger" in connection with Pyra Labs' Blogger product.

Blogs add creative value and originality to the concept, making it unique and special.

It instills a community feel among the group, sharing knowledge and experiences - posting text extracts, photos, videos, writings and artwork, etc. keeps it visually alive and interactive. Everything stays focussed and connected, with the steady inflow of relevant contributions. The entries are usually in reverse chronological order. A typical blog combines text, images and links to other blogs, web pages, and other media related to its topics.

Personal blogs are special – like a spider's web. It is a way to reflect on life. Some personal blogs quickly garner an extensive following, like the rain drops that glitter on the delicately woven threads. Blogging can have a sentimental quality and the blogger usually takes pride in his posts.

A Reverse Blog is composed by its users rather than a single blogger. This system has the characteristics of a beehive, which represents a regional community – with each individual contributing to the whole. There is typically some limit to the number of entries. At the international level, this type of community-building is similar to a nesting site, where birds from all corners of the world flock together for a common purpose.

Blogs have also had an influence on minority languages, bringing together scattered speakers and learners; this is particularly so with blogs in Gaelic languages. Minority language publishing (which may lack economic feasibility) can find its audience through inexpensive blogging.

Many bloggers, particularly those engaged in participatory journalism, differentiate themselves from the mainstream media. The first known use of a blog on a news site was in August 1998, when Jonathan Dube of The *Charlotte Observer* published one chronicling Hurricane Bonnie.

Some bloggers have moved over to other media like radio and television: Duncan Black (known widely by his pseudonym, Atrios), Glenn Reynolds (Instapundit), Nate Silver (Five Thirty Eight.com), and Ezra Klein (Ezra

Klein blog in *The American Prospect,* now in the *Washington Post*). Established authors like Mitzi Szereto and Chetan Bhagat have started using blogs to not only update fans on their current works but also to expand into new areas of writing.

Blog-based books have been given the name blook. A prize for the best blog-based book was initiated in 2005, the Lulu Blooker Prize· The book based on Julie Powell's blog "The Julie/Julia Project" was made into the film *Julie and Julia,* apparently the first to do so.

Blog themes have an amazing variety - studies, hobbies, travel, food... the list is endless.

Information is continuously updated, usually with a regional flavor. Fresh aspects are discovered that pave the way for discussions. New schools of thought arise, enriching the current scenario. Blogs have emerged highly successful in creating interactive communities in their respective fields. Future generations stand to gain a lot from the creative bloggers of today!

(d) You Tube

YouTube is an online public communications site. Registered users upload or share videos for public viewing. The quality and content of these videos vary from amateur to professional.

YouTube was designed and released in 2005 by Chad Hurley, Steve Chen, and Jawed Karim. They came up with the novel idea of individuals reaching out to the public with their creative works. Google, sensing its potential in public communications, took over YouTube. The launch witnessed a great following. The product spoke for itself and very little was spent on marketing.

YouTube is a great tool to update information on new products or services- a cost effective way of advertising. Registered users can upload videos and seek public response. The range of themes is endless – initiating the process of community building, almost instantaneously.

Apart from creative pursuits, Youtube plays a key role in education. Video lectures by professors from Universities around the world are readily accessible to students. This knowledge-sharing creates specific learner-groups– the focus being either the subject or the University itself. On the other hand, there are interesting video lessons on languages, dialects, culture, music and etiquette presented with native flavour. These are especially useful for those travelling abroad for studies or on business and carry a lot of value even from the tourist perspective.

5. The Observer/Participant

The spectator becomes the *observer/participant* when he is made conscious of the bombardment of visual imageries and the multiple viewing choices presented. The luminal experience and the multi layered audio accompaniment kindles the senses.

Justin Gardner and his colleagues set out to put the hypotheses on sensitivity enhancement and efficient selection to the test and determine which of them plays a dominant role in perception. The study by researchers at RIKEN Brain Science Institute (BSI) provides valuable insights on how our brains achieve such focus and on how this focus can be disrupted, suggesting new ways of presenting information that augment the brain's natural focal capabilities.

Our brain achieves the ability to focus due to two distinct processes, referred to as 'sensitivity enhancement' and 'efficient selection' Sensitivity enhancement corresponds to improvements in how neurons in the cortex represent sensory information like sounds and lights, similar to the volume control or reception control on a television set. Efficient selection is more like a filter, routing important sen-sory information to higher-order perceptual areas of the brain while suppressing disruptions from irrelevant information.

6. Sensory Perception and Image Processing

Blogs and youtube content has text, images and videos thus simulating visual cortex, auditory cortex, and somatosensory cortex. Content and image processing takes place in the *association cortex-* a structure characterised by extensive connections with other areas of cerebral cortex and specialized in holding *mental images.* This may result in a new vision of, or the discovery of a new casual relationship between data sets. Such a process may result in

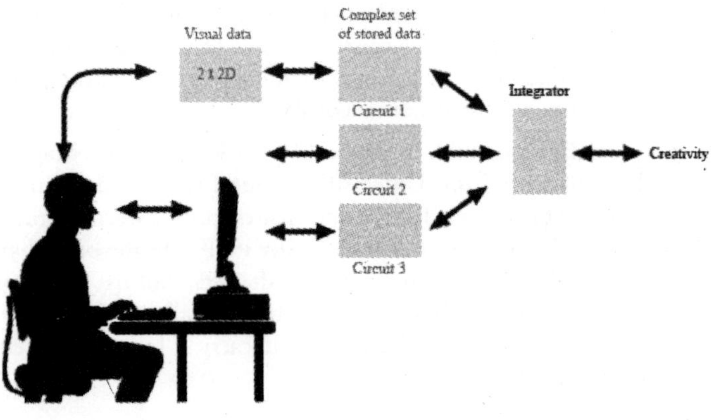

Fig. 6.(a) Narrative structures being processed as information packages into enabling a higher level of perception in an individual.

creativity, new vision and intelligence depending on the development. This is further illustrated in the Fig. 6.(a) where complex sets of data are processed and stored in a brain.

7. Conclusion

The relative space between the presenter and observer/participant has literally shrunk and virtual communities have become a common phenomenon. Unlike traditional media, which required a physical presence, today's technology has made instantaneous sharing across the world a possibility, irrespective of location. The focus of communities has shifted from mere entertainment towards more educating purposes – a healthy process that holds a lot of promise in the future.

References

1. Azri, W.; Chambon, C.; Herbette, S. P.; Brunel, N.; Coutand, C.; Leplé, J. C.; Ben Rejeb, I.; Ammar, S. D. et al..: "Proteome analysis of apical and basal regions of poplar stems under gravitropic stimulation". J. Physiologia Plantarum 136 (2): 193–208.(2009).
2. Birdwhistell, R.: Kinesics and Context. University of Pennsylvania Press, Philadelphia (1970).
3. Caldwell, John Thornton.: Televisuality: Style, Crisis, and Authority in American Television. Rutger's University Press. New Jersey (1995).
4. Davis, Erik.: Techgnosis: myth, magic and mysticism in the information age. Harmony Press. New York (1998).
5. Hall, Stuart.: The Silent Language. Double Day. New York (1959).
6. Canuto, Marcello A. and Jason Yaeger, eds. (2000) The Archaeology of Communities. Routledge, New York.
7. Patanjali Dharma Sutra. Divya Prakashan. New Delhi.
8. Rajanayagam, Dr. S: Carnival 'Dreama'. J. Culture and Communication, Loyola Press. Chennai (2004).
9. Vatsyayan, Kapila. : Bharata: The Natyasastra. Sahitya Akademi, New Delhi (1996).
10. Brown, J.S. and Duguid, P. Keeping It Simple: Investigating Resources in the Periphery *Solving the Software Puzzle*. Ed. T. Winograd, Stanford University.
11. Gibson, J. The Ecological Approach to Visual Perception. New York: Houghton Mifflin, 1979.

5

Family Vs Friends: Who take the Top Spot?

An Analysis of the Status Updates of Teenagers in Facebook

Titto Varghese

Introduction

There is always a conflict between peers and parents in the case of the adolescents. Psychologists are of the opinion that usually adolescents go for peers when it comes to choose choice. Social Media play a very significant role in the lives of teenagers today. Twitter, blogs and facebook are ways they find to keep in touch with their loved ones and to make new friends. This is done through messages, scraps and frequent status updates. The teenagers and children are using it very frequently and lively for certain gratification needs too. It gives them immense chances to keep their inner thoughts posted and updated.

Early adolescence or teenage is a critical period of change in children's relationships. There is a tendency seen in the teenagers for more closeness to the peer group and a resulting distancing from the parents and family. But this "waxing of peer orientation and the waning of closeness with parents" is not a permanent phenomenon but just a temporary one (*source:* http://www.oppapers.com/essays/Adolescent-Relationships-With-Parents-And-Peers/*502768*). Though the teenagers do not wish to withdraw completely from their family, they would love to have more freedom and greater control over their own lives. It is clear that if the teenagers get both these (freedom and control over their lives) somewhere they would love to be part of it. The social media platforms provide such an occasion for them.

Researchers and Psychologists are of the opinion that it is erroneous to assume that parents have little or no influence on their adolescent children

(Hayes, L. et.al, 2004). Both parents and peers act as a dual force in the development of the children's socialization. Evidence suggests that well-adjusted adolescents tend to have high quality relationships with their peers (Armsden & Greenberg 1987). Research on decision-making has shown that importance of parents or peers depends on the quality of the parent-adolescent relationship (Noller, 1994, *source: h*ttp://www.aifs.gov.au/institute/pubs/resreport10/parentpeer.html.)

Lindsay Clandfield says that the members of many social networking sites have the option of keeping their friends informed of their current circumstances by posting a brief 'status update'. If somebody likes to update, people are eager to know what their friends are up to. (Clandfield, 2011, *source:* http://www.onestopenglish.com/teenagers/teen-talk/does-your-status-need-an-update/.)

Review of Literature

The study by Carla Seal reveals that teenagers go to certain media in order to find their own 'personal space' (Wanner, 2006). This issue of personal space is very important for teenagers since at this age they want to have some degree of personal freedom and privacy, no matter which culture they are coming from. Here the teenagers are finding this 'space' in their 'facebook' or 'mySpace' accounts.

In the Report of a research titled 'A Day without Media', Research conducted by ICMPA and students at the Phillip Merrill College of Journalism, University of Maryland, College Park, USA, the teenagers were asked to write about their ideas on Media Dependence. The teenagers then wrote about the role of media in establishing and cementing social connections – how they used their laptops and phones and myriad devices to communicate with friends, families, and others in their lives (*source:* http://withoutmedia.wordpress.com/). Some of the comments are worth reading:

> "This technology craze has become so deeply ingrained in each of us we know no other way of living our lives, but to rely on our cell phones, laptops, televisions, and iPods to keep us occupied and connected with the world around us. I find it [difficult] to fathom someone not being connected through media, because I know no other way".

"It's funny," wrote another, "but I realized we are a social species, and the use of media today helps us to establish a connection with one another."

In her article 'The Mass Media and Family Communication', Barbara J Wilson says that Mass communication technologies permeate the homes of American families today. The average child in this country lives in a house hold with three television sets, 3 tape recorders, 3 radios, 2 VCRs, 2 CD players, one video game player and one computer (Roberts, Foehr, Rideout & Brodie, 1999). Moreover children spend almost 6 ½ hr each day using these media (Woodard and Gridina, 2000). In many American homes, the television occupies a central space in the main gathering area. Today the Computer with its Internet facilities occupies that centre stage at home. Given the prominence, the media are clearly an integral part of the daily routines of family life. But mass media can be used to avoid family interactions as well. The media strongly shape the rhythms of family life. In many families, the architecture of the house, evening meals and even conversations are structured around large-screen TV. But there are changes happened in the last decade which caused a change of focus from the traditional and electronic media to the new media. That too, especially to the Social Media Sites. As families structure their activities around the media, the technologies themselves become part of how family members negotiate their social reality.

A study, conducted by Pew Research Center's Internet and American Life Project, found that the use of social media is most widespread among teens 95% of the respondents who participated in the survey use the Internet regularly. Among them more than 80% said they use social media sites daily. "Social networking sites have created new spaces for teens to interact. For most teens, these are exciting and rewarding spaces. Teens in the survey reported that parents were also the biggest influence on shaping what they think is appropriate or inappropriate behaviour when going online". *(source*-http://netaddictionrecovery.blogspot.com/).

Teenaged students can "develop relationships online devoid of the anxiety found in face-to-face relationships," and they "can take on any persona (mask) they desire, without fear of judgment on appearance or personal mannerism, and can avoid racial and gender prejudice" reveals a study published in the website of Centre for Internet Addiction as part of their series of researches on this issue *(source*-http://netaddiction-recovery.blogspot.com/). The study clarifies again that this type of adaptive behaviour tends to diminish the social capacity of teenagers, leaving them unprepared for the development of real world relationships.

Sonia Livingstone's book 'Half a Century of Television in the Lives of Our Children' reviews evidence over five decades regarding the changing place of television in children's lives in the families. It argues that the family relied more on television as the medium of instruction for the children in these decades. Now it has become the stage for the Social Networking Media (Livingstone, 2007). Another article by William Douglas titled 'The Role of the Media in Our Lives' acknowledges that the presence of the media profoundly influences family patterns of interaction, by virtue of the quantity of their daily consumption by children and parents, alone and together, and by their presence in family life (Douglas, 1996).

Professor Bernard Cañaveral, a lecturer on media literacy observed that "80 per cent of the waking time of the youth is influenced by media." He added that "Television has changed the family life patterns of people and it has stolen the 'quality time' supposed to be shared by family members so they can interact with each other" (Cañaveral, 2009).

The article titled 'Television and Mediating Effects of Family Communication' by Desmond Roger describes that outcomes such as increases in aggressive behavior, decreases in family communication, lowered academic achievement, and motor restlessness have been associated with excessive amounts of media use, including TV viewing and movies, video games, and computer use by children (Roger, 2004).

Another interesting study was conducted by the Ypulse Research on the Status Updates and the facebook fatigue. They came out with findings as stated below:

1. Most of the female teenagers were tired of facebook whereas their male counterparts were trying for some other related sites like twitter.
2. Many have decided to leave facebook just because their mom or dad has already created accounts in facebook.
3. Though many have opined that they are suffering from facebook fatigue and depression, they are just a minority. There are still a lot of facebook fanaticswhere 53% of female teenagers said they cannot live without facebook. Many are curious to know what would be the next status update of their friends.
4. Status updates are only second to chatting, another relatively recently added feature, in favorite activities among high school students. (*source:* http://www. ypulse.com/ypulse-research-status-update-facebook-fatigue).

Many teenagers feel that they cannot be their original self if their parents are there in facebook. Many remarked that it is 'embarrassing', 'invasive' or 'distasteful' that their parents too are watching them online through facebook. They regard facebook as a place for the students and youngsters and not for the parents or the older ones. On the website MyParentsJoined Facebook.com, there are numerous examples of parents over-sharing their daily lives in status updates and wall posts made on their offspring's wall, which many children find very embarrassing. There were many petitions by students sent to Facebook creator Mark Zuckerberg to prevent nonstudents from joining the site. "For instance, the creator of the Facebook group "Don't Let My Parents onto Facebook!!" sent an e-mail to Zuckerberg before the change to general admission, detailing the reasons why parents shouldn't be allowed on the site. (*Source:* http://www.freeonlineresearchpapers.com/facebook-isnt-everybody).

The teenagers and the youth have a marked sense of privacy, says Nick Eaton. They get this privacy through facebook, twitter and myspace. But most of the parents see Facebook as a public space and are afıaid that their children are posting personal information to a wide world through their status updates in it. According to Microsoft researchers Danah Boyd and Alice Marwick, teenagers tailor specific messages to specific audiences (likely not to their parents), and expect them to be received that way (Eaton, N. 2011. *Source:* http://blog. seattlepi.com/microsoft/2011/05/09/do-teens-of-the-facebook-generation-value-privacy/).

Social media can go to the other extreme by hurting people which may even lead them to commit suicide. Jarom Loosle and Anderson in their study about the teenage suicide found, that the major cause of teenage suicide nowadays is the cyber bullying (Loosle and Anderson, 2011). This is a form of frightening or terrorizing someone online about some of their activities. It usually happens through the social networking sites. Michael Ollore coined a term "bullycide", a term increasingly finding its way into the educational lexicon as a result of several teen suicides that were attributed at least in part to bully-ing, (Ollore, 2010). (*Source:* http://www.facebook.com/notes/inspire/teen-depression-and-suicide-reasearch-paper-i-wrote/187901821249294).

Methodology

The study was conducted using a content analysis method, in which the facebook status updates of 30 teenagers were analyzed for the months of October, November and December 2011 and January 2012. These teenagers were followed online daily to read and assess the content of their posts and status updates. Among the 30 teenagers followed 21 of them were heavy users of facebook, i.e., they were logged in to facebook more than once a day. Three others were visiting facebook at least once daily. Four of them were seen in facebook once in two or three days and that too for a very limited time. The other two were not frequent visitors of facebook. They post something or change their status once in a month or so. These details about the usage patterns were obtained from the respondents through a mail.

Analysis and Findings

The Study reveals that many of the teenagers are talking mainly to their friends regularly through social media sites. Some of them talk with their distant relatives too. Here, the cases of chat options are not taken into account. There was not much talk (in the form of posts) about the members of or issues in their families. Instead many were seen having interactions with friends or classmates through social media. Only very few had talks with their parents or family members using the social media platform. This was particularly seen in the case of teenagers whose parents or siblings are abroad. More than 80% of the teenagers had status updates related to their own thoughts or states of mind. They also have status updates related to their friends. But only less than 10% of the teenagers had status updates connected with their parents and family members. Their updates related to family were mainly about the family outings and pilgrimages or family functions like marriage.

Subjects of Status Updates

Teenagers had a wide range of subjects for their status updates. It ranged from their inner thoughts (most number of entries) to the family outings (least number of entries). Here we display them according to their ranks in the Teenagers' Status Updates.

1. **About their inner thoughts**: The most common subject of their status updates were their own inner thoughts in the form of poetry or prose or some simple phrases. Again there were different subjects for their thoughts. Some of them had written on the natural calamities, some others on the plight of their own life, some on ways in which God takes their life through and some others on an imaginary world of theirs.

   "My new year resolution is to make better bad decisions"

   "Loneliness is d most difficult and pain staking period in our lifetime. I think nw 'm having somebody 2 get rid of d situation! Most of d time if v hav any bitter xperiencez, n if v r alone it will make our mind perplexed n could b doing some thing crazy. It wil b always make our mind lighter wen v share our difficulties to other, so that @ least v could get some relaxation 4 that situation.)"

2. **Philosophy of Life**: teenagers have their own philosophy of life. They view life in a different angle. There were many quotes posted as status updates. There were quotes from great philosophers, hit music albums, dialogues in their favourite movies or from some books they read.

   "Sometimes, you really just don't know what to say. Because, what you really want to say; is something that you just cannot say."

   "some one askd god "If everything is already written in destiny, thn y sholud we wish for somthing?" God smiled and said may b in few places i have written "AS YOU WISH"

   "Hopes keeps on life going...on and on and oon..."

3. **About the boredom of studies and exams**: Another usual theme of comments was regarding the boredom of studies. The repetition of studies and exams make them think that they cannot have an escape from this. Somebody commented:

   "Class, tuition, study, exams….. it is a vicious circle…. When can I get out of this?"

   "I love my facebook…..but I don't like to face my book"

4. **About their friends**: another major subject was their friends. They discussed openly about many of their friends with or without mentioning their names. In case of appreciation they mentioned their friends' names. If it was for open criticism, they used some clues which gave others an indication about the name of the 'friend' in question.

   "realizing lyf wot i am, i am totally imperfect

   thankz to ma frndz

   they r helpin me understand thingz..........!!!!!!!!!!"

   "I may lose something today I may get anything else tomorrow. But, I can never lose ... and ever get one thing and thats 'YOU' So, be d bst f minE !!"

   "going to miss all of u....................:(....................can`t belive i have to stay for 10 days wid out seeing or talking to u guys..:"

5. **About their love failures**: Love failure was a leading subject for both boys and girls. Many had the courage to openly discuss their romantic life. Many were seen asking for help from others who are regarded as 'experts' in this field. Many were sad that their love life didn't click as they wanted.

   "Missing someone special in life is only due to two reasons♥ "Either that person was always with you" ♥OR ♥ "You always wanted to be with that person"

   "I love how I am loved by the person I love. :) ♥♥♥"

   "If You Can't FOrget YOur 'EX' YOu Will Never Trust YOur 'next'"

6. **Life Sucks**: Many comments were seen in a melancholic note which says that *"life sucks"*. Many of the teenagers seem to be affected badly by even a very simple incident in their lives. They were not able to digest certain dialogues by their friends or parents. Many teenagers who posted many things good about their friends and school/college were seen on a negative tone when speaking about their family issues. There was a comment:

"I am not lazy i am highly motivated to do NOTHING :D"
"fone bill jus came!!!!!! no fone again.....n gt busted by princi.........awsum..."

7. **About Freedom**: One of the major complaints the teenagers post in the facebook pages is their lack of freedom even in their personal matters. Teenagers would love to have freedom at least in deciding what to wear. When parents make decisions even on dressing styles, they feel that they are regarded as little kids. On the Republic Day one of the respondents put a status update which brought out all these emotions. The post read like this:

   "what republic? what independence? who is independent? I am not any way....don't know when I can be independent????"

8. **Eating out with friends**: There were pictures and comments posted about their outing with friends and having food from some leading restaurants. There were pictures of friends having a cup of tea and snacks from a local tea shop on the way side too. Many had the courage to post their pictures in front toddy shops or beverage stores.

   "love those MOMENTS buddies...after the school days these will be the only MEMORIES...."

9. **About the school days**: Once they left the school they started commenting on the glorious days in the school. Only when they started studying in some colleges many of them could realize the beauty of the school days. Most of them confessed that they were posting bad comments about the school when they were in the school. There was a comment put by some of the respondents in another respondent's page when the former commented about the agony of finishing the school life. The comment went like this:

   "Only when you come out of this school you will realise that it was not a school but a real COLLEGE".

10. **About a Sports star they like**: There were many who made status updates about Sachin's 100th century. Many were seen sad because he couldn't achieve the feat in Australia. A leading 'online war' was between the fans of cricket icon Sachin Tendulkar and his Australian counterpart Ricky Ponting. There were slogans in favour of Tendulkar saying:

    "East or west Sachin is the best....Day or Night Ponting is to Rest"

11. **About a film they watched**: There were many discussions related to the performance of their favourite stars in a recently released movie. There were fights even in the name of these super stars. Fans of one

star will attack the other star and his fans through pictures or comments. In Kerala an interesting online crusade is seen for Super stars Mammootty and Mohanlal. When the big budget Mohanlal film produced by the Confident Group turned out to be a flop in the theatres, the fans of Mammootty came up with posts and comments like:

"Confident Group has started new project of building toilets after the release of the film Casanova.......what a confidence??? OMG!!!"

12. **Family outings**: The last theme of discussion, according to the popularity or number of entries in the teenagers' posts, was related to their families. There were only very few comments or posts about the family members or their whereabouts. There were exceptions too. But in general the only updates about the family were the news or pictures of some family outing to some places of interest.

In all these updates, the youngsters revealed their mind and their attitude towards life. Though we may discard them as teenage talks, there were many comments with clear vision about life and world.

Specialties of the Updates

1. **Seems to be natural**: There were not many instances of artificiality in the comments and status updates of the teenagers. They seemed to be flowing from their inner hearts. This may be because they feel social media platforms are more secured or they are having an element of privacy in their talks here. They might have blocked the unwanted people (especially their parents or 'problematic' relatives) from seeing their comments and updates.
2. **Spontaneous responses to a life situation**: There was spontaneity to the responses. It is a specialty of the social media site itself. This spontaneity is seen not in the case of responses to certain comments by others but also in the case of certain life situations they are undergoing. They don't keep things for tomorrow. They settle accounts then and there.
3. **Not bothered about the after effects**: Whatever came to their minds they poured out as it is. They were not bothered about the consequences of their comments posted in the social media pages. This is one of the characteristic features of the adolescence. Elders may call it the teenager's carelessness or disrespect for others. But the teenager in turn might not have thought about it in that way. They just wanted to express themselves; and they did it in their own way.

4. **Expressing their original selves without fear**: One element seen in almost all the posts was that they were posted without any fear. This fearlessness can be seen as an outcome of the teenagers' urge to become an adult. This fearlessness again makes them post comments which in turn may cause some troubles later.
5. **Ready to ask for forgiveness if they said /did something wrong**: The teenagers were ready to ask forgiveness if they think that they said or did something wrong. They were prompt in doing so especially if their words or comments hurt someone.
6. **Bold enough to discuss many things in public**: One of the interesting factors seen here is that there is no taboo for any subject. They discussed freely and openly about their sexual interests and crushes towards somebody. They found it convenient to discuss about their teachers, parents and friends.
7. **Melancholic in nature**: Though the charm and thrill of the teenage was seen in many comments, there was an underlying melancholic tone for many comments and updates. Many have commented about different subjects in a pessimistic way. They were cynic about the chance of attitude change in their parents.
8. **Basically Apolitical**: Teenagers in general seemed to be apolitical in their discussions and status updates. There were not many posts related to any of the political leaders except for some funny pictures which were shared as innocent jokes. Some teenagers who were residing in the northern part of India put some slogans in support of Anna Hazare for a few days. But there was no political inclination seen in any of these.

Conclusion

The facebook and its status update provision play very important role in the teenagers' socialization process today. They use this updating function to let others know about their whereabouts, what they are thinking or doing, what they like the most and what not. In this process they regard certain topics or subjects as more important compared to others. As it is evident from the findings more than 80% of the teenagers consider family as the least important factor to be added in the status update section. They were fearless in expressing themselves without being bothered about the consequences of their posts.

What can be the cause of such a phenomenon? As psychologists say adolescents tend to have their own 'personal fables' and they try to create more and more stories about themselves. And in all human beings there can be seen an ego-centric personality within the projected self. Here, the most important factor of status updates is the "inner thoughts" of the teenagers. This is a clear manifestation of the psychological concepts like personal fable and the ego centrism. These are two concepts which are part of the Adolescent Psycho Social Development theory.

Though we see many negative elements in these findings, we should accept that these are some of the true facts about social media usage of teenagers. There is no point in considering the social media or the teenagers' usage patterns of these media as something to be avoided. Instead what we need today is a better Social Media Culture, where everyone respects everyone.

This takes our attention to the fact that our teenagers are not having much freedom at home, in school or in the society. They cannot take their own decisions in many situations. They have to largely depend upon their parents. They need to vent their frustration somewhere and they find facebook as their best companion at least for the time being and at least for this catharsis.

References

Armsden, G.C. & Greenberg, M.T. (1987). The Inventory of peer and parent attachment: Individual relationships and their relationships to psychological well-being in adolescence. *Journla of Youth and Adolescence*, 16, 427 – 454.

Bauer, Laura. (2009). "Cyber Bullying case brings big changes". *Kansas City Star* 25 May.

Boyd, danah. (2011). Retrieved from http://digitalyouth.-ischool.berkeley.edu/book-friendship.

Cañaveral, Bernard. (2009). The ill effects of Media on Family Interactions: paper presented on The Symposium for Media and Family, Philipines.

Clandfield, Lindsay. (2011). Teen Talk: Does your status need an update? Retrieved from http://www.onestopenglish.com/teenagers/teen-talk/does-your-status-need-an-update/.

Douglas, William. (1996). The Fall From Grace: The Modern Family on Television. *Communication Research December* 1996 Vol. 23 no. 6 675-702.

Eaton, Nick. (2011). (Retrieved from http://blog.seattlepi.com/microsoft/2011/05/09/do-teens-of-the-facebook-generation-value-privacy/).

Hayes, Louise, Smart, Diana, Toumbourou, John, W. and Sanson, Ann. (2004). Research report no.10 2004, Parenting influences on adolescent alcohol use.

Livingstone, Sonia. (2007). Half a Century of Television in the Lives of Our Children, paper presented at the Department of Media and Communications at the London School of Economics and Political Science.

Loosle, J. & Anderson. (2011). Teen Depression and Suicide published in Inspire on March 2.

Noller, P. (1994). Relationships with parents in adolescence: Process and Outcome. In R Montemayor, G.R. Adams & T.P. Gullotta (Eds), Personal Relationships during Adolescence: *Advances in Adolescent Development* (Vol. 6, pp. 37 – 77). Thousand Oakes, CA: Sage.

Ollore, Michael. (2010). "Bullying and Teen Suicide: How do we adjust to School climate?". *Christian Sience Monitor*. 28 April.

Roberts, Foehr, Rideout and Brodie. (1999). Generation M: Media in the lives of 8-18 year olds. Retrived from https://docs. google.com/viewer?a=v&q=cache:jj4QHzw1RkcJ: www.kff.org /entmedia/upload/Generation-M-Media-in-the-Lives-of-8-18-Year-olds

Roger, Desmond. (2004). Television and Mediating Effects of Family Communication, 16-Oct.

Sydell, Laura. Retrieved from http://www.npr.org/2011/11/09/142166055/teen-study-social-media-is-positive-experience..

Wanner,C.S., (2006). e Teens: Teens and Technology: A Perfect Storm, in Television Quarterly, Retrieved from https://doc-08-94-docsviewer.googleusercontent.com/viewer/.

Wilson, B.J. (2008). The Mass Media and Family Communication. In A.L. Vangelisti (Ed.). *Handbook of Family Communication* (pp. 5-33). New Jersy: Lawrence Erlbaum Associates, Inc., Publishers.

Woodward, E.H., and Gridina, N. (2000). Media in the home in 2000: The Fifth Annual Survey of Parents and Children. Philadelphia: Annenberg.

Ypulse Research Status Update: Facebook Fatigue, (Retrieved from http://www.ypulse.com/ypulse-research-status-update-facebook-fatigue).

Retrieved from http://www.oppapers.com/essays/Adolescent
Relationships-With-Parents-And-Peers/502768.

Retrieved From http://www.aifs.gov.au/institute/pubs/res-report10/parentpeer.html.

Retrieved from http://www.facebook.com/notes/inspire/teen-depression-and-suicide-reasearch-paper-i-wrote/18790-1821249294.

Retrieved from http://www.onestopenglish.com/teenagers/teen-talk/does-your-status-need-an-update/.

Retrieved from *http://netaddictionrecovery.blogspot.com/.*

Retrieved from http://www.freeonlineresearchpapers.com/facebook-isnt-everybody))

Retrieved from http://www.facebook.com/notes/inspire/teen-depression-and-suicide-reasearch-paper-i-wrote/18790-1821249294.

Retrieved from http://withoutmedia.wordpress.com/.

6

The Relationship between Culture and Communication in the Context of Social Change and its Conflicts

Ms. Anjali Pundhir, Ms. Mridula Singh

> "Society is not merely a select body of spiritual or intellectual persons, but a great organism composed of all kinds of members, a net containing bad and good."
>
> *Robert Hugh Benson*

Indian society and culture are undergoing constant changes under the effects of globalisation which also bring rapid development in technology and communication. These changes are spreading innovative ideas, values, knowledge and producing a shift in society from industrialisation towards an information-based society. It reflects the effect on culture and brings about a new form of cultural imperialism. The rise of new cultural imperialism is shaping children, the future citizens of the world into 'global citizens', intelligent people with a broad range of skills and knowledge to apply to a competitive, information based society. The internationalisation of our society can be linked to various internal and external changes in the international system because of the advancement in technology and communicative skills.

Globalisation is a process, which has affected many areas of human life. It is an invaluable opportunity for the people of the developing countries to raise their skills in every possible field. Internet technology has an enormous impact on the globalisation of culture and ideas. It has considerably increased the speed of social change. It is also a valuable tool for *social change organisations*.

India contains a large number of different regional, social and economic groups, each with distinctive or dissimilar customs and cultural practices. Region-wise, differences between social structures of India's north and south are marked, especially with respect to kinship systems and family relationships. Religious differences are pervasive throughout the country. A highly noticeable feature of India's social structure is highly inequitable division of the nation's wealth. Access to wealth and power varies sharply. Extreme differences in socio-economic status are glaringly visible among the smallest village communities to metropolitan cities and mega-towns. The poor and the rich live side by side in urban and rural areas.

Prosperous, well-fed, perfumed men or women in chauf-feured luxury cars passing and even living in narrow streets with poor, starving, ill-nourished, ill-clad or even half-naked men, women, children dwelling on their pavements and bathing in dirty water of its flowing or even clogged drains are common sights. Contrasting extreme poverty and enormous wealth and obvious class distinctions are egregiously visible in almost every settlement in India.

Every individual expresses its thoughts and carries out its affairs through the medium of communication. It should be evident by now that the trends of globalization and informatisation have important implications at the foundational level of the society for intercultural communication which is highly influencing to our very understanding of culture, society, and communication.

A second significant issue associated with the convergence of global values, technology, and communication is the ability of technologies to truly fulfil the promises made for it, both in the encouragement of intercultural interaction as well as its effectiveness in the development of new political, social, or cultural movements.

Intercultural competence is the ability of successful communication with people of other cultures. A person who is inter-culturally competent captures and understands, in inter-action with people from foreign cultures, their specific concepts in perception, thinking, feeling and acting. Earlier experiences are considered, free from prejudices; there is an interest and motivation to continue learning.

"He who knows, does not speak. He who speaks, does not know."

Lao Tzu

Specifically, the issues of the impact of culture on computer-mediated communication and other communication issues, the effectiveness of communication technologies to actually fulfil some of the political and social promises made for them, and the role of intercultural communication skills for professional success.

Cross-cultural communication (also frequently referred to as intercultural communication, which is also used in a different sense, though) is a field of study that looks at how people from differing cultural backgrounds communicate, in similar and different ways among themselves, and how they endeavour to communicate across cultures. New communi-cations and information technologies have created a global revolution in communications, access to information, and media delivery.

"The way we communicate with others and with ourselves ultimately determines the quality of our lives."

Anthony Robbins

Aspects of Cross Cultural Communication

There are several parameters that may be perceived differently by people of different culture. These may include:

- High and Low Context Cultures: Culture is the most important dimension of any civilized society. Basically culture can be categorized into two dimensions: High and Low context cultures. Context refers as the stimuli, environment or ambiance surrounding the environ-ment. Low-context cultures assume that the individuals know very little about what they are being told, and therefore must be given a lot of background information. High-Context cultures assume the individual is know-ledgeable about the subject and has to be given very little background information.
- Non Verbal, Oral and Written: The main goal behind improving intercultural audiences is to pay special attention to specific areas of communication to enhance the effectiveness of the intercultural messages. These specific areas are broken down into three sub categories;

  (i) Non-Verbal,

  (ii) Oral

  (iii) Written messages.

In today's globalized environment, more and more of us are required to understand people who come from countries and cultures different from our own. While there is no short and easy way to learn about a given culture in any depth, there are some general principles that lead to success in communi-cating and conducting business with people of backgrounds unlike our own.

Cultures are always changing, especially as they interact with each other. Even from within, cultures move and flow and change through time, even when they think they don't. But the pace of change is accelerated when cultures that reinforces different styles of communication, and which accent different binding customs and values, interact with each other. The result is often disorienting to the societies which causes different kind of conflicts between an individual of different society.

Forms of Conflict

Conflict is the inherent incompatibility between the objectives of two or more characters or forces. By its nature, conflict is unstable. Conflict is competition by groups or individuals over incompatible goals, scarce resources, or the sources of power needed to acquire them. This competition is also determined by individuals' perceptions of goals, resources, and power and such perceptions may differ greatly amongst individuals. One determinant of perception is culture, the socially inherited, shared and learned ways of living possessed by individuals in virtue of their membership in social groups. Conflict that occurs across cultural boundaries thus is also occurring across cognitive and perceptual boundaries, and is especially susceptible to problems of intercultural miscommunication and misunderstanding. These problems exacerbate the conflict, no matter what the root causes of it—including strictly material interests—may be. In this sense culture is an important factor in many sorts of conflicts that at first may appear to be exclusively about material resources or negotiable interests.

Disagreement - Generally, we are aware there is some level of difference in the positions of the two (or more) parties involved in the conflict. But the true disagreement versus the perceived disagreement may be quite different from one another. In fact, conflict tends to be accompanied by significant levels of misunderstanding that exaggerate the perceived disagreement considerably. If we can understand the true areas of disagreement, this will help us solve the right problems and manage the true needs of the parties.

Parties involved - There are often disparities in our sense of who is involved in the conflict. Sometimes, people are surprised to learn they are a party to the conflict, while other times we are shocked to learn we are not included in the disagreement. On many occasions, people who are seen as part of the social system (e.g., work team, family, company) are influenced to participate in the dispute, whether they would personally define the situation in that way or not. In the above example, people very readily "take sides" based upon current perceptions of the issues, past issues and relationships, roles within the organization, and other factors. The parties involved can become an elusive concept to define.

Perceived threat - People respond to the perceived threat, rather than the true threat, facing them. Thus, while perception doesn't become reality but people behaviours, feelings and ongoing responses become modified by that evolving sense of the threat they confront. If we can work to understand the true threat (issues) and develop strategies (solutions) that manage it (agreement), we are acting constructively to manage the conflict.

Needs, interests or concerns - There is a tendency to narrowly define "the problem" as one of substance, task, and near-term viability. However, workplace conflicts tend to be far more complex than that, for they involve ongoing relationships with complex, emotional components. Simply stated, there are always procedural needs and psychological needs to be addressed within the conflict, in addition to the substantive needs that are generally presented and the durability of the interests and concerns of the parties transcends the immediate presenting situation.

Intercultural communication principles guide the process of exchanging meaningful and unambiguous information across cultural boundaries, in a way that preserves mutual respect and minimizes antagonism. For these purposes, culture is a shared system of symbols, beliefs, attitudes, values, expectations, and norms of behaviour.

Improvements in communication and transportation technology have made it possible for previously stable cultures to meet in unstructured situations, e.g. the internet opens lines of communication without mediation, while budget air-lines transplant ordinary citizens into unfamiliar *milieux*. Experience proves that merely crossing cultural boundaries can be considered threatening, while positive attempts to interact may provoke defensive responses. Misunderstanding may be compounded by either an exaggerated sensitivity to possible insight, or an exaggerated and over-protective fear of giving offence; some groups believe that the phenomenon of globalisation has reduced cultural diversity and so reduced the opportunity for misunderstandings. One product or brand.

What can go wrong?

People from different cultures encode and decode messages differently, increasing the chances of misunderstanding, so the first step for safety should be the assumption that everyones thoughts are different. Wrong thoughts that stem from potentially devastating ignorance and can lead to much frustration for members of both cultures. Entering a culture with this type of ethnocentrism, the assumption your own culture is correct, is another by product of ignorance and cultural misunderstanding. Main types of misunderstanding are: –

Rights, Values and Needs

Some cultural characteristics will be easy to identify, e.g. whether people are conscious of status or make displays of material wealth. But many rights are assumed, values are implied, and needs are unspoken, (e.g. for safety, security, love, a sense of belonging to a group, self-esteem, and the ability to attain one's goals).

For example, issues of personal security, dignity, and control will be very different as between able and a disabled person. Similarly, there may be problems of respect when a person from a rigidly class-based culture meets a meritocratic, or where there is racism, sexism or religious intolerance in play. In such situations, identity is fundamental when disputing the proper role or "place" of the other, about who is in control of their lives, and how they present themselves to the outside world. But the reality is more deeply rooted in power relationships: about who is on top of the social, economic, and/or political hierarchy. Family members or long term rivals may be obsessed with their mutual competition. The relationships between racial or ethnic groups may be affected by economic jealousy. Nations may assert that their political systems are superior. Such conflicts are difficult to resolve because no-one wants to be the loser, and few are willing to share the winnings. Stereotyping can aggravate these problems and prevent people from realising that there is another way to interpret a situation, or that other groups may define their rights in a different way. Hence, what may appear just or fair to one group can often seem *unjust* to an opposing group.

Improving Intercultural Communication

It is essential that people research the cultures and communication conventions of those whom they propose to meet. This will minimize the risk of making the elementary mistakes. It is also prudent to set a clear agenda so that every-one understands the nature and purpose of the interaction. When language skills are unequal, clarifying one's meaning in five ways will improve communication:

1. Avoid using slang and idioms, choosing words that will convey only the most specific *denotative* meaning;
2. Listen carefully and, if in doubt, ask for confirmation of understanding (particularly important if local accents and pronunciation are a problem);
3. Recognize that accenting and intonation can cause meaning to vary significantly; and
4. Respect the local communication formalities and styles, and watch for any changes in body language.
5. Investigate their culture's perception of your culture by reading literature about your culture through their eyes before entering into communication with them. This will allow you to prepare yourself for projected views of your culture you will be bearing as a visitor in their culture.

Social Issues

By cultural factors we refer mainly to ideas, knowledge, values, beliefs, inventions and exchange. Culture provides the base for inventions and discoveries.

Social systems are directly or indirectly the creations of cultural values. Any change in values or belief systems on the part of social group affect social institutions. New social values and beliefs can also produce social change.

Nowadays India is facing various social, cultural, educational, economical, political and environmental issues. Media and other communicative technologies played a very vital role in making people concerned with all these issues.

Over Population

Many people in different profession began to recognize that there may well be too many beings in the world. Is it possible that the dominant species has been too successful for its own good? History has shown that human beings are ingenious and adaptable. But sometimes human activities have pressed against and exceeded environmental limits. The traditional *Malthusian* view also follows the same track. According to *Malthus* an unchecked population growth leads to a heavy degradation in the quality of life and ultimately checked by rising mortality. In the twentieth century this argument has been extended to the availability of energy and minerals, the effect of rising environmental pollution, and so on. In *The Limits to Growth,*Though it is believed that there are no real natural resource limits, because population growth itself brings the adjustments that continually put off the doomsday.

Poverty

Poverty is "pronounced deprivation in well-being." The conventional view links well-being primarily to command over commodities, so the poor are those who do not have enough income or consumption to put them above some adequate minimum threshold. This view sees poverty largely in monetary terms. Poverty may also be tied to a specific type of consumption; thus someone might be house poor or food poor or health poor. These dimensions of poverty can often be measured directly, for instance by measuring malnutrition or literacy.

Corruption: Causes, Consequences and Cures

There is a growing worldwide concern over corruption at the present time. Several factors are responsible for this. First, a consensus has now been reached that corruption is universal. It exists in all countries, both developed and developing, in the public and private sectors, as well as in non-profit and charitable organisations. Second, allegations and charges of corruption now play a more central role in politics than at any other time. Governments have fallen careers of world renowned public figures ruined, and reputations of well-respected organisations and business firms badly tarnished on account of it.

The international mass media feeds on it and scandals and improper conduct, especially of those in high places, are looked upon as extremely newsworthy, and to be investigated with zeal and vigour. The rising trend in the use of corruption as a tool to discredit political opponents, the media's preoccupation with it as a highly marketable commodity, and the general public' fascination with seeing prominent personalities in embarrassing situations have brought scandalous and corrupt behaviour, a common human frailty, into the limelight of international attention.

Third – and the main issue is that corruption can be a major obstacle in the process of economic development and in modernising a country. Many now feel that it should receive priority attention in a country's development agenda. This greater recognition that corruption can have a serious adverse impact on development has been a cause for concern among developing countries. Countries in the Asia and Pacific region are also very worried about this problem and they are in substantial agreement that corruption is a major constraint that is hindering their economic, political and social development, and hence view it as a problem requiring urgent attention at the highest level.

There are still wide gaps in the current state of information and knowledge on the matter and much more remains to be done. Nevertheless, theoretical and empirical research that has been conducted thus far has yielded fresh insights into the problem. We now have a clearer understanding of the underlying causes of corruption, its consequences, and ideas and approaches on possible measures to combat it. At the same time, a better perspective has been obtained on the reasons why corruption persists in so many countries, and why it is difficult to deal with, although people throughout the world view it with disfavor. Against corruption society awakened by the revolt of Anna Hazare on Jan Lok Pal Bill.

Terrorism

"The terrible thing about terrorism is that ultimately it destroys those who practise it. Slowly but surely, as they try to extinguish life in others, the light within them dies".

Terry Waite, London

Terrorism is a very big issue in front of our country as well as other nations of the world. The term "international terrorism" means terrorism involving citizens or the territory of more than one country. The intention of terrorists is to cause fear and terror among a target audience rather than the harm caused to the immediate victims.

Impact of Terrorism on Society and Economy

Terrorism poses a serious law and order problem and leads to disintegration of society. The incident of murder, torture, mutilation, kidnapping, arson and extortion create atmosphere of suspicion, fear and panic all around. Life becomes uncertain. The terrorists kill unarmed civilians including women and children.

Organised crime and violence cause social disharmony. The inter relationship among various insurgent groups and their foreign linkages bring illegal money and encourages smuggling. Many insurgent groups collect certain percentage of money from the employees and businessmen on regular basis. Economic development of the area comes to an end. Our government has to make heavy expenditure to meet the challenges of terrorism. The media reports contribute to the "fear factor" experienced by the public during and after a terrorist events.

Caste based Discrimination

More than 160 million people in India are considered "Untouchable"—people tainted by their birth into a caste system that deems them impure, less than human. Discriminatory and cruel, inhuman, and degrading treatment of a vast global population has been justified on the basis of caste. Caste imposes enormous obstacles to their full attainment of civil, political, economic, social, and cultural rights. Caste is descent-based and hereditary in nature. It is a characteristic determined by one's birth into a particular caste, irrespective of the faith practiced by the individual. Caste denotes a system of rigid social stratification into ranked groups defined by descent and occupation. Under various caste systems throughout the world, caste divisions also dominate in housing, marriage, and general social interaction-divisions that are reinforced through the practice and threat of social ostracism, economic boycotts, and even physical violence. These communities share many features; features that have allowed even the most appalling practices to escape international scrutiny.

Sanitation

Lack of sanitation is one of the biggest problems in the developing nations like India. Officially it has been given some priority, but for common people it seems something remote, something that doesn't have anything to do with them. But it affects each and everybody. If any strata of our society remains poorly sanitized, it may physically or socially contaminate the whole society.

For basic sanitation, Government of India will have to ensure that public funds are allocated principally to the promotion and stimulation of demand

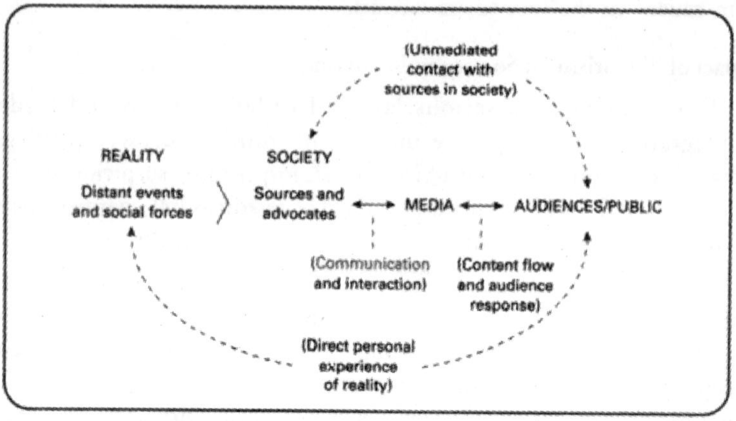

www.schulersolutions.com/cross_cultural_communication.html

for sanitation. Public financing for sewage, drainage, and wastewater treatment and garbage is warranted, as they produce benefits for society as a whole, as well as better services to households.

Media: Creator and Destructor of Society

In today's world Media is changing and shaping people's beliefs and system in both the ways. Therefore it is a major element of the social change movement.

Older technologies, like television and cable are now combined with modern technologies to create new ways of delivering information, news, and entertainments. Information, Education and Communication (IEC) is dealing with bridging with the digital divide, gender divide and knowledge using different communication tools at different levels.

Media develops in response to the contact and interaction between human beings and their material, social and intellectual environment.

In the modern world inspite of cultural diversity at international level, the work culture, socio-economic policies of various nations have shown uniformity to a great extent. And thus created an atmosphere of unity in diversity. the "Global Village" has created theoretical and practical awareness towards diversified cultures. knowing each other's cultures and respecting emotions, belief and traditions of other. it's a proof of global understanding. this is Cultural Senstiveness. Cultural Consciousness depends on the values, beliefs and traditions of various communities.

Media on macro scale, shape all of our major social institutions (economics, politics, religion, family, education, science/technology, military, legal system, and so on. On a micro scale, it shapes our values, attitudes, beliefs and behaviors. In sum, it influences our ways of life tremendously.

Now a days the word Media has been changed and it becomes The New media. It has changed the world dramatically. The new media has changed the social behavior of human in terms of information, communication, and entertainment. Newspapers, magazines, paper journals and books were the old media of information. However, due to the grace of technology and internet, people replace the old media and start using e-words. The means of information are digital, such as, e-news, e-books, blogs, and e-magazines. The information in new media can be shared and redistributed among millions of people. In terms of communication, in old media we use post mails, radio, and TV. However, people communicate lively on chat, Skype, messenger, VOIP, cell phones, and other digital medias. Both the sender and receiver are actively participate in communicating. The social networking sites has changed the communication among the people socially as it is way easier to communicate with people. People can view the favorite programs whenever they want. You tube and other live videos sites are great contribution in terms of entertainment in new media in society.

On the contrary When you try to imitate your role models of the glamour industry, are you thoughtful enough to distinguish between the right and the wrong? It is often seen that young girls and boys imitate their role models blindly. The negative things the celebrities do are often talked about. The controversies in the lives of the celebrities are often highlighted by the media. This leads to a blind imitation of what appears in the news.

Media often hypes the scintillating things about the celebrities. The negatives in society are highlighted with an intent to awaken the people about the society of the modern days. But this hype is actually having a negative effect on society. Masses are seeing only the negatives around them. Controversies are constantly being bombarded on them.

Some say that it is media to be blamed for the eating disorders in the youths of society as also for the unhealthy lifestyle that has recently emerged. Be it television, magazines or the Internet, media is almost omnipresent, affecting various aspects of our life. The products advertised by the media and the ways they are advertised are bound to affect the practices of our livelihood.

The negative effects of media on children are manifested in terms of their changing mental setup and the declining quality of their lifestyle. Children, who should invest their time in reading good books, studying, playing outdoors, exercising and engaging in social activities, today, spend their evenings glued to the television. The Internet that is easily accessible to even small children exposes them to things they need not know and will not understand.

The negative psychological effects of media are seen in terms of media changing the people's outlook of looking towards life. Media being one of the prominent sources of looking at the outside world has changed the cultural and moral values of society. A majority of the audiences believe in what is depicted by the media. Many think all of it as true. Youngsters and children are bound to mix the reel and the real world and get highly influence by the media.

Sexual exploitation of women and children is a global human rights crisis that is being escalated by the use of new technologies. Using new technologies, sexual predators and pimps stalk women and children. New technical innovations facilitate sexual exploitation of women and children because they enable people to easily buy, sell and exchange millions of images and videos of sexual exploitation of women and children.

The Critical Analysis

Unlike the skill or attitude that may be specific to a particular physical activity or social context, values tend to be more universal in their application. They express in everything we do. Values can be described as the essence of the knowledge gained by humanity from past experiences distilled from its local circumstances and specific context to extract the fundamental wisdom of life derived from these experiences. Values give direction to our thought processes, sentiments, emotional energies, preferences, and actions.

In this article we have attempted, from a general perspective, to address the issue of how culture is conceptualiseds and manifests itself in the application of qualitative research methodology to cross-cultural and intercultural communication. Despite the numerous definitions of culture it can be asserted that the conceptualisation applied in cross-cultural and intercultural communication studies is characterised by its complexity, dynamism and inter-subjective character, and that in this conceptualization it is possible to identify a multiplicity of components of which the individual is not always aware. It has become clear throughout this article that culture constantly makes its presence felt in the research process, and especially in the context of qualitative research, starting with the theoretical-epistemological foundations of such research, as well as in the process of approaching and generating empirical data and in its analysis and interpretation.

The media's role in contributing to cognitive, attitudinal and behavioural change on a large scale is unique. Conflict prevention and peace building professionals can use the media in harmony with their other programmes – if they know when, why, and how to use the media for the most strategic impact in lessening the polarization between groups. On the other hand, media professionals still have much to learn about why and when their work can contribute to preventing violent conflict and building peace between groups. The media and peace professionals both have their limitations and share an interest in the dynamism of conflicts.

So the challenges of the current developments of globalisation open some new ways in front of media and communication. These crucial developments have coincided with the electronic revolution together which have transformed communication media tremendously. Media plays very important role in shaping the society in this era of explosion of Information Technology. It is media, which can give new heights of the society and make it more progressive so that our nation will be able to get very suitable place in the international arena.

Hence we can say that in Indian society Media is a major component to resolve the conflicts and communication-gaps. Education is helping us in turning into a civilized society and media is providing definite structure by acting like a backbone.

References

Altheide DL (1991) The Impact of Television News Formats on Social Policy. Journal of Broadcasting and Electronic Media 35: 3-21.

Alatas, Hussein S., 1999. *Corruption and the Destiny of Asia* (Singapore, Simon and Schuster (Asia) Pvt. Ltd.).

Geoffrey Nunberg (October 28, 2001). "Head Games / It All Started with Robespierre / "Terrorism": The history of a very frightening word". San Francisco Chronicle. http://articles.sfgate.com/2001-10-28/opinion/17622543_ 1_terrorism-robespierre-la-terreur. Retrieved 2010-01-11.

Grabe ME, Zhou S, Barnett B (2001) Explicating Sensationalism in Television News: Content and the Bells and Whistles of Form. Journal of Broadcasting and Electronic Media 45:635-655.

Haralambos, M and Holborn, M (2004). *Sociology: themes and perspectives.* London: Harper Collins Publishers Ltd.

James Alfred Aho. 1990. Politics of Righteousness: Idaho Christian Patriotism. Washington: University of Washington Press. ISBN 0295969970.

Kiltgaard, Robert, 1998. "International cooperation cooperation against corruption", IMF/World Bank, *Finance and Development,* 35(1): 3.

Kitsantas, A. (2004). Studying abroad: the role of college students' goals on the development of cross-cultural skills and global understanding. *College Student Journal,* 38(3). Retrieved July 9, 2007 from ERIC database.

Meadows, Donella H., and others, *The Limits to Growth: A Report for the Club of Rome's Project on the Predicament of Mankind,* New York: Universe Books, 1972.

Planning Commission of India. "Health and Family Welfare and AYUSH : 11th Five Year Plan".http://planningcommission.nic.in/plans/planrel/fiveyr/11th/11_v2/11v2_ ch3.pdf. Retrieved 19 September 2010, p. 78.

Pressat, R., *Dictionary of Demography,* Paris: Blackwell Reference, 1985.

Schramm, W. (1954). How communication works. In W. Schramm (Ed.), *The process and effects of communication* (pp. 3-26). Urbana, Illinois: University of Illinois Press.

World Bank, 1998. *World Development Report 1998* (New York, Oxford University Press); table 1, pp. 190-191.

7

POKE ME: Social Networking Sites; A Weapon, A Threat and A Target

Yashaswee Bharadwaj

Why people prefer Social Networking sites is the biggest research topic nowadays and from past studies we came to the conclusion that through social networking, people can use networks of online friends and group memberships to keep in touch with current friends, reconnect with old friends or create real–life friendships through similar interests or groups. Besides establishing important social relationships, social networking members can share their interests with other like–minded members by joining groups and forums. Some networking sites can also help members find a job or establish business contacts.

Most social networking websites also offer additional features. In addition to blogs and forums, members can express themselves by designing their profile page to reflect their personality. The most popular extra features include music and video sections. Members can read bios of their favorite music artists from the artist's profile page as well as listen to their favorite songs and watch music videos. The video section can include everything from member–generated videos from hundreds of subjects to TV clips and movie trailers.

Today the popularity and use of social networking sites is at its peak and at this stage of penetration social networking is not just a medium but today it can be use as a weapon, a threat or as a target because "Social networking will change the nature of warfare just as surely as the telegraph, the radio and the telephone did", does that states that social networking is a new battle ground? That only terrorists and bad guys use social media and using it to promote your company would send the wrong message, which was the old saying about guns in its initial days of use.

Its all about the perception and psychology of an individual that he or she must decide how to use the power of social networking, it has positive influence if used with positive intensions and even adverse effect if use in a negative way.

Weapon

It is difficult to ignore the impact of social networking on the legal industry. Social networking has become an indispensible tool for many career-related activities such as job-hunting, networking, sharing knowledge and marketing your services. More recently, lawyers, paralegals, investigators and other professionals have turned to social networking in seek of more opportunity. Social Networking is an open platform to express and share one's view. There is no boundation as such and this right of expression can be used in raising voice against injustice and other activities which are unethical and against the law.

Social networking as a weapon can be understood by the current trend of raising voice against unjust acts of either some individual or of the government.

Threat

As the availability of social networking is very easy, just because of this quality of social networking sites it is used in other way also by terrorist and other bad guys to promote their company and expand their empire, its also used for requirement in their company and the seriousness of this issue has to be considered else it will be too late to react on it.

Social Networking as a threat can be understood by the example set by US Army which is likely to be adopted by Indian Army very soon, i.e.

The Indian Army has reportedly asked all its personnel to quit social networking websites with immediate effect. It has directed them to refrain from joining social networking websites including Facebook, Orkut, and Google+ in future too. The move comes as an effort to "safeguard the well-being" of army personnel.

According to sources, the Indian Army had been monitoring the social networking activities of its officers to find out if they posted uniformed photos of themselves, weaponry, or other units for the past few months. It has now decided to issue a blanket ban on all such websites throughout the ranks. It is not yet clear if the army will rely on self-censorship to be practised by its men or if it will restrict access at its end. Howcver, it has been said that violations to this directive will be dealt with strictly.

Incidentally, it is not only the Indian Army that has imposed such restrictions. A couple of days ago, US Army personnel were also advised by their top brass to exercise restring in using FB. It has been posited that this information can be used by terrorist organizations such as Al Qaeda to target army units. They suggested certain strategies, duplicated below:

Adjust the privacy settings to Only Me or Friends.

Remove any personally identifiable data that gives away too much information about you or your family.

Avoid sharing details about bases and capabilities by not posting photos of or details about formations, quarters, armored vehicles, and \ or weapons.

Disable the GPS feature on your mobile device or turn off tagging or tracking applications on your Facebook account that give your exact location.

Educate yourself, your friends and your family about what is and isn't safe to share on Facebook or any other social networking platform.

These measures could also apply to the Indian armed forces in order to secure themselves against terrorist elements. Indeed, it would be a better way to go, rather than issuing a total ban on social networking. That being said, there is a difference between how the internet is viewed by both armies. This is evident from the fact that the US Army has an official FB page, while the Indian Army does not.

Target

The popularity and use of social networking sites is on height of its penetration and due to its easy availability it attracts the mass audience. There are different sets of segment of audience but these sites have been such designed and are modified from time to time according to the requirement that they focuses on all set of segments and in whole targets everyone who ever is possible and in result succeed in doing so.

By help of this special and specific group of peoples can be also targeted, as they can divided in different segments in terms of age, profession etc and according to the need target can be set and can be used in every possible way.

Social networking sites are used as target can be understood with the example of Linkedin.com, which is a professional social site generally used for recruitments of employees in different fields according to the needs and wants.

Conclusion

"SOCIAL NETWORKING IS JUST A TOOL AFTER ALL BUT IS MIGHTIER THAN THE SWORD", this is not just a statement but is the reality of the power of influence of social networking on the perception of mass audience. Social Networking has positive influence else well as can have adverse effect on an individual's psychology depending upon the perception of that individual. Social Networking can be used in every possible way depending upon the needs, wants and desire for the outcome.

References

Top 15 Most Popular Social Networking Sites, February 2012.

Alexa Global Traffic Rank, and U.S. Traffic Rank.

How Social Networks Can Both Help and Harm Our Kids, by Larry D. Rosen, PhD, California State University, Dominguez Hills.

Social Media: The Three Big Myths, by Blaise James and Jim Asplund.

U.S. Army's official page on Facebook.

8

Social Concern's and Role of Media: With Reference to Conversion Disorder

Sonali Sengar, Neha Gupta, Abid Rizvi and Prashanta Kumar Pal

Introduction

Conversion disorder is a psychological disorder which falls under the category of somatoform disorders. This disorder is neurological in nature and is spurred by a stressful event. Considering that it is a somatoform disorder there are physical symptoms that manifest themselves with no obvious causes. Conversion disorder is a neurosis marked by the appearance of physical symptoms such as partial loss of muscle function without physical cause but in the presence of psychological conflict.

Symptoms include numbness, blindness, paralysis, or fits without a neurological cause. It is thought that these problems arise in response to difficulties in the patient's life, and conversion is considered a psychiatric disorder in the Diagnostic and Statistical Manual of Mental Disorders 4th edition (DSM-IV).

Formerly known as "hysteria", the disorder has arguably been known for millennia, though it came to greatest prominence at the end of the 19th century, when the neurologists Jean-Martin Charcot and Sigmund Freud and psychiatrist Pierre Janet focused their studies on the subject. The term "conversion" has its origins in Freud's doctrine that anxiety is "converted" into physical symptoms. Though previously thought to have vanished from the west in the 20th century, some research has suggested it is as common as ever. In summary, conversion disorder is a challenging psychiatric disorder that requires a careful clinical approach. In particular, in developing countries the present situation may be somewhat different to what is normally described in texts. Clinicians in developing world settings should be wary of the differences in presentations of conversion disorder. Further research is needed to fill information gaps in this somewhat baffling condition.

Symptoms

The symptoms of conversion disorder can vary in their severity and frequency. They can be categorized under many different symptoms and their longevity is also dependent on the physical appearance. Sensory issues are present in a loss of sensation such as tingling, blurred vision, or even blindness. The loss of sensation can appear in extremities or in the head and can be temporary or become a long lasting neuropathy. Paralysis can also occur which exceeds an episode of numbness or imbalance. Temporary blindness can be a symptom experienced in rare cases as well. Aside from sensory issues, motor dysfunction is also a concern as imbalance, delays in mobility, severe shaking, or even tics can be signs of conversion disorder. Visceral manifestations present themselves in uncontrollable fits of coughing, throat restrictions, and vomiting. Seizures, deafness, and even the inability to speak are all additional signs of the disorder and can be mistaken symptoms because of their sudden appearance.

Causes

This psychological disorder is caused by a stressful event or environment and promotes physical symptoms which can range in severity depending on the level of trauma. Emotional imbalance or hysteria can often trigger an episode which results in physical responses and are considered to be at the minor end of the spectrum. More severe experiences such as witnessing a tragedy or cases of abuse can be identified as extreme means which generate physical responses that can prove to be debilitating. Considering that conversion disorder is psychological in disposition, depression, and other common psychological disorders often accompany this illness. These factors compound the disorder and can lead to misdiagnosis. Repressed memories, inability to cope with stress, personality disorders, and phobias can also lead to episodes where the physical responses are prevalent. An example would be if someone has a fear of speaking in public, their voice would weaken or even cease to produce sound as a response to their fear.

Statics Related To Conversion Disorder

Karachi: Patients with conversion disorder (n=109) represented 5.1% of the 2120 psychiatric admissions over the study period. Of the 97 records available for review, there were Major depressive disorder was the most common psychiatric diagnosis, seen in 40% of patients, followed by personality disorder (7%), anxiety (5%), adjustment disorder (3%), psychosis (1%), acute stress reactions (1%), and bipolar disorder (1%). A majority (79%) of patients recovered from symptoms during their hospital stay, while 7% continued to have symptoms at the time of discharge. In 13 cases (13%), status of symptoms at discharge could not be ascertained. Organic illness was diagnosed in 6 patients during hospital stay and in another 4 patients after discharge. Seventy two per cent of patients were discharged after completing hospital stay. However 11% left against medical advice prematurely, while 6% were discharged on request. In all, 43% of patients were lost to follow up.

This presents a variety of statistics about Conversion Disorder. The term 'prevalence' of Conversion Disorder usually refers to the estimated population of people who are managing Conversion Disorder at any given time. The term 'incidence' of Conversion Disorder refers to the annual diagnosis rate, or the number of new cases of Conversion Disorder diagnosed each year. Hence, these two statistics types can differ: a short-lived disease like flu can have high annual incidence but low prevalence, but a life-long disease like diabetes has a low annual incidence but high prevalence.

India: The clinical profile, commonly involved precipitating factors, comorbid conditions, treatment options and outcome of conversion disorder in 40 children in a tertiary level hospital in North India were studied, retrospectively. Majority of the patients were from rural India. Most common presenting symptom was psychogenic non-epileptic seizures; depression and anxiety were among the commonest comorbid conditions. Precipitating factors were predominantly scholastic problems. Treatment option included either psychotherapy only or combination of psychotherapy and pharmacotherapy. No significant difference was found in terms of outcome between the in-patient and out-patient treatment groups. This observation could be cost effective for developing countries like India, where the resources are very limited.

The *Diagnostic and Statistical Manual for Mental Disorders, Fourth Edition, Text Revision (DSM-IV-TR)* includes a specific category for somatic symptoms related to psychiatric origins called the somatoform disorders. Specific somatoform disorders include (1) somatization disorder, (2) conversion disorder, (3) pain disorder, (4) hypochondriasis, and (5) body dysmorphic disorder. Somatization disorder is a relatively rare disorder that is associated with high medical resource utilisation. More common somatization syndromes may not reach the diagnostic threshold for somatization disorder but may be clinically and functionally significant.

Conversion Disorder At Different Stages of Life

The lifetime prevalence rates of conversion disorder in the general U.S. population are estimated to fall between 11 and 300 per 100,000 people.

The differences in the estimates reflect differences in the method of diagnosis as well as some regional population differences. In terms of clinical populations, conversion disorder is diagnosed in 5%–14% of general hospital patients; 1%–3% of outpatient referrals to psychiatrists; and 5%–25% of psychiatric outpatients.

Among adults, women diagnosed with conversion disorder outnumber men by a 2:1 to 10:1 ratio; among children, however, the gender ratio is closer to 1:1. Less educated people and those of lower socio-economic status are more likely to develop conversion disorder; race by itself does not appear to be a factor. There is, however, a major difference between the populations of developing and developed countries; in developing countries, the prevalence of conversion disorder may run as high as 31%.

The doctor can also use a list of factors known to be associated with conversion disorder to assess the likelihood that a specific patient may have the disorder:

- Age. Conversion disorder is rarely seen in children younger than six years or adults over 35 years.
- Sex. The female to male ratio for the disorder ranges between 2:1 and 10:1. It is thought that higher rates of conversion disorder in women may reflect the greater vulnerability of females to abuse.
- Residence. People who live in rural areas are more likely to develop conversion disorder than those who live in cities.
- Level of education. Conversion disorder occurs less often among sophisticated or highly educated people.

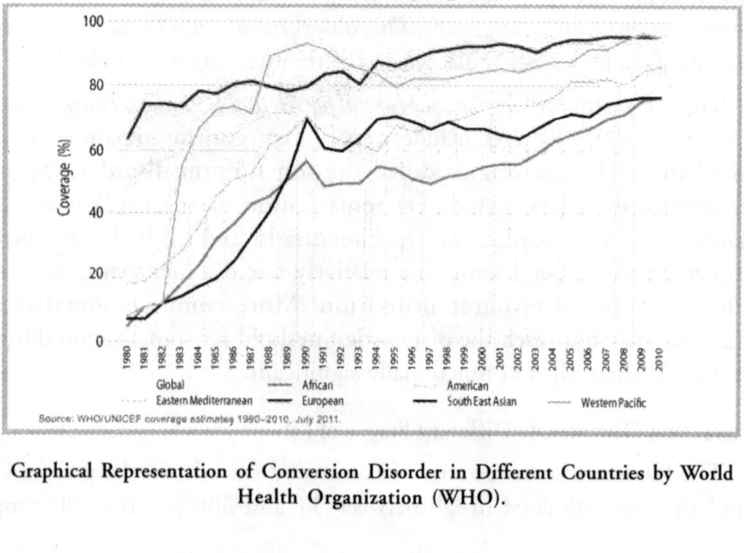

Graphical Representation of Conversion Disorder in Different Countries by World Health Organization (WHO).

- Family history. Children sometimes develop conversion disorder from observing their parents' reactions to stressors. This process is known as social modeling.
- A recent stressful change or event in the patient's life.

Conversion Disorder and Workplace

Predisposing causes include prior physical disorders, exposure to people with real physical symptoms, and severe psychosocial stressors. Onset is usually between ages 10 and 35. It is more frequent in women (anywhere from 2 to 10 times more prevalent than in men), and in rural settings, lower socioeconomic groups, and military personnel exposed to combat. Studies indicate that conversion disorder may be found in between 1% to 14% of general medical and surgical inpatients (DSM-IV-TR). The individual may also benefit from the symptoms in other ways (secondary gain) such as gaining attention or support from family and friends, a reward of some kind, or avoidance of unwanted responsibilities. Although most individuals appear unconcerned emotionally about their illness and are unaware of any psychological conflicts, some experience anguish over their new symptoms. The symptoms are not intentionally or consciously faked but there is no known medical condition to account for the findings. Instead of corresponding to any known anatomic or neurological patterns typical of illness having a physical basis, the symptoms may instead correspond to the individual's concept of a disease.

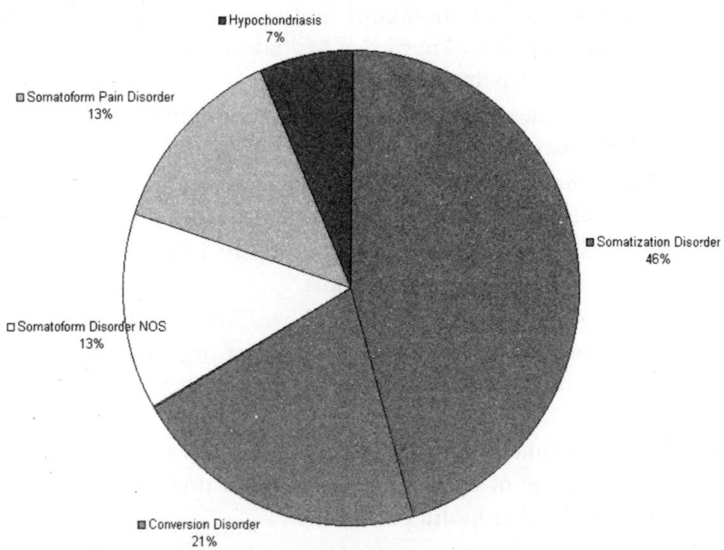

Somatoform Diagnoses in a Series of University Hospitals Psychiatric Consultations in USA.

Conversion disorder is diagnosed only after a thorough medical examination fails to find a physical explanation for the symptoms. Some diseases take years for diagnosis so conversion disorder should be considered a tentative, working diagnosis. Even when a known disease is present, conversion disorder can still exist if the symptoms cannot be explained by the medical illness. Workplace should be sensitive about these issues.

Human resource (HR) departments should also be sensitive to employees with conversion disorder. Situations are improving in corporate sectors especially MNCs as they have structured medical benefit system with work.

Role of Mass Media and Health Promotion

1. Raise public awareness about a particular problem or issue related to this disorder.
2. Create a climate of opinion sharing
3. Stress out the ill effects of unhealthy behaviour and benefits of preventive behaviour.
4. Planned campaigns and advertising. This has the advantage of target a wide range of audience.
5. Unpaid publicity and media advocacy. This may be low cost campaigns that may seem to provide greater credibility to the target audience.
6. Expression and promotion of healthy behaviours through the adoption of healthy knowledge, attitude and practices by media through advertisement.
7. Media can use emotional and psychological content in discussing health issues.
8. Making health issues more relevant to the audience and to the social cultural settings at locally, regionally and internationally.
9. Promotion can be done by community radio station being promoted by government of India.
10. Institute of higher education along with relevant department of a hospital can be integrated with media organisation for free lectures and coverage of the program and further sharing to large masses.
11. Health channels airing their programmes on television should have coverage of conversion disorder and psychiatric problems along with other health problems.
12. Short Messaging Service (SMS) can be structured by media organization(s) with the help of clinicians with having telecom

partners and reaching out to every knock and corner of the country in vernacular languages.

13. Use of vernacular language should be a motto with media to be effective and for success of specific communication language.

Conversion disorder promotion activities are strongly linked with the social context, among others with the mass media, which is a powerful companion in health promotion actions. Beside explicit health-communication there is also plenty of implicit health information in the media, messages which unintentionally and unconsciously are related to health. Talking about health promotion, i.e. health promotion discourse in the media is influenced by cultural determinants, such as societal values, norms and beliefs by proposing a selected day for conversion disorder like diabetes day or epilepsy day.

The appropriateness of mass media as a vehicle for conversion disorder promotion or as generators of health insight is subject to debate. Since 1970s it is gaining popularity as a strategy for delivering preventive health messages. Mass media programmes appear to have a number of advantages over traditional public health strategies. On the other hand, the public health community has long been concerned about the mass media as a source of problems. Various types of advertising and the portrayal of health-compromising behaviours and products in the media have been identified as promoting disease rather than health. The potential influence of movies, advertising media, and television programming; and various other public health threats (MacDonald 1998, Smedley 2000).

The advantages of mass media programmers include the ability to reach a large proportion of the population. Although it is important to bear in mind that a conversion disorder promotion "exhibition" will probably only draw in people who are interested, the people who are motivated, and most probably not the people who are not aware of any need for health promotion. Perhaps more to the point, mass media interventions are a relatively inexpensive method of exposing the population to health information. The mass media can make use of 'visually potent images' to invent a hard-hitting and powerful message which is more often than not available to other avenues. However, the role of the media in initiating widespread and long-lasting behaviour change may be overrated. Some communications experts have concluded that, although mass media may increase knowledge, they are ineffective in changing attitudes and behaviour.

References

1. Katon W, Lin E, Von Korff M, Russo J, Lipscomb P, Bush T. Somatization: a spectrum of severity. *Am J Psychiatry.* 1991; 148:34-40.
2. Smith GR, Monson RA, Ray DC. Psychiatric consultation letter in somatization disorder. *N Engl J Med.* 1986; 314: 1407-1413.
3. Mayou R, Kirmayer LJ, Simon G, Kroenke K, Sharpe M. Somatoform disorders: time for a new approach in *DSM-V. Am J Psychiatry.* 2005;162:847-855.
4. Woolfolk RL, Allen LA. *Treating Somatization: A Cognitive-Behavioral Approach.* New York, NY: Guilford. In press.
5. Allen LA, Woolfolk RL, Lehrer PM, Gara MA, Escobar JI. Cognitive behavior therapy for somatization: a pilot study. *J Behav Ther Exp Psychiatry.* 2001; 32:53-62.
6. First MB, Spitzer RL, Gibbon M, Williams JBW. *Structured Clinical Interview for DSM-IV Axis I Disorders (SCID-I).* Washington, DC: American Psychiatric Press; 1997.
7. Ware JE, Sherbourne CD. The MOS 36-Item Short-Form Health Survey (SF-36). *Med Care.* 1992; 30:473-483.
8. McHorney CA, Ware JE, Lu JFL, Sherbourne CD. The MOS 36-Item Short-Form Health Survey, III: tests of data quality, scaling assumptions, and reliability across diverse patient groups. *Med Care.* 1994; 32:40-66.
9. Wolfe F, Hawley DJ, Goldenberg DL, Russell IJ, Buskila D, Neumann L. The assessment of functional impairment in fibromyalgia (FM): rasch analyses of 5 functional scales and the development of the FM Health Assessment Questionnaire. *J Rheumatol.* 2000; 27:1989-1999.
10. Looper KJ, Kirmayer LJ. Behavioral medicine approaches to somatoform disorders. *J Consult Clin Psychol.* 2002; 70:810-827.
11. Kroenke K, Swindle R. Cognitive-behavioral therapy for somatization and symptom syndromes: a critical review of controlled trials. *Psychother Psychosom.* 2000; 69:205-215.
12. Blais MA, Smallwood P, Groves JE, Rivas-Vazquez RA. Personality and personality disorders. In: Stern TA, Rosenbaum JF, Fava M, Biederman J, Rauch SL, eds. *Massachusetts General Hospital Comprehensive Clinical Psychiatry.* 1st ed. Philadelphia, Pa: Mosby Elsevier; 2008:chap 39.

9

Face Book or Book Face

Dr Sandeep Shandilya

1. Introduction

Social sites have their origin in recent times but they have witnessed stupendous growth in very less time. Their emergence and growth can be attributed to the developments in computer networking. Development in the field of USENET, ARPANET, LISTERV and bulletin board services (BBS) has greatly contributed in this direction[1]. In initial stages social networking on the www started with the inception of generalized online communities like theglobe.com (1995), Geocities (1994) and tripod.com (1995)[2]. These earlier developments were mainly confined to bringing people together through chat rooms so as to promote interaction and sharing of personal information through personal web pages. Easy to use publishing tools were also added to it. Face book was launched in 2004[3] and it went on to become the largest social networking site in the world during 2009[4] and still enjoys the same position.

Above information taken from various sources amply reflect two things- first, emergence of social sites is of recent origin and second, computer networking and strides of morden man in the field of information technology lies at the core of this unprecedented development. Through a number of social websites are in vogue but in contemporary times face book scores maximum points when it comes to number of users and popularity world over. Social sites have gained worldwide popularity and their place in overall social fabric of various nations can be very well felt and appreciated. Emergence and widespread popularity of these sites has transformed into an interesting social phenomenon with certain merits as well as demerits. No one can deny the recent Anna movement in India. Long strides in the area of information technology by Modern science lie in the backdrop of emergence of this unique social phenomenon. For a developing nation with wide varieties of socioeconomic problems. Present paper is a humble effort by author to analyse some such aspects of these social sites in general and face book in particular which are of far reaching impact and consequences for humanity and the social structures world over.

2. Social Sites May Convert into Social Parasites

Social and the way its members behave and interact remains an unsolved puzzle for social thinkers and scientists. This puzzle becomes even more complex when complicated intrusion of developments like the one of the nature of social sites takes place. The remarkable role played by these sites in some mass movement of grave concern for humanity including the one in India recently which was guided by Anna, a well known social activists, cannot be undermined by any means. However, the developments like tarnishing the image of personalities like Baba Ramdev or Sonia Gandhi are some of the notorious acts which were championed by face book. Emergence of social sites is a sophisticated issues and needs to be carefully evaluated otherwise it will invite many troubles to society and humanity as a whole. Efforts must be taken in time to prohibit the transformation of these social sites into social parasites.

A parasite lives in a close relationship with another organism, its host, and causes it harm. The parasite has to be in its host for its life functions. For example, viruses are common parasites. The parasite has to be in its host to live, grow and multiply. Parasites rarely kill their host. A common, well-known type of a parasite is a hookworm. It is possible for humans on their pets to get them. Hookworms attach themselves in the lining of the small intestine, and cause diseases, and malnutrition as well, as they eat the nutrients and keep them from going to the host. Just like hookworm prevents nutrients to reach to the host body, these social sites if not controlled and used widely will cause society to become weak and full of social evils and diseases as does the parasites like hookworm to host's body. The passion for social sites has already taken shape of an epidemic. This wide spread popularity of social sites will become detrimental to humanity if their harmful effects on society are not checked or amicably or amicably addressed.

3. Social Sites are Backed by Killer Technologies

Modern technology is sometimes also referred to as killer technology. Following excerpt is taken from an article by James champy[6]. "It is a now accepted wisdom that information technology can accelerate everything you do. It can also kill your business quickly. A slew of spectacular technology caterings make the point-giving the term "killer technologies a whole new meaning:

Crash: Snap-on Inc. Close five manufacturing plants, lays off 1,000 workers and writes off $50 millions in lost sales when foul-ups in a new computer system make it nearly impossible for franchisers to order products.

Smash: For Meyer *health Corp. Lands* in bankruptcy after paying Andersen consulting $30 million for a new SAP system. For Meyer's bankruptcy trustees claim that the new system handles only 10,000 orders a day, compared with the 420,000 processed by Unisys mainframe. The trustees are seeking $500 million in damages from Andersen.

Kaboom: oxford health plan elaborate that the IT systems somehow fail to catch millions of dollars in medical care cost. Results: a $300 million loss. Executives depart and the formerly highflying stock tumbles 75%.

Crunch: home runs, a two year old online grocery delivery service o use in Boston, ceased operation for six weeks after a "construction mishap" crashed the computer system at the warehouse where the Hannaford brothers Co. Subsidiary took orders.

The faster and more elaborate your computer technology, the quicker things can go wrong. This is because of a little interaction between you and your customer, and increased involvement of computer system intransactions. Call centres, reservation systems, on-line order system are all a couple of electron impulses away from the disaster and that to say nothing of the business intranets and electronic data interchange (EDI) networking linking you to suppliers and partners".

Fast speeds with which information can traverse in Morden times can have disastrous consequences also because a slight mismanagement of fast moving electrons can let humanity down. Perhaps information also requires its own gestation period before acquiring shape of a true and reliable friend of society and humanity. Killer technologies like in the backdrop of social sites and their killer instinct needs to be channelized in favour of society and in no case otherwise.

4. Face Books or Book Face: What is the Truth

social sites including face book have given a readymade platform to every user to interact with each other, project and presents his/her ideas to entire world. These sites are being rampantly used to make one's presence felt online. Earlier we use to have very few autobiographies but today each one of us can present his/her autobiography to entire world through these social sites. Face book is infact not face book because rather than presenting his true face value, a face book user generally tends to overstate his capabilities. He tries to project and match himself with the great characters and heroes which can perhaps be found only in the books of history. Social sites do promote interaction with the members of society (its users) but this face book interaction adds to the artificiality in human relations which is already marred by consumerism and materialism of modern times. It appears that correct explanation of face book is its book face characteristics. So it will be better to remain it as book face. This artificiality can cause sere damage to social system across the globe. Recently there was a news that a lady kept posting on his account about the steps she was going to follow to commit suicide. None of her friends' took it seriously as they through social sites are becoming a sources of sources for their users as a person using these sites consider others happier than him or her after evaluating the posts of others.

5. Conclusion: beauty V/s Reality

"To appear beautiful is not bad but to hide reality is. There can be numerous varieties of response possible to above question. Some of you may say that world is becoming more beautiful and attractive. I will add only few worlds to above response and these are"but by artificial means".

If we analyse general character of social sites like facebook, they appear more like psychological cosmetics rather than messengers of simplicity and originality. Hiding reality to look beautiful is an act which is full of ugliness. It is not the intention of social networking sites to promote the culture of hiding reality among the members of society (its users). But it is just a by product of morden technology and can be extremely disastrous. Its peaceful use can substantially contribute toward the betterment of society and humanity. The same can be implied and said about these social networking sites including facebooks.

It is quite interesting to draw parallel between fashion technology and the unique feature of character of social sites, the paper has attempted to diagnose. In fashion technology also we are suggested ways and means to hide our ugliness by artificial means. However truth remains as it is. Sometimes guided by this artificiality and so called fashionable behaviour, we tend to motivate towards nudity ending up with even bigger frustration to share with. After nudity there is only place you can think to go and it is the soul. May be this rampant competition to look and/or appear attractive and beautiful by behaving book face way while working with face book will make humanity about something which is really beautiful-**Our Soul**.

References

1. Michael Haubenn, Ronda Haubenn, and Thomas Truscott (1997-04-27). Netizens: on the history and impact of Usenet and the internet (perspectives). Wiley-IEEE computer society P.ISBN 0-8186-7706-6
2. Cotriss, David (2008-05-29). "Where are they now: TheGlobe.com".

The industry standard. Shttp://www.thestandard.com/news/2008/05/29/where-are-they-now-theglobe-com.

3. "Social graph-iti": Face book's social network graphing: article from *The Economist's website. Retrieved on January 19, 2008.*
4. *Ibid.*
5. www.extramarks.com/ask-explore-answer/....parasite...../7/?pn
6. James champy. Killer technologies, The times of India, New Delhi, September 23, 1998@ forbes.
7. Sandeep shandilya, restructure business education says Shandilya, 1999 Aditi publications Aligarh.

10

NEW MEDIA AND SOCIETY

FACEBOOK ADDICTION: A NEWBORN PSYCHOLOGICAL PROBLEM

Aditya Kumar Shukla and
Shraddha Tripathi

1. Introduction

Originally psychiatrists used the term 'addiction' with reference to the use of alcohol or other substances. Addiction refers to the presence of tolerance and withdrawal that hinder affective or psychological functioning. Internet addiction or internet addiction disorder (IAD) is excessive computer use that interfaces with daily life or results in certain problems to its users. It is proposed as a disorder in a satirical hoax[1].

Like any other chemical addiction, Internet addiction disorders describe various types of successive and independent stages through which the individual progresses into an addiction to Internet. The addictive behaviours may not be limited to a single cause, namely, media use but there is a clear relationship with the use of Internet.[2]

Internet addiction is described as an 'impulsive control problem' (Dr. Kimberly Young, IAT)[3]. It is defined as four subtypes:

(A) **Cyber Sexual Addiction:** They typically engage in viewing, downloading and trading online pornography or involved in adult fantasy role-play chat rooms.

(B) **Cyber Relationship Addiction:** They suffer from an addiction to chat rooms; Internet message or social network sites-over involved in online relationship or may engage in adultery. Online friends become more important to them at the expenses of real life relationships.

(C) **Net Compulsions:** Addictions to online gaming, online gambling and eBay, which may disrupt other job or education related duties or significant relations.

(D) Information Overload: Excessive web surfing and data base researches as enormous amount of information available on Internet, individual will spend greater of time searching and collecting data.

The second part of Internet addiction includes cyber relationship addiction which involves mainly the addiction of social sites (SSAD). The word social sites include facebook, twitter, google+ etc. The excessive use of all these sites affects our mind, body and soul. So due to this giving up the technology was considered by some to be hard as quitting smoking or drinking.

According to paper presented at the 119th Annual Convention of the American Psychological Association, pre-teens and teenagers who use technology, like the Internet and video games, on a regular basis will have more stomach aches, sleeping problem, anxiety and depression. In this paper entitled, "Poke Me: How Social Networks Can Both Help and Harm our Kids", Larry D. Rosen, Ph.D, professor of psychology at California State University, found positive and negative effects of social networking sites on children and teenagers. According to Rosen, Teens who use Facebook continuously may show narcissistic tendencies and young adults show more signs of other psychological disorders. Spending more time on Facebook may also bring health related problems[4].

2. Facebook: World Scenario

In February 2004, Mark Zuckerberg, with the help of Andrew McCollum and Eduardo Saverin, launched a website www.facebook.com that would change online social interaction forever. The Facebook started on the campus of Harvard University, where the three friends were students, Zuckerberg being a psychology major of all things. Within 24 hours of going live, The Facebook was a community of 1200 Harvard University students.

Now it is a biggest network for social interaction having more 800 then million active users. In which 50% if active users log on to Facebook in any given day. They are spending more than 55 minute on Facebook. Average users have almost 150 friends. You can find here More than 900 million objects that people interact with (pages, groups, events and community pages). Average user is connected to 80 community pages, groups and events.On average; more than 3 billion photos and 14 million videos are uploaded per day. More than 3.5 million events are created each month. On average, sends 8 friend requests per month, writes 25 comments on Facebook content each month.More than 70 languages available on this site. More than 75% of users are outside of the United States. More than 350 million active users currently access Facebook through their mobile devices More than 475 mobile operators globally work to deploy and promote Facebook mobile products. More than 6 billion minutes are spent on Facebook each day (worldwide). That is twice as much as the time spent on Google. So due to this Mark Zukerberg is the youngest billionaire according to Forbes list[5].

So now days Facebook is becoming a tool to spark, stir, and set in motion social movements. Proponents argue that Facebook is encouraging young people to become involved like never before. For example, President Obama used Facebook and other social media sites to rally support for his Presidential run. As politicians and businesspeople are starting to realize, Facebook represents a lucrative avenue for connecting with people of all ages. In India ANNA Movement is the latest example of most successful social nedia campaign India against corruption. Facebook helped in making it globel with 1.5 lacks supporters[6].

But now the side effects of also coming in studies. Studies are saying that once you are a member, Facebook can be hard to avoid. Facebook is so attractive that more and more of the population is spending time on its site. However, the increasing popularity of facebook has both positive and negative implications, leading to unity and action on the positive end and prompting addiction and disorder on the negative end[7].

3. Facebook Addiction or Facebook Addiction Disorder (FAD)

According to Medilexicon's medical dictionary Addiction is Habitual psychological or physiologic dependence on a substance or practice that is beyond voluntary control. Withdrawal has many meanings, one of which is a psychological and/or physical syndrome caused by the abrupt cessation of the use of a drug in a habituated person. People with an addiction do not have control over what they are doing, taking or using. Their addiction may reach a point at which it is harmful. Addictions do not only include physical things we consume, such as drugs or alcohol, but may include virtually anything, such abstract things as gambling to seemingly harmless products, such as chocolate. The addictions classifies mainly in two types, the first one is a Substance dependence (e.g. drug addiction) or Behavioural addiction (e.g. gambling addiction, sex activities, internet addiction, working or shopping)[8].

Any activity, substance, object, or behaviour that has become the major focus of a person's life to the exclusion of other activities, or that has begun to harm the individual or others physically, mentally, or socially is considered an addictive behavior[9].

In psychiatry, the only disorders that have been considered addictions are those involving alcohol or other drugs. Now, proposed revisions for the

American Psychiatric Association's Diagnostic and Statistical Manual of Mental Disorders (DSM-V) include for the first time "Behavioural addictions"—a change some say is long overdue and others say is still premature. So far, only one behaviour has made the cut: gambling, which under the new proposal would join substance-use disorders as a full-fledged addiction[10].

3.1. Causes of Addictive Behaviors: There is no consensus as to the etiology (cause), prevention, and treatment of addictive disorders. A United States government publication, "Theories on Drug Abuse: Selected Contemporary Perspectives," came up with no less than forty-three theories of chemical addiction and at least fifteen methods of treatment! As an example of this confusion, many people consider addictive behaviours such as gambling and alcoholism as "diseases," but others consider them to be behaviors learned in response to the complex interplay between heredity and environmental factors. Still others argue for a genetic cause. Some researchers point out that, unlike most common diseases such as tuberculosis, which has a definite cause (a microbe), and a definite treatment model to which everyone agrees, there is no conclusive cause or definite treatment method to which everyone agrees for most of the addictive behaviors.

3.2. Facebook addiction or Facebook Addiction Disorder (FAD): Facebook Addiction Disorder (FAD) is a term introduced by US phychologists for those who are addicted to facebook and their life is really affected by their uncontrolled activities on Facebook. According to US psychologists the number of patients suffering from FAD is increasing. Not only US but also millions of South Africans may also be at risk as they search for long-lost friends and relatives, share photo albums and stay abreast of gossip.

Lynlee Howard-Payne, a psychology lecturer at the University of the Witwatersrand, said: "While there are no official statistics available regarding South Africans who have been diagnosed as having or being treated for FAD, based on the large number of universities, schools and companies blocking access to Facebook … there could very well be an uncontrolled dependence." Howard-Payne added: "Universities, schools and companies are forced to limit accessibility to Facebook because some people seem to be unable to perform other tasks if they have access to this online social network. While Facebook is often a great way of maintaining both social and professional relationships, it seems to take on a destructive force with certain personalities[11]."

3.3. Phases of Facebook Addiction: The facebook addiction has mainly three phases. The first one is engagement, which is primary stage, in which the person just starts to learn about facebook, second is substitution, in which the facebook becomes a substitute for users what he/she could not find in life and the last one is escape, in which the person starts to escape from real world and their problems.

4. Facebook Addiction: Sign and Symptoms

As a substance and behavioural addicted person Facebook addicted persons also show some symptoms, which are given below:

4.1. Tolerance: This term is used to describe the desperate behaviour of a Facebook addict. They spend an increasing amount of time on the site, coming to a stage where they need it in order to obtain satisfaction or on the other extreme, it is having a detrimental effect on them as a person and their life.

4.2. Withdrawal symptoms: These become obvious when one is restricted from using Facebook because they have to participate in normal everyday activities. Common signs are anxiety, distress and the need to talk about Facebook and what might have been posted on their wall in their absence.

4.3. Reduction of normal social/recreational activities: Someone suffering from FAD will reduce the time spent catching up with friends, playing sport or whatever it is they used to enjoy doing, to simply spend time on Facebook. Instead of catching up with a friend for coffee, they will send a Facebook message.

4.4. Virtual dates: It is obvious that things are extreme when real dates are replaced with virtual dates. Instead of going to the movies or out for dinner, they tell their partner to be online at a certain time.

4.5. Fake friends: If 8 out of 10 people shown on their Facebook page are complete strangers, it is undeniable: they have a serious case of FAD.

Some other symptoms of Facebook addiction to help users in realizing whether they are really addicted to Facebook or not[12]:

(A) Users and their siblings communicate through Facebook wall and messages, even if they stay in the same house.

(B) Users check Facebook for updates and comments after every hour at their workstation or on their cell phone.

(C) Users wake up in the morning, and log onto their Facebook account first.

(D) Users' Facebook wall is full of status updates, comments, and applications that they just used.

(E) Users give priority to Facebook over their commitments in professional and personal life.

(F) Users spend over an hour on Facebook at a stretch or in short episodes over regular intervals.

(G) Users can not stop thinking about Facebook updates and comments when they are offline.

(H) Users look forward to get home in the evening so that they can see what is happening in cyberspace. (On Facebook to be precise)

(I) Users can not go for a day without using Facebook, and even this thought makes them go into sort of depression.

(J) Users' day ends with checking Facebook for that one last time bidding people 'good night' through their Facebook status update.

If users are facing any of these activities, then they are suffering from Facebook addiction disorder. Facebook addiction disorder contains the tendency to affect some serious problem of their mental health and social life. Therefore they need to throw away this habit as soon as possible.

5. Facebook Addiction: Effect on kid's

Social networking sites Facebook, Orkut, Myspace and the microblogging site Twitter have become popular among teenagers in most of the countries. Even though Facebook has an age limit of 13, minors give wrong age to get to this site. The use of social networking sites is common among children. In May, Consumer Reports announced that 7.5 million kids age 12 and younger are on Facebook[13]. But the much use of Social networking websites are causing alarming changes in the brains of young users, an eminent scientist has warned. Sites such as Facebook, Twitter and Bebo are said to shorten attention spans, encourage instant gratification and make young people more self-centred[14].

Rosen presented preliminary findings from several research projects during a talk titled "Poke Me: Kids and Social Networking" at the American Psychological Association Convention in Washington, D.C., this weekend. His was not the only talk to address this issue; "social media and technology" was one of the key subject areas of this year's convention, which gathered leading researchers from around the world. Rosen's work is part of a broader debate over what effect the Internet is having on our minds. Rosen's work focuses on the differences between generations, and on the way technology affects kids. "All of these technologies have to be evaluated as they impact your life," he says. Adults can evaluate and reject various technologies—he offers the example of people turning down Google+ invites—but kids lack the experience and self-control to do so. Zeynep Tufekci, an assistant professor of sociology at the University of North Carolina, Chapel Hill, who specializes in the social impact of technology, suggests that parents' worries about the effects of social networks on children may be overblown[15].

5.1. Damaging child Brain: A neuroscientist Susan Greenfield said that most people spend at least two hours each day in front of a computer, and living this way will result in minds very different from those of past generations. Our brains are changing in unprecedented ways. We know the human brain is exquisitely sensitive to the outside world - this so-called 'plasticity' is famously illustrated by London taxi drivers who need to remember all the streets of the city, and whose part of the brain related to memory is generally bigger than in the rest of us as a result.

Indeed, one of the most exciting concepts in neuroscience is that all experience leaves its mark on your brain. But while adults' brains can change, it is children who are most at risk, for their brains are still growing - and may not have yet had a full range of experiences in three dimensions. Yet 99 per cent of children and young people use the internet, according to an Ofcom study. In 2005, the average time children spent online was 7.1 hours per week. By 2007, it had almost doubled to 13.8 hours. Now think about the condition of 2011[16].

5.2. Mental Risks: Social site may be harmful for the mental health of your kids. Children growing up alongside the rise of social networking websites may have a "potentially dangerous" view of the world, says a leading psychiatrist. Dr Himanshu Tyagi said said that people born after 1990 did not know a world without the widespread use of the internet. He warned that the current crop of psychiatrists was perhaps not fully prepared to help young people with internet-related problems. "People used to the quick pace of online social networking may soon find the real world boring and unstimulating[17]".

5.3. Effect on Grades: Regular columnist Bill Thompson probes media reports that Facebook usage affects grades. The examination period is always stressful. During this period students used to have email, instant messaging and of course Facebook and other social network sites to keep in touch with their school mates and share revision tips and exam guidance. Some revising school children probably found their access to Facebook severely curtailed last month, however, after The Sun revealed that those who checked the site every day dropped a grade in their studies while heavy users were doing as little as an hour of school work a week. The story was far from exclusive to The Sun, as a quick search of Google News reveals. It made dozens of papers and websites, including The Times, The Calgary Herald, and The Australian, which told its readers that "Facebook fixation harms student grades" and referred worried readers to a Sydney University-based group called "I want to sue Facebook if I fail university"[18].

5.4. Fear of Meeting with Strangers: children's are meeting with strangers online. So due to this parents spy children's Facebook profile to know about their relationship and contacts. A report of daily mail said that 55 percent mother and fathers are logging to social networking site Facebook to spy on their children's[19].

So due to all these problems President Obama doesn't like kids to use Facebook and other social media sites even though he made full use of Facebook to get vote from young generation in the presidential election and had raised lot of money for his election campaign with the help of his 24 million followers on his Facebook page. And now its been reported that President Obama has banned his daughters from using Facebook. In an interview Mr. President said: "Why would we want to have a whole bunch of people who we don't know knowing our business? That doesn't make much sense. We'll see how they [his daughters] feel in four years"[20].

6. Facebook Addiction: Effect on youths

Facebook is accessed by over 350 million users through their cell phones. The entire world spent up to a whopping 6 billion minutes a day on Facebook. The number of Facebook users boosts up day by day. Facebook has negative effects. Teens, youngsters and youth who use Facebook more often shows narcissistic tendencies and some signs of Psychological disorders, including antisocial behaviours, mania and aggressive tendencies. Facebook can be distracting and can negatively impact on learning. Studies found that middle class, high school and college student who checked Facebook account at least once during a 15-minute period achieved lower grades[21].

A large mass of Facebook users belong to the 35+ age groups. People favor instant messaging over face-to-face conversation these days. Oxygen Media and Lightspeed Research conducted a study that shows Facebook is checked in the morning by one-third of women in the age group of 18-34. 21 per cent of them wake up in the middle of the night to check Facebook[22]. Apart from all these problems youth are facing many problems due to overuse of Facebook, some of them are given below:-

6.1. Cause of depression, anxiety and stress: A recently published American Academy of Pediatrics (AAP) paper made a major splash when it described Facebook depression: a condition said to result when teens spend too much time on social media, leading them to turn to "substance abuse, unsafe sexual practices, or aggressive or self-destructive behaviors." Dr. Catriona Morrison, from the University of Leeds, said: "The Internet now plays a huge part in modern life, but its benefits are accompanied by a darker side. 'Internet addicts' spent proportionately more time browsing sexually gratifying websites, online gaming sites and online communities. Excessive use of the Internet could be a warning signal for depressive tendencies.[23]"

Meera Neelkanthan, a student of psychology from Coimbatore, presented a paper titled 'Relatedness between Facebook Addiction and Self-Regulation' at the ongoing national meet of Indian Association of Clinical Psychologists (IACP). In her study, she observed that greater the time users spend on the site, higher are the chances that they will lose control over their urge to log in. In her study, she studied 160 participants with 60 adolescents, 60 youngsters and 40 middle-aged adults. She found out that the ratio of those getting hooked to the site was higher in adolescents and youngsters than other users. She also pointed out that due to peer pressure; the networking sites a large number of users below 18 years of age[24].

6.2. Cyberbullying: "Cyberbullying is bullying that occurs through e-mail, instant messages, text messages, social networking or Web sites, or through images or videos posted online or sent via cell phone," says Patricia Agatston, PhD, a licensed professional counselor and co-author of *Cyber Bullying in the Digital Age.* It's important for parents to be on the watch for signs of cyberbullying: don't assume your child will confide in you. Such clues include symptoms of depression (including irritability, unexplained aches and pains, feelings of hopelessness, and fatigue or lack of energy), avoiding school or peer groups, and looking upset after viewing text messages or spending time online[25].

6.3. Sexting: In a new study, researchers discovered that display of sexual references on teens' Facebook profiles is associated with their intention to have sex. Moreno from the University of Wisconsin-Madison. "Our study suggests that if sexual content is noted on a teen's social networking site profile, it's definitely time for that talk." Dr. Moreno's team previously found that 54 percent of MySpace profiles contained high-risk behavior information, with 24 percent referencing sexual behavior. In the current study, researchers investigated what sexual displays on social networking sites represent in the offline world. They identified publicly available Facebook profiles of college freshmen, 85 of whom completed a survey measuring sexual experiences, risky sexual behavior, and for that not yet sexually active, sexual intention. Researchers found a strong association between display of sexual references on Facebook and self-reported intention to initiate sexual intercourse. The authors concluded that social networking sites present innovative opportunities for clinicians, educators and parents to identify adolescents who may benefit from targeted education regarding safe sex practices prior to sexual initiation[26].

6.4. Digital Footprint: Sexting, along with posting inappropriate messages, photos, or other content, can affect adolescents' digital footprint: the online record of a user's Internet activity. While sharing a scandalous picture or making an off-color remark online may not seem like a big deal to your kid, it could come back to haunt her later when she applies to jobs or college. (Yep, bosses and college admissions officers check Facebook profiles). To keep your kid's digital footprint pristine, parents should monitor privacy and make sure your kids understand the concept of "what goes online stays online."

6.5. Poor Social Adjustment: People make a lot of friends in Facebook and interact with them at internet. But in the real world, they have no time to interact with others. Actually, people spend most of their time with the internet and the result is they are reducing their social skills, communication skills as well as verbal skills[27]. In a recent study of 70 undergraduate students at Assumption College in Massachusetts, researcher Maria Kalpidou found that the number of Facebook friends you have can predict social adjustment to college. Freshmen with 200 or more friends scored with lower levels of self-esteem and personal and academic adjustment than freshmen with less than 200 friends. That's right: he more "friends" you have on Facebook, the less likely you are to have, well, actual friends[28].

6.6. Psychical Encounters: Drs. Diane Kholos Wysocki and Cheryl Childers, both sociologists, investigated the behaviours of infidelity on the Internet and sexting: sending sexually explicit text messages and photographs via e-mail or cellphone. In order to explore both sexting and infidelity and understand how people use the Internet to find sexual partners, Kholos Wysocki and Childers placed a survey on a website aimed at married people looking for sexual partners outside their marriage (Ashley Madison). A total of 5,187 adults answered questions about Internet use, sexual behaviors, and feelings about sexual behaviors on the Internet[29]."

6.7. Narcissistic Tendencies: Teen who use Facebook frequently may become narcissistic. Dictionary.com describes narcissism as an, "inordinate fascination with oneself; excessive self-love; vanity." Most likely these are not the character traits you desire for your child[30].

6.8. Reduce the Time for Study: Facebook attract people by allowing them to do time pass with their family, friends, and relatives, whole time. Students also browse Facebook after coming from school and this way, they reduce the time for their study.

6.9. Possibility of Conflict: Many immature people create stupid status, upload embarrassing picture and many other ridiculous actions. By these actions, definitely conflicts can be set up with others. So users need to be aware from these kinds of problems.

6.10. Privacy Blow Up: Facebook is a social networking website so many people use it to connect with lots of people. In those people, many people can be their identified people but surely some people may be totally new for them. Users can not keep any information private due to any of the people can get their personal information. So, users must not place their detailed personal data on Facebook.

6.11. Does not Care about His/Her Surroundings: Someone who previously connected to Facebook, doesn't care about **His/Her Surroundings.** They only cares about his/her world. They Facebook users check their Facebook profile to see who has written on their wall commented on their photos or commented on their status, etc; this activity takes them away from spending time with friends and family.

7. Facebook Addiction: Impact on Relationships

While many people view social media sites as time wasters, others find them to be beneficial. Social media users view these sites as a good way to keep in touch with friends and family reconnect with people from their past, or find love. But due to this media our relationships today often have a third-party, and it's causing some issues. Social networking sites are heavily incorporating themselves into our relationships and we're hurting from it. So now days much use of social site like Facebook lead its user to these given problems:-

7.1. Less Family Concern: Facebook becomes a trend so people are interested to be Facebook users. Users give importance to their Facebook friends and community in comparison to their family members. Actually the words, "Family comes first" are losing their meaning for Facebook users[31].

7.2. Leads to Divorce: In USA, $1/5^{th}$ divorce cases are due to Facebook, According to American Academy of Matrimonial lawyers survey, during divorce cases different sites used for judicial prove are; Facebook-66%, MySpace-14%, Twitter-5%, others-15%. In India, IIM girl Malini Commits suicide over her boy friend's comment on Facebook that- Feeling cool today, dumped my girl friend, Happy Independence Day. Apollo Hospital psychiatrist, Dr. Sandeep Bohra – For the adolescents' addicted to net, difference between real and virtual life has vanished. Addiction to virtual world is making them psychopath[32]. According to a mainstream magazine survey, 8 out of 10 school children in metros are on social network site[33]. Studies on Internet addiction said, over 50% of respondents said that they suffered marital problems because of their Internet use[34].

According to a study conducted recently by the American Academy of Matrimonial Lawyers, more than 80% of the divorce attorneys polled have seen an increase in the number of divorce cases using social networking evidence. "Social media has changed the way infidelity is discovered[35]."

7.3. Leads to Jealousy: Social media has attained such a pivotal role in today's lifestyle that social interactions and relationships are directed by it. The amount of private information shared on these platforms lead to feelings of eventual jealousy and mistrust. The present study investigated the levels of influence of Facebook in creating and accentuating such emotions, specifically in romantic relationships. This effect is attributed largely to the ease of availability of personal information that would not otherwise be accessible[36].

8. Facebook Addiction: Impact on Moral Values

Bite-size news fed to us on social-networking sites like Facebook and Twitter can make us immoral, says a new study by the Brain and Creativity Institute at the University of Southern California. According to the scientists who did tests on 13 volunteers measuring how long it took to emotionally respond to real stories of pain and heartache, we can't reflect properly on sad news that comes to use in quick micro chunks."If things are happening too fast, you may not ever fully experience emotions about other people's psychological states and that would have implications for your morality," claims the report. "In a media culture in which violence and suffering becomes an endless show, be it in fiction or in infotainment, indifference to the vision of human suffering gradually sets in," said Manuel Castells, a leading sociology expert at USC[37].

Digital media may take direct users away from traditional avenues for learning about humanity, such as literature or face-to-face social interactions, said Ms Immordino-Yang. We need to understand how social experience shapes interactions between the body and mind, to produce citizens with a strong moral compass."

Mr Antonio Damasio director of BCIU, S. California Barack Obama, who was inspired by his father, showed how admiration could drive a person onto great things, adding: "We actually separate the good from the bad in great part thanks to the feeling of admiration. It's a deep physiological reaction that's very important to define our humanity[38]."

9. Facebook Addiction: Impact on Physical Health

More recently social networks have been gaining increasing attention in healthcare and medicine.

9.1. Risk of Obesity: Obesity is among the negative effects of Facebook. If people will sit in front of the monitor all the time and will eat snacks then their physical activities will reduce and certainly they will be fatter. Researchers found that an individual's chances of becoming obese increased by 57% if they had a friend who became obese. Adult siblings also influenced one another, increasing the chance of obesity by 40%. The risk of becoming obese increased by 37% if an individual's spouse became obese. Additionally, the sex of friends and siblings was also important[39].

9.2. Risk of Cancer: Social networking sites such as Facebook could raise your risk of serious health problems by reducing levels of face-to-face contact, doctor claims. Emailing people rather than meeting up with them may have wide-ranging biological effects, said psychologist Dr Aric Sigman. Increased isolation could alter the way genes work and upset immune responses, hormone levels and the function of arteries. It could also impair mental performance. The number of hours people spend interacting face-to-face has fallen dramatically. This could increase the risk of problems as serious as cancer, strokes, heart disease and dementia, Dr Sigman says in Biologist, the journal of the Institute of Biology. Some genes, including ones involved with the immune system and responses to stress, acted differently according to how much social interaction a person had with others. Their activity may account for higher rates of inflammatory disease and other health problems seen in socially isolated individuals[40].'

9.3. Eating Disorders: The more time adolescent spent on the social networking site, the more likely they were to develop eating disorders such as anorexia, bulimia, and extreme dieting, Israeli researchers recently found. Exposure to online fashion and music content, as well as watching TV shows like Gossip Girl, were also associated with an increased risk for eating disorders. But researchers aren't saying that social networking sites necessarily cause eating disorders; as with Facebook depression, it may be that people prone to eating disorders spend more time online. What's more, the researchers found that parents can help protect their daughters from harmful effects of media: The children of parents who were aware of what their daughters were viewing online — and talked to them about what they saw and how much time they spent: were less prone to develop eating disorders, according to study authors[41].

Professor Yael Latzer and Ruth Katz of Haifa Faculty of Social Welfare and Health Sciences and their colleague Zohar Spivak conducted a study on 248 girls, aged between 12 to 19 years. For this purpose, researchers took into account two factors that they thought might lead to development of eating disorders in teen girls. The results showed that the more time girls spent on Facebook, the more they suffered from conditions like bulimia, anorexia. They also had poor physical self-image, negative approach to eating, and a greater urge to be on a crash diet[42]."

10. Ways to Cure Facebook Addiction Disorder (FAD)

If you are addicted to Facebook you need to get yourself some recovery tools. The given 10 strategies are presented here are some simple ways you can beat the Facebook addiction Disorder (FAD):-

10.1. Realise that you have a problem: Frist Step to cure from FAD is that you should realise that you have a Problem. If you ought to know it, the 50% work will be comleted.

10.2. Treat Internet as a tool: Use Internet as a tool of gathering information. Stay focused on the fact that the Internet is a means to an end. Plan your strategy: whether you're looking for information or entertainment: with the end in mind and you'll save valuable time.

10.3. Facebook, don't make it Personal: Facebook is a social networking Site, so it should be used socially not personally. Because when we are using it personally, we have an attachment with it and it leads to FAD.

10.4. Write down exactly how much time you are spending on Facebook: It is hard work; we should do it for our health care. Write down the hours or minutes which you are spending on Facebook in a day. At the end of the day add them and note down it on note book. The reason it is important to know how long you have been on the sites is because it gives you a solid measure of how bad your addiction is. After a few days, weeks and months this number should decrease.

10.5. Meditation: Realize that spending time on these sites is not a bad thing. Done in the right amounts it can be a lot of fun and even quite healthy. Use time to meditate. For example you might give yourself the first 20 minutes of the work day for the security of your health.

10.6. Make Work Schedule everyday: Everyday you should make your work schedule. Put the most important work on the top, with all this decide the hours for the use of social networking sites.

10.7. Turn of e-mail notifications: Email notifications are like little red devils coming to sit on your shoulder and begging you to come back and visit Facebook. Turn them off. You don't need to be notified every time someone sends you a message.

10.8. Get off the computer: Really… do you need to spend that much time on the computer? Honestly ask yourself that. Instead of getting home, pouring a beer and sitting in front of the computer to check your updates you could go for a walk, hit the gym or go and see a movie[43].

10.9. Find other people to talk to. Many people become hooked on the Internet through talking with others online. Find people in "real life" to talk to by joining a club, going to a concert, dining out with friends, or attending a training class[44].

10.10. Stay connected to the offline world. Visit newsstands, book and music stores, and participate in entertainment such as dance, museums, music, and live theater. Long novels and poetry readings are hard to experience online. Spend time with your real life friends.

11. Conclusion

Now we can conclude that over use of Facebook is harmful for us. In India **Facebook penetration** is **3.53%** compared to the country's population and **51.11%** in relation to number of Internet users, having 3rd number in the world. The **total number of FB users in India** is reaching **41402420** and have grown more than **12821860** in the last 6 months. The largest age group is currently **18 - 24** with total of 19,873,162 users, followed by the users in the age of **25-34**. There are **73% male** users and **27% female users**[45]. If we see the growing statistics of Facebook users in India, we can say the FAD is a big concern for us. So for the bright future of India use Facebook as a tool of Social interaction not for personal revelations. Also don't let Facebook become an addiction as it harms our mind, body and soul. So follow the techniques given by the experts, we can easily get rid of Facebook addiction disorder (FAD), if any and use Facebook as an effective tool of personal growth and excellence.

References

1. http://www.treatment-centers.net/internet-addiction.html.
2. Jose, Jolly, Bhavani, V.Durga. (2010). Internet addiction among adolescents-The enfaced reality: Media Mimansa, Bhopal: volume-4, April-June, pp-63-70.
3. Young KS. (1998). Caught in the Net. New York: John Wiley & Sons.
4. http://news.oneindia.in/2011/08/09/tech-negative-positive-effects-of-facebook-part-1.html, August 9, 2011.
5. http://www.facebook.com/press/info.php?statistics.
6. Pandey, Piyush. 2011. Ladten hain aur hath mein talwar bhi nahin: Kadambani. May, p.72.
7. http://danielsethics.mgt.unm.edu/pdf/Facebook%20DI.pdf.
8. http://www.medicalnewstoday.com/info/addiction/.
9. http://www.indiana.edu/~engs/hints/addictiveb.html.

10. Holden, Constance. (2010). Behavioral Addictions Debut in Proposed *DSM-V: Science Magazine.* 19 February. 2010: Vol. 327 no. 5968 p. 935.

11. *Summers, Amy. (2011).* Facebook Addiction Disorder: The 6 Symptoms of F.A.D. May 2, http://socialtimes.com/facebook- addiction-disorder-the-6-symptoms-of-f-a-d_b60403.

12. http://thurs.hubpages.com/hub/Negative-Effects-of-Facebook-Addiction.

13. *BAZELON, EMILY. Just how bad is Facebook for you? Why Facebook Is After Your Kids, October 12, 2011.*

14. Social websites harm children's brains: Chilling warning to parents from top neuroscientist, David Derbyshire, 24th February 2009.

15. Status Update: What's Facebook's Effect on Kids?, August 9, 2011, Vezina, Kenrick.

16. GREENFIELD. B. Susan, how Facebook addiction is damaging your child's brain: A leading neuroscientist's Chilling warning, 23rd April 2009.

17. 'Mental risk' of Facebook teens, July 3, 2008, http://news.bbc.co.uk/ 2/ hi/7487723.stm.

18. Just how bad is Facebook for you? May 5, 2009, http:// news.bbc.co.uk/ 2/hi/technology/8033466.stm.

19. 55 pct of parents spy children's Facebook profile, July 20, 2011, http:// news.oneindia.in/2011/07/20/tech-55-percent-parents-spy-children-facebook-profile-aid0102.html.

20. President Obama Banned His Daughters to Use of facebook, December 19, 2011,http://sickfacebook.com/president-obama-banned-his-daughters-to-use-facebook-total-respect/

21. Facebook may cause psychological disorders: Study, August 9, 2011, http://news.oneindia.in/2011/08/09/tech-negative-positive-effects-of-facebook-part-1.html.

22. Block, Jamie. Study: A Whole Lot of Women Are Addicted to Facebook, July 8th, 2010.

23. Nauert PhD, R. (2010). Obsessive Web Browsing Linked to Depression. *Psych Central.* Retrieved on October 8, 2011, from http:// psychcentral.com/news/2010/02/05/obsessive-web-browsing-linked-to-depression/11223.html.

24. Shastri, Parth, 'Facebook addiction causes anxiety, depression in youngsters', Jan 24, 2011.

25. 4 Biggest Online Risks for Kids, http://www.everydayhealth.com/kids-health/0328/biggest-online-risks-for- kids.aspx, **March 28, 2011**

26. Nauert PhD, R. (2010). Social Networking Sites Reveal Teens' Sexual Intent. *Psych Central.* Retrieved on October 8, 2011, from http://psychcentral.com/news/2010/05/03/social-networking-sites-reveal-teens-sexual-intent/13428.html.

27. Negative Effects of Facebook, http://thurs.hubpages.com/hub/Negative-Effects-of-Facebook-Addiction.

28. Facebook Friends = Poor Social Adjustment, John M. Grohol, PsyD, *Founder & Editor-in-Chief*.

29. Nauert PhD, R. (2011). Online Cheating Usually Leads to Physical Encounters. *Psych Central.* Retrieved on October 8, 2011, from http://psychcentral.com/news/2011/06/21/online-cheating-usually-leads-to-physical-encounters/27109.html.

30. Effects of Facebook on Teens: A New Study, http:// ktrapp.hubpages.com/hub/Teens-and-Facebook.

31. Impact on marriage, http://thurs.hubpages.com/hub/Negative- Effects-of-Facebook-Addiction, February 06, 2008.

32. http://www.deshnama.com/2011/09/blog-post_23.html.

33. India Today, 9 March, 2011, p. 20.

34. http://netaddictionrecovery.blogspot.in/2008_02_01_archive.html.

35. Nauen, Rachel. February 4, 2011, the Effects of Social Networking Sites on Relationships.

36. Facebook Leads to Relationship Jealousy, FYI Health Writer, July 2007, 2011.

37. Chacksfield, Marc, Facebook hurting moral values, says study: http://www.techradar.com/news/internet/facebook-hurting-moral-values-says-study-591753, April 14th 2009.

38. http://www.telegraph.co.uk/science/science-news/5149195/Twitter-and-Facebook-could-harm-moral-values-scientists-warn.html, 13 April 2009.

39. The United Health Foundation's 2006 edition of "America's Health Rankings: A Call to Action for People and Their Communities".

40. http://www.dailymail.co.uk/health/article-1149207/How-using-Facebook-raise-risk-cancer.html: How using Facebook could raise your risk of cancer, February 2009.
41. Day, Ashley. The Facebook Effect: Good or Bad for Your Health? http://www.everydayhealth.com/healthy-living/0406/the-facebook-effect-good-or-bad-for-your-health.aspx, Ashley Day.
42. Chandvani, Silly. (2011). Facebook addiction linked to eating disorders: http://www.themedguru.com/node/43592.
43. http://www.thedailymind.com/productivity/facebook-syndrome-8-ways-to-beat-your-facebook-addiction.
44. Self-help strategies adapted from Goldstein, D. and Flory, J. Best of the Net Online Guide Book Series. Toronto, Canada: Irwin Professional Publishing, 1998, and from Jonathan Kandell, Ph.D., Psychologist and Assistant Director of the University Counseling Center, University of Maryland—College Park, 1996.
45. http://www.socialbakers.com/facebook-statistics/india, India Facebook Statistics.

11

Reflection on New Media

Dr. Minal

Introduction

New media is a broad term in media studies that emerged in the latter part of the 20th century. For example, new media holds out a possibility of on-demand access to content any time, anywhere, on any digital device, as well as interactive user feedback, creative participation and community formation around the media content. Another important promise of new media is the "democratisation" of the creation, publishing, distribution and consumption of media content. Another aspect of new media is the real-time generation of new, unregulated content.

Wikipedia, an online encyclopedia, is an example of combining Internet accessible digital text, images and video with web-links, creative participation of contributors, interactive feedback of users and formation of a participant community of editors and donors for the benefit of non-community readers. Facebook is an example of the social media model, in which most users are also participants.

Most technologies described as "new media" are digital, often having characteristics of being manipulated, networkable, dense, compressible, and interactive. Some examples may be the Internet, websites, computer multimedia, video games, CD-ROMS, and DVDs. New media does not include television programs, feature films, magazines, books, or paper-based publications – unless they contain technologies that enable digital interactivity.

History

In the 1960s, connections between computing and radical art began to grow stronger. It was not until the 1980s that Alan Kay and his co-workers at Xerox PARC began to give the power of a personal computer to the individual, rather than have a big organisation be in charge of this. "In the late 1980s and early 1990s, however, we seem to witness a different kind of parallel relationship between social changes and computer design. Although causally unrelated, conceptually it makes sense that the Cold War and the design of the Web took place at exactly the same time."

Until the 1980s media relied primarily upon print and analog broadcast models, such as those of television and radio. The last twenty-five years have seen the rapid transformation into media which are predicated upon the use of digital technologies, such as the Internet and video games. However, these examples are only a small representation of new media. The use of digital computers has transformed the remaining 'old' media, as suggested by the advent of digital television and online publications. Even traditional media forms such as the printing press have been transformed through the application of technologies such as image manipulation software like Adobe Photoshop and desktop publishing tools.

Andrew L. Shapiro (1999) argues that the "emergence of new, digital technologies signals a potentially radical shift of who is in control of information, experience and resources" (Shapiro cited in Croteau and Hoynes 2003: 322). W. Russell Neuman (1991) suggests that whilst the "new media" have technical capabilities to pull in one direction, economic and social forces pull back in the opposite direction. According to Neuman, "We are witnessing the evolution of a universal interconnected network of audio, video, and electronic text communications that will blur the distinction between interpersonal and mass communication and between public and private communication" (Neuman cited in Croteau and Hoynes 2003: 322). Neuman argues that New Media will:

- Alter the meaning of geographic distance.
- Allow for a huge increase in the volume of communication.
- Provide the possibility of increasing the speed of communication.
- Provide opportunities for interactive communication.
- Allow forms of communication that were previously separate to overlap and interconnect.

Consequently it has been the contention of scholars such as Douglas Kellner and James Bohman that new media, and particularly the Internet, provide the potential for a democratic postmodern public sphere, in which citizens can participate in well informed, non-hierarchical debate pertaining to their social structures. Contradicting these positive appraisals of the potential social impacts of new media are scholars such as Ed Herman and Robert McChesney who have suggested that the transition to new media has seen a handful of powerful transnational telecommunications corporations who achieve a level of global influence which was hitherto unimaginable.

Scholars, such as Lister et al. (2003) and Friedman (2005), have highlighted both the positive and negative potential and actual implications of new media technologies, suggesting that some of the early work into new media studies was guilty of technological determinism – whereby the effects of media were determined by the technology themselves, rather than through tracing the complex social networks which governed the development, funding, implementation and future development of any technology.

Definition

Although there are several ways that New Media may be described, Lev Manovich, in an introduction to The New Media Reader, defines New Media by using eight simple and concise propositions:

1. New Media versus Cyberculture – Cyberculture is the various social phenomena that are associated with the Internet and network communications (blogs, online multi-player gaming), whereas New Media is concerned more with cultural objects and paradigms (digital to analog television, iPhones).
2. New Media as Computer Technology Used as a Distribution Platform – New Media are the cultural objects which use digital computer technology for distribution and exhibition. e.g. (at least for now) Internet, Web sites, computer multimedia, Blu-ray disks etc. The problem with this is that the definition must be revised every few years. The term "new media" will not be "new" anymore, as most forms of culture will be distributed through computers.
3. New Media as Digital Data Controlled by Software – The language of New Media is based on the assumption that, in fact, all cultural objects that rely on digital representation and computer-based delivery do share a number of common qualities. New media is reduced to digital data that can be manipulated by software as any other data. Now media operations can create several versions of the same object. An example is an image stored as matrix data which can be manipulated and altered according to the additional algorithms implemented, such as color inversion, gray-scaling, sharpening, rasterizing, etc.
4. New Media as the Mix Between Existing Cultural Conventions and the Conventions of Software – "New Media today can be understood as the mix between older cultural conventions for data representation, access, and manipulation and newer conventions of data representation, access, and manipulation. The "old" data are representations of visual reality and human experience, and the "new"

data is numerical data. The computer is kept out of the key "creative decisions, and is delegated to the position of a technician." e.g. In film, software is used in some areas of production, in others are created using computer animation.

5. New Media as the Aesthetics that Accompanies the Early Stage of Every New Modern Media and Communication Technology – "While ideological tropes indeed seem to be reappearing rather regularly, many aesthetic strategies may reappear two or three times ... In order for this approach to be truly useful it would be insufficient to simply name the strategies and tropes and to record the moments of their appearance; instead, we would have to develop a much more comprehensive analysis which would correlate the history of technology with social, political, and economical histories or the modern period."
6. New Media as Faster Execution of Algorithms Previously Executed Manually or through Other Technologies – Computers are a huge speed-up of what were previously manual techniques. e.g. calculators. "Dramatically speeding up the execution makes possible previously non-existent representational technique." This also makes possible of many new forms of media art such as interactive multimedia and video games. "On one level, a modern digital computer is just a faster calculator, we should not ignore its other identity: that of a cybernetic control device."
7. New Media as the Encoding of Modernist Avant-Garde; New Media as Metamedia – Manovich declares that the 1920s are more relevant to New Media than any other time period. Meta-media coincides with post-modernism in that they both rework old work rather than create new work. New media avant-garde "is about new ways of accessing and manipulating information" (e.g. hypermedia, databases, search engines, etc.). Meta-media is an example of how quantity can change into quality as in new media technology and manipulation techniques can "recode modernist aesthetics into a very different postmodern aesthetics."
8. New Media as Parallel Articulation of Similar Ideas in Post-WWII Art and Modern Computing – Post WWII Art or "combinatorics" involves creating images by systematically changing a single parameter. This leads to the creation or remarkably similar images and spatial structures. "This illustrates that algorithms, this essential part of new media, do not depend on technology, but can be executed by humans."

Globalisation and New Media

The rise of new media has increased communication between people all over the world and the Internet. It has allowed people to express themselves through blogs, websites, pictures, and other user-generated media.

Flew (2002) stated that as a result of the evolution of new media technologies, globalisation occurs. Globalisation is generally stated as "more than expansion of activities beyond the boundaries of particular nation states". Globalisation shortens the distance between people all over the world by the electronic communication (Carely 1992 in Flew 2002) and Cairncross (1998) expresses this great development as the "death of distance". New media "radically break the connection between physical place and social place, making physical location much less significant for our social relationships" (Croteau and Hoynes 2003: 311).

However, the changes in the new media environment create a series of tensions in the concept of "public sphere". According to Ingrid Volkmer, "public sphere" is defined as a process through which public communication becomes restructured and partly disembedded from national political and cultural institutions. This trend of the globalised public sphere is not only as a geographical expansion form a nation to worldwide, but also changes the relationship between the public, the media and state (Volkmer, 1999:123).

"Virtual communities" are being established online and transcend geographical boundaries, eliminating social restrictions. Howard Rheingold (2000) describes these globalised societies as self-defined networks, which resemble what we do in real life. "People in virtual communities use words on screens to exchange pleasantries and argue, engage in intellectual discourse, conduct commerce, make plans, brainstorm, gossip, feud, fall in love, create a little high art and a lot of idle talk" (Rheingold cited in Slevin 2000: 91). For Sherry Turkle "making the computer into a second self, finding a soul in the machine, can substitute for human relationships" (Holmes 2005: 184). New media has the ability to connect like-minded others worldwide.

While this perspective suggests that the technology drives– and therefore is a determining factor – in the process of globalisation, arguments involving technological determinism are generally frowned upon by mainstream media studies. Instead academics focus on the multiplicity of processes by which technology is funded, researched and produced, forming a feedback loop when the technologies are used and often transformed by their users, which then feeds into the process of guiding their future development.

While commentators such as Castells espouse a "soft determinism" whereby they contend that "Technology does not determine society. Nor does society script the course of technological change, since many factors, including individual inventiveness and entrpreneurialism, intervene in the process of scientific discovery, technical innovation and social applications, so the final outcome depends on a complex pattern of interaction. Indeed the dilemma of technological determinism is probably a false problem, since technology is society and society cannot be understood without its technological tools." (Castells 1996:5) This, however, is still distinct from stating that societal changes are instigated by technological development, which recalls the theses of Marshall McLuhan.

Manovich and Castells have argued that whereas mass media "corresponded to the logic of industrial mass society, which values conformity over individuality," (Manovich 2001:41) new media follows the logic of the postindustrial or globalised society whereby "every citizen can construct her own custom lifestyle and select her ideology from a large number of choices. Rather than pushing the same objects to a mass audience, marketing now tries to target each individual separately." (Manovich 2001:42).

As Tool for Social Change

Social movement media has a rich and storied history (see Agitprop) that has changed at a rapid rate since New Media became widely used (Chris Atton). The Zapatista Army of National Liberation of Chiapas, Mexico were the first major movement to make widely recognised and effective use of New Media for communiques and organizing in 1994. Since then, New Media has been used extensively by social movements to educate, organise, share cultural products of movements, communicate, coalition build, and more. The WTO Ministerial Conference of 1999 protest activity was another landmark in the use of New Media as a tool for social change. The WTO protests used media to organise the original action, communicate with and educate participants, and was used as an alternative media source. The Indymedia movement also developed out of this action, and has been a great tool in the democratisation of information, which is another widely discussed aspect of new media movement. Some scholars even view this democratisation as an indication of the creation of a "radical, socio-technical paradigm to challenge the dominant, neoliberal and technologically determinist model of information and communication technologies." A less radical view along these same lines is that people are taking advantage of the Internet to produce a grassroots globalisation, one that is anti-neoliberal and centered on people rather than the flow of capital. Of course, some are also skeptical of the role of New Media in Social Movements. Many scholars point out unequal access to new media as a hindrance to broad-based movements, sometimes even oppressing some within a movement. Others are skeptical about how democratic or useful it really is for social movements, even for those with access. There are also many New Media components that activists cite as tools for change that have not been widely discussed as such by academics.

New Media has also found a use with less radical social movements such as the Free Hugs Campaign. Using websites, blogs, and online videos to demonstrate the effectiveness of the movement itself. Along with this example the use of high volume blogs has allowed numerous views and practices to be more widespread and gain more public attention. Another example is the on-going Free Tibet Campaign, which has been seen on numerous websites as well as having a slight tie-in with the band Gorillaz in their Gorillaz Bitez clip featuring the lead singer 2D sitting with protesters at a Free Tibet protest. Another social change seen coming from New Media is trends in fashion and the emergence of subcultures such as Text Speak, Cyberpunk, and various others.

National Security

New Media has also recently become of interest to the global espionage community as it is easily accessible electronically in database format and can therefore be quickly retrieved and reverse engineered by national governments. Particularly of interest to the espionage community are Facebook and Twitter, two sites where individuals freely divulge personal information that can then be sifted through and archived for the automatic creation of dossiers on both people of interest and the average citizen.

Interactivity and New Media

Interactivity has become a term for a number of new media use options evolving from the rapid dissemination of Internet access points, the digitalization of media, and media convergence. In 1984, Rice defined new media as communication technologies that enable or facilitate user-to-user interactivity and interactivity between user and information. Such a definition replaces the "one-to-many" model of traditional mass communication with the possibility of a "many-to-many" web of communication. Any individual with the appropriate technology can now produce his or her online media and include images, text, and sound about whatever he or she chooses. Thus the convergence of new methods of communication with new technologies shifts the model of mass communication, and radically reshapes the ways we interact and communicate with one another. in "What is new media?" Vin Crosbie (2002) described three different kinds of communication media. He saw Interpersonal media as "one to one", Mass media as "one to many", and finally New Media as Individuation Media or "many to many".

When we think of interactivity and its meaning, we assume that it is only prominent in the conversational dynamics of individuals who are face-to-face. This restriction of opinion does not allow us to see its existence in mediated communication forums. Interactivity is present in some programming work, such as video games. It's also viable in the operation of traditional media. In the mid 1990s, filmmakers started using inexpensive digital cameras to create films. It was also the time when moving image technology had developed, which was able to be viewed on computer desktops in full motion. This development of new media technology was a new method for artists to share their work and interact with the big world. Other settings of interactivity include radio and television talk shows, letters to the editor, listener participation in such programs, and computer and technological programming. Interactive new media has become a true benefit to every one because people can express their artwork in more than one way with the technology that we have today and there is no longer a limit to what we can do with our creativity.

Interactivity can be considered a central concept in understanding new media, but different media forms possess different degrees of interactivity, and some forms of digitized and converged media are not in fact interactive at all. Tony Feldman considers digital satellite television as an example of a new media technology that uses digital compression to dramatically increase the number of television channels that can be delivered, and which changes the nature of what can be offered through the service, but does not transform the experience of television from the user's point of view, and thus lacks a more interactive dimension. It remains the case that interactivity is not an inherent characteristic of all new media technologies, unlike digitisation and convergence.

Terry Flew (2005) argues that "the global interactive games industry is large and growing, and is at the forefront of many of the most significant innovations in new media" (Flew 2005: 101). Interactivity is prominent in these online video games such as World of Warcraft, The Sims Online and Second Life. These games, which are developments of "new media," allow for users to establish relationships and experience a sense of belonging that transcends traditional temporal and spatial boundaries (such as when gamers logging in from different parts of the world interact). These games can be used as an escape or to act out a desired life. Will Wright, creator of The Sims, "is fascinated by the way gamers have become so attached to his invention-with some even living their lives through it". New media have created virtual realities that are becoming virtual extensions of the world we live in. With the creation of Second Life and Active Worlds before it, people have even more control over this virtual world, a world where anything that a participant can think of can become a reality.

New Media changes continuously because it is constantly modified and redefined by the interaction between users, emerging technologies, cultural changes, etc.

Industry

The new media industry shares an open association with many market segments in areas such as software/video game design, television, radio, and particularly movies, advertising and marketing, through which industry seeks to gain from the advantages of two-way dialogue with consumers primarily through the Internet. The advertising industry has capitalized on the proliferation of new media with large agencies running multi-million dollar interactive advertising subsidiaries. Interactive websites and kiosks have become popular. In a number of cases advertising agencies have also set up new divisions to study new media. Public relations firms are also taking advantage of the opportunities in new media through interactive PR practices. Interactive PR practices include the use of social media to reach a mass audience of online social network users.

Conclusion

The novelty of "new media" is mainly an experienced novelty, where the use of a new technology seems to imply that this is an entirely new kind of medium. The "new media" is more than something real.

References

1. Flew, 2008.
2. Manovich, Lev. "New Media From Borges to HTML." The New Media Reader. Ed. Noah Wardrip-Fruin and Nick Montfort. Cambridge, Massachusetts, 2003. 13-25.
3. Wardrip-Fruin, Noah and Nick Montfort, ed (2003). The New Media Reader. The MIT Press, ISBN 0-262-23227-8.
4. Lev Manovich, New Media from Borges to HTML, Wardrip-Fruin, Noah and Nick Montfort, ed (2003). The New Media Reader. pp.16-23. The MIT Press, ISBN 0-262-23227-8.
5. Thompson, John B. (1995). The Media and Modernity. Cambridge: Polity Press, p. 150.
6. Violaine Hacker, "Buiding Media's industry while promoting community of values in the globalisation", Politické Vedy, Journal of International Affairs, Policy and Security, 2/2011, http://www.fpvmv.umb.sk/politickevedy.
7. Volkmer, Ingrid (1999) News in the Global Sphere. A Study of CNN and its impact on Global Communication, Luton: University of Luton Press.

8. Williams, Raymond (1974) 'Television: Technology and Cultural Form, London, Routledge.
9. Durham, M & Kellner, Douglas (2001) Media and Cultural Studies Keyworks, Malden, Ma and Oxford, UK, Blackwell Publishing.
10. Lister, Martin, Dovey, Jon, Giddings, Seth. Grant, Iain. & Kelly, Kieran (2003) "New Media: A Critical Introduction", London, Routledge.
11. Castells, Manuel, (1996) Rise of the Network Society, The Information Age: Economy, Society and Culture volume 1, Massachusetts, Blackwell Publishing.
12. Lister, Martin, Dovey, Jon, Giddins, Seth. Grant, Iain. & Kelly, Kieran (2003) New Media: A Critical Introduction, London, Routledge.
13. McLuhan, Marshall (1962) The Gutenberg Galaxy: The Making of Typographic Man, London, Routledge and Kegan Paul.
14. McLuhan, Marshall (1964) Understanding Media: The Extensions of Man, Toronto, McGraw Hill.
15. Manovich, Lev (2001) The Language of New Media MIT Press, Cambridge and London.
16. Atton, Chris "Reshaping Social Movement Media for a New Millennium." Social Movement Studies, 2, (2003).
17. *Ibid.*
18. Reed, television, "Will the Revolution be Cybercast?"
19. Kellner, Douglas, "New Technologies, TechnoCities, and the Prospects for Democratization."
20. Preston, Paschal "Reshaping Communications: Technology, Information and Social Change," London:Sage, 2001.
21. Kellner, Douglas, "Globalization and Technopolitics."
22. Wasserman, Herman, "Is a New Worldwide Web Possible? An Explorative Comparison of the Use of ICTs by Two South African Social Movements," African Studies Review, Volume 50, Number 1 (April 2007), pp. 109–131.
23. Marmura, Stephen, "A net advantage? The Internet, grass-roots activism and American Middle-Eastern Policy," New Media Society 2008; 10; 247.
24. http://www.wikileaks.org/wiki/Mind_Your_Tweets:_The_CIA_Social_Networking_Surveillance_System
25. Schorr, A & Schenk, M & Campbell,W (2003), Communication Research and Media Science in Europe, Mouton de Gruyter, Berlin, p. 57.
26. Croteau, David & Hoynes, William (2003) Media Society: Industries, Images and Audiences (third edition), Pine Forge Press, Thousand Oaks, p. 303.

27. Crosbie, V. (2002). What is New Media? Retrieved from http://www.sociology.org.uk/as4mm3a.doc
28. Rafaeli, Sheizaf (1988). "Interactivity: From new media to communication". Beverly Hills, CA. Pg. 110.
29. Flew, Terry (2002), New Media: An Introduction, Oxford University Press, UK, p. 13
30. Feldman, Tony (1997) An Introduction to Digital Media, Routledege, London.
31. The Sun Newspaper Online.
32. http://secondlife.com/whatis/#Be_Creative.
33. http://mashable.com/2010/03/16/public-relations-social-media-results/

12

Obsessive Compulsive Disorder, Relevant Social Conditions and Role of Media

Dinesh Chaudhary, Zainul Abdeen, Abid Rizvi* and *Prashanta Kumar Pal

Introdction

Obsessive-compulsive disorder (OCD) is one of the more disabling and widespread, yet least understood, mental disorders. This disorder is characterised by two central features — obsessions and compulsions. Both the features need to be present and to such a degree that they interfere with your normal daily functioning to be diagnosed with OCD. Many people have traits of compulsiveness and "being compulsive" which should not be confused with OCD.

Obsessions are unwanted ideas or impulses that repeatedly pop up in a person's mind. According to the National Institute of Mental Health (NIMH), "Persistent fears that harm may come to self or a loved one, an unreasonable concern with becoming contaminated, or an excessive need to do things correctly or perfectly, are common."

Examples of common obsessions include: "My hands may be contaminated — I must wash them"; "I may have left the gas on in the house"; or "I am going to injure my child." These thoughts are often intrusive, unpleasant and produce a high degree of anxiety. Sometimes the obsessions are of a violent or a sexual nature, or concern illness.

Compulsions, on the other hand, are repetitive behaviours to which people who suffer from OCD resort. The two most common compulsions are washing (hands, usually) and checking (e.g., gas is off on stove). Other common compulsions include counting (often while performing another compulsive action such as hand washing), repeating, hoarding and endlessly rearranging objects in an effort to keep them in precise alignment with each other.

A person who has OCD often believes that these behaviors will keep harm away from them or their loved ones and that if they fail to complete a compulsive behaviour, harm is imminent.

Also, according to the NIMH, "Some people with OCD have regimented rituals while others have rituals that are complex and changing. Performing rituals may give the person with OCD some relief from anxiety, but it is only temporary."

"OCD is sometimes accompanied by depression, eating disorders, substance abuse disorder, a personality disorder, attention deficit disorder or another of the anxiety disorders," states the NIMH. "Co-existing disorders can make OCD more difficult both to diagnose and to treat."

One of the more frustrating aspects of OCD is that people who have it are often very much aware of how ridiculous or silly some of their behaviours may seem. This insight, however, is usually of little help to them in their treatment.

The causes of OCD remain as murky as do the causes for most mental disorders. It is probably a complex combination of genetic, biological, psychological and social factors which go to make up what we label "OCD." There may be a problem with how a person develops their information processing skills. But to a great extent, we simply do not yet know what causes OCD.

Specifically, according to the NIMH:" Clinical trials in recent years have shown that drugs that affect the neurotransmitter serotonin can significantly decrease the symptoms of OCD."

SIGNS AND SYMPTOMS

Obsessions often have themes to them, such as:

- Fear of contamination or dirt
- Having things orderly and symmetrical
- Aggressive or horrific impulses
- Sexual images or thoughts.

Obsession symptoms and signs may include:

- Fear of being contaminated by shaking hands or by touching objects others have touched
- Doubts that you've locked the door or turned off the stove
- Thoughts that you've hurt someone in a traffic accident
- Intense stress when objects aren't orderly or facing the right way
- Images of hurting your child
- Impulses to shout obscenities in inappropriate situations
- Avoidance of situations that can trigger obsessions, such as shaking hands
- Replaying pornographic images in your mind
- Dermatitis because of frequent hand washing
- Skin lesions because of picking at your skin
- Hair loss or bald spots because of hair pulling.

As with obsessions, compulsions typically have themes, such as:

- Washing and cleaning
- Counting
- Checking
- Demanding reassurances
- Performing the same action repeatedly
- Orderliness.

Compulsion symptoms and signs may include:

- Hand washing until your skin becomes raw
- Checking doors repeatedly to make sure they're locked
- Checking the stove repeatedly to make sure it's off
- Counting in certain patterns
- Arranging your canned goods to face the same way

Symptoms usually begin gradually and tend to vary in severity throughout your life. Symptoms generally worsen during times when you're experiencing more stress. OCD is considered a lifelong illness.

Treatment

"The first of these serotonin reuptake inhibitors (SRIs) specifically approved for the use in the treatment of OCD was the tricyclic antidepressant clomipramine (Anafranil^{R}). It was followed by other SRIs that are called "selective serotonin reuptake inhibitors" (SSRIs). Those that have been approved by the Food and Drug Administration for the treatment of OCD are flouxetine (Prozac^{R}), fluvoxamine (Luvox^{R}) and paroxetine (Paxil^{R})."

"Another that has been studied in controlled clinical trials is sertraline (Zoloft^{R}). Large studies have shown that more than three-quarters of patients are helped by these medications at least a little. And in more than half of patients, medications relieve symptoms of OCD by diminishing the frequency and intensity of the obsessions and compulsions. Improvement usually takes at least three weeks or longer.

If a patient does not respond well to one of these medications, or has unacceptable side effects, another SRI may give a better response. For patients who are only partially responsive to these medications, research is being conducted on the use of an SRI as the primary medication and one of a variety of medications as an additional drug (an augmenter)."

"Medications are of help in controlling the symptoms of OCD, but often, if the medication is discontinued, relapse will follow. Indeed, even after symptoms have subsided, most people will need to continue with medication indefinitely, perhaps with a lowered dosage."

Medications are rarely enough to help overcome a serious mental disorder such as OCD. According to the NIMH, "Studies of behaviour therapy for OCD have found it to be a successful treatment for the majority of patients who complete it. For the treatment to be successful, it is important that the therapist be fully trained to provide this specific form of therapy. It is also helpful for the patient to be highly motivated and have a positive, determined attitude."

"The positive effects of behavior therapy endure once the treatment has ended. A recent compilation of outcome studies indicated that, of more than 300 OCD patients who were treated by exposure and response prevention, an average of 76 per cent still showed clinically significant relief from three months to six years after treatment (Foa & Kozak, 1996)."

It should be kept in mind that "OCD affects not only the sufferer but the whole family. The family often has a difficult time accepting the fact that the person with OCD cannot stop the distressing behaviour. Family members may show their anger and resentment, resulting in an increase in the OCD behavior. Or, to keep the peace, they may assist in the rituals or give constant reassurance."

"Education about OCD is important for the family. Families can learn specific ways to encourage the person with OCD to adhere fully to behavior therapy and/or pharmacotherapy programs. Self-help books are often a good source of information. Some families seek the help of a family therapist who is trained in the field. Also, in the past few years, many families have joined one of the educational support groups that have been organised throughout the country" (NIMH).

OCD can be successfully treated. But it must first be properly recognized and diagnosed by a trained mental health professional, such as a psychologist, psychiatrist or clinical social worker. Treatment should be multi-faceted, addressing not only the biological aspect (through appropriate medication), but also the psychological and social aspects of this disorder (through psychotherapy).

In the hands of skilled professionals, most people with OCD can enjoy relief from their symptoms and the ability to live free of most obsessions and compulsions.

Literature Review

Now all know about Depression and besides that, many talk-shows directly try to address Mental Disorders.

So when will it be OCD's turn to success? Well it has been a busy few years for OCD in the Media. While a T.V.- show with high ratings depicted a detective with OCD in the T.V. Series "Monk" a movie (based on the book) named "MatchStick Men" came out that showed a criminal with OCD and all this while a Hollywood star wrote a book "The Pleasure of My Company: A Novel". One more movie "The Beautiful Mind" is a great example of such disorders based on OCD.

Will OCD's Fame end here or not? Maybe the media will have to explore a new Mental Disorder that will aid them to give their characters some quirkiness and depth. So OCD makes for a good story. Here are some of those OCD (and other) moments gathered .

OCD Famous People

There is quite a big list on famous people with a variety of Mental Disorders and often it seems to have somehow contributed to their qualities.

Here are people who had or have **OCD.**

- Marc Summers.
- Howard Hughes.

Short List of people who had or have **depression.**

- Albert Einstein
- Sir Winston Churchill
- Abraham Lincoln (and his wife)
- Marilyn Monroe (and her mother)
- Elvis Presley (and his mother)
- Franklin D. Roosevelt
- Vincent Van Gogh
- William Shakespeare

Gary Schwitzer

The Media May be the Most Important Source of Health Information for the General Public.

Health reporting does involve "telling a story," but it also requires writers to take on additional responsibilities through the story cycle—finding the story, collecting information, and writing it.

Standard news criteria such as, timeliness and impact, may be used to pick stories. But in health reporting, context is crucial. Research advances to be reported need to be placed in context. This may be achieved by citing earlier research on the topic and seeking out comments from independent experts who could put a new finding in perspective. Sometimes health research throws up contradictory findings. Is a gene linked to a disease? One study finds a link. Another does not. Such situations demand interpretative and analytical skills on the part of health writers. Otherwise, writers may mislead readers, or leave them confused.

Health reporters need to find out who has funded the research and who might be likely to gain. And reporters must always double-check claims or else they may end up in embarrassing situations. Let me illustrate with an example. A top international science magazine last year reported that a novel stem cell therapy had cured patients with chronic aplastic anemia in Bombay, India. The story was apparently based on claims made by the developers of the therapy, a private British company. A little more patience and investigation would have led the magazine to the real story: none of the patients had responded to the treatment, and the clinical collaborators in India had terminated the study.

When a public health situation is involved, health writers and the media can certainly play a role in quickly delivering important messages to the public In a sense, then, they do serve as a component of the health provider community. And this makes it all the more important for health writers to ensure that they get it absolutely right. Given that most people do not interact with their doctors on a regular basis, the media is possibly the most significant source of health information for the general public. But health information in the media cannot substitute for personal medical advice. It is important that the public understands this.

Regulatory mechanisms may be lax in some developing countries. India, for instance, has had a long history of unethical or illegal clinical trials. Drug regulatory authorities in India allow the sale of drugs—including pediatric formulations—that have never been approved in Western countries. This opens up opportunities for investigative health journalism, an opportunity for reporters to take up the traditional watchdog role of the press to find and report wrongdoing.

Ganapati Mudur: The Media May Be the Most Important Source of Health Information for the General Public

Health reporting does involve "telling a story," but it also requires writers to take on additional responsibilities through the story cycle—finding the story, collecting information, and writing it.

David Henry and Amanda Wilson: Health Journalists Should Discuss Benefits and Harms of New Treatments and Use Independent Expert Sources

Health reporting is a major growth area for the media, probably because it is in demand by the public and it is profitable. However, media coverage of medical news is generally of poor quality, particularly stories about new treatments.

Media Doctor is a web site where the quality of stories in the Australian press is reviewed (www.mediadoctor.org.au). We rate articles using ten evaluation criteria(www.mediadoctor. org.au/content/ratinginf ormation.jsp). In February/March 2005 articles that we rated achieved an average of only 52% on our "satisfactory" score (www.mediadoctor.org.au/content/sourceinf o.jsp). This was an improvement on the score from one year ago, but it is still inadequate. North American analyses of the quality of health reporting have had similar results. The print media are clearly superior to the online news services. The greatest differences between print and online services are in the use of independent information sources, and the quantification of the benefits and the coverage of potential harms of new treatments.

Box 1. Criteria Used by Media Doctor to Evaluate News Stories

- Whether the treatment is genuinely new
- The availability of the treatment in Australia
- Whether alternative treatment options are mentioned
- If there is evidence of disease mongering in the story
- If there is objective evidence to support the treatment
- How the benefits of the treatment are framed (in relative or absolute terms)
- Whether harms of the treatment are mentioned in the story
- Whether costs of the treatment are mentioned in the story
- Whether sources of information and any known conflicts of interest of informants are disclosed in the article
- Whether the journalist relied only on the press release for the story

We recognise that there are different depths of journalism and that journalists face constraints, including commercial pressures and deadlines that give little time to reflect on stories, which are usually written on the same day as the press release arrives. Some journalists argue that the media are the messengers and not the message, and it is up to others to interpret their reporting. To a reporter who might otherwise exercise more caution, a well-written media release from a large public relations company describing a new pharmaceutical product must be attractive when a deadline is imminent. There is no danger that the company will allege plagiarism if it appears, almost intact, under the journalist's by-line.

And even when they do have the time, journalists face two major challenges—understanding the clinical science and epidemiology, and dealing with powerful vested interests. Vested interests are not unique to medicine, but reporting on a new drug is different from, say, an MP3 player or a dishwasher. People will be intensely interested in a story about a new drug if it purports to treat a condition that they or their relatives have, and the story may become the basis of discussions with their physician and subsequent treatment decisions. We believe that in writing this type of story journalists have special responsibilities to ensure that they provide balanced information for their readers. In Australia, the Press Council believes the matter is of sufficient importance to provide advice to journalists.

In our view journalists will meet their responsibilities if they cover certain key issues when writing stories about new medical treatments. These include the accurate reporting of the comparative benefits, harms, and costs of the treatment and the extent to which their informants have ties with the manufacturer. It is helpful if journalists use independent expert sources to answer questions about the novelty of the treatment and the availability and efficacy of alternatives, although we acknowledge the practical difficulties in finding independent sources when time is limited. Journalists have indicated to us that they are concerned about these issues and are prepared to look critically at their own practices. It is unclear whether their editors and producers hold the same views and will provide the necessary resources, particularly time to do the job properly.

Researchers and medical journal editors have responsibilities too. When reading medical news stories, it is sometimes possible to tell whether the researchers and journals have done a good or bad job in communicating the essential facts to journalists. A number of medical journals issue press releases, and these have been found wanting. Researchers should consider carefully what they wish to convey about the results of a new study and should ask to see and edit any press releases. We believe that the criteria used by Media Doctor to evaluate news stories are a good starting point for researchers and editors.

Merrill Goozner: Medical Reporters Must Get Beyond the Hype and Hope When Reporting on the Latest "Breakthrough"

When I broke into the news business, the financial desk's primary source of breaking news was a Dow Jones wire clack-clack-clacking in the corner of the room. A bell rang whenever a major story broke. Sometimes two bells would go off, signaling a really big story. The day the stock market crashed in 1987, the newsroom sounded like St. Peters Square on Easter.

I imagine something comparable occurs these days when the advance copies of leading medical journals cross science editors' computer screens. Stories from the frontiers of medical research can make it onto page one—

the most coveted real estate in daily journalism. News magazines have bolstered their sagging bottom lines with an endless stream of cover stories touting the latest breakthroughs in medicine.

But is this news all that it is cracked up to be? Have the reporters properly weighed the importance of the studies they're touting? Have they asked the tough questions to the researchers and their sponsors to figure out the significance of the results? Have they presented the data in a fashion that is meaningful to health-care consumers? And in an age when most clinical trials are sponsored by private companies, have they fully informed their readers of the researchers' conflicts of interest?

Too often, the answer to these questions is no. Take recent reports from the American Society of Clinical Oncology, which met in mid-May in Orlando. One leading paper reported on a Veterans Administration review of the experience of over 40,000 women in the south central US. "The women taking statins were half as likely to have breast cancer as women who were not taking the drugs," the paper reported. Put that way, it sounds like a dramatic reduction. But elsewhere in the story, it was reported that 12 percent of the women were taking the cholesterol-lowering medications and that only 1.4 percent of the total group contracted breast cancer. Only by messaging the numbers could one figure out that physicians would need to put 700 women on statins to eliminate one cancer case (in medical parlance, this is called number needed to treat). It sounds a lot less impressive that way. But the number needed to treat would be a lot more meaningful to women, especially those on tight budgets wondering if it is worth $1,000 a year for a prescription.

Reporting of surrogate endpoints instead of primary endpoints is another way that readers get misled. Reports on cancer drug trials often fall into this trap. A "lifesaving" drug that shrinks tumors by 50 percent sounds a lot better than a chemotherapy agent that prolongs life by two months. The same can be said for bone density and fractures, blood pressure and strokes, and cholesterol levels and heart attacks. While there may be a minor yet statistically significant reduction in the primary endpoint, the trial sponsors prefer to promote the more dramatic-sounding secondary endpoint. Too many reporters prominently feature the less meaningful number, while leaving out or delaying until late in the story the real bottom line.

Sadly, the media have only lately come around to taking seriously the issue of conflicts of interest in medical science. Last July, the National Heart, Lung, and Blood Institute's National Cholesterol Education Project updated its guidelines for cholesterol management. The update, touted in the front page of every major US paper, called for a dramatic reduction in the cholesterol levels now considered optimal for people who have never had heart disease but are considered moderately at risk. Prescribing physicians using these guidelines will likely put millions more Americans on these drugs in the next few years.

Yet three days after the report came out, reporters at *Newsday* broke the story that eight of nine physicians on the National Cholesterol Education Project panel had financial ties to statin manufacturers, which had the most to gain from the new guidelines. Writing in the *Washington Post*, former *New England Journal of Medicine* editor Jerome Kassirer asked, "Why should we swallow what these studies say?" The ensuing uproar contributed to a change in policy at the *New York Times*, which last fall circulated a memo to all reporters encouraging them to always report conflicts of interest of quoted sources in science stories, a policy that leading science and medical journals have had in place for many years.

In recent years the pharmaceutical and biotechnology industries have responded to complaints about the high cost of drugs by claiming they are needed to finance the medical miracles that are just around the corner. Meanwhile, the increase in life expectancy in the US has slowed and still remains far below other advanced industrial countries. The number of new drugs coming out of industry labs, despite a slight uptick last year, is actually down from a decade ago. In a health-care environment that is increasingly cost-constrained, it shouldn't be too much to ask that medical reporters get beyond the hype and hope when reporting on the latest "breakthrough."

Maria Simbra: Whatever News Managers Want, Viewers Get—As Medical Reporters Are Pressed to Feed the Media Beast Top

Reporters are surpassing doctors as a source of medical information. It's no secret health news sells. Producers and news directors take advantage of this to attract an audience for their newscasts. And viewers respond.

In a survey by Rodale Press, 39% of the respondents said they turn to TV for health and medical information, and 37% said they would ask a health professional.

So as audience-appointed proxies for "health professionals," television medical reporters have a daunting task. They must be accurate, authoritative, and compassionate. They also need to understand the terminology, physiology, epidemiology, study design, and statistical analysis to keep health news in context for the viewer.

But typically, this doesn't happen. The medical industry churns out volumes of information for medical reporters to quickly sift through every day. There's a lack of special training for medical journalists (the general assignment reporter can expect to get thrown into the medical beat from time to time). Usually local news reports are under 90 seconds. The pressure for ratings compounds the problem.

Medical news is often simplified, or worse, sensationalized, because of industry pressures. Because health news sells, it can be and will be promoted—and in the process, distorted.

What is a medical reporter to do? Well, alone, there's not much a reporter can do. Like medical errors, the problems with medical journalism are system wide. At the root is a clash of cultures.

Medicine tends to be very methodical, slow, and subject to change. But the media want information that's definitive, they want it now, and, boy, it better be sensational. Also, people who go into journalism and ascend to management, tend to be more inclined toward writing and creative interests. They may not understand (or may be openly hostile toward) the scientific process.

TV reporters rarely cover medicine exclusively—one day it's finance, the next it's health

(Illustration: Giovanni Maki)

doi:10.1371/journal.pmed.0020215.g002

For TV reporters who are committed to the medical beat, educational opportunities are available through organizations such as the Association of Health Care Journalists (www.ahcj.umn.edu) and the National Association of Medical Communicators (www.ibiblio.org/namc). Journalists can learn how to interpret studies and present evidence-based balance in order to help viewers understand and make up their own minds about the latest developments in medicine, rather than just show the gee-whiz side of new technology.

Unfortunately, it's rare to find a TV reporter who exclusively covers medicine. Stations view this as a luxury. It is more common for medical reporters to also be general-assignment reporters or anchors, and they have other priorities with their combination jobs.

It's also rare to find management that's supportive of continuing education for their reporters. Even with the large profit margins at many TV stations, news directors generally do not provide financial support and ask that reporters interested in attending educational meetings use their own vacation time to do so. Furthermore, news directors, producers, and promotions staff don't seem to be themselves interested in learning about medical reporting.

An article in *JAMA* says that viewers are acting on and making personal medical decisions based on health information in the mass media. This trend has led some TV medical reporting experts, such as Gary Schwitzer (formerly of CNN, now at the University of Minnesota, and a contributor to this *PLoS Medicine* debate) and Dr. Timothy Johnson *(ABC News)*, to call for credentialing of medical journalists. After all, some meteorologists are credentialed. Are personal health decisions less important than the weather?

There's a disconnect between what station management values, what the reporters need, and what the viewers get. Right or wrong, the audience looks to TV medical reporters to educate and guide them on medical issues. It's an important responsibility that medical reporters and the mass media in general need to take seriously.

Melissa Sweet: Remember the Commercial Imperative when Examining Media Coverage of Health Top

Many people make the mistake of using the terms "journalists" and "the media" interchangeably. They speak, in the same breath, of the terrible failings of journalists and the media in covering health or other issues. In so doing, they fail to make a distinction between the craft or profession of journalism and the competitive industry that is the media. They fail to understand that the goals and drivers of journalism are often in conflict with those of the media industry.

The foremost goal of the media industry is, not surprisingly, to make profit. Many journalists are too idealistic to admit, even to themselves, that their job is to make money for their employers. Some believe they are there for the public interest, or even to interest the public. Some simply love to tell a yarn, to get the buzz that comes with uncovering a great story and breaking news. Some no doubt also come to enjoy the reflected glory of associating with the famous and the powerful. Indeed, many journalists have become celebrities themselves. Not coincidentally, this has benefits for their employers—nothing sells like celebrity.

But only a brave, naïve, or foolhardy journalist would publicly admit these days that one of their roles is to provide a voice to those who otherwise have difficulty having their voices heard, such as the disadvantaged. It is not a career-enhancing move at a time when many media proprietors have decided that a key to improving profits lies with their so-called AB audiences.

For those not up-to-date with marketing jargon, AB is shorthand for the affluent professionals so beloved by cashed-up advertisers. The theory goes that media outlets that attract audiences at the AB end of the socioeconomic scale are more likely to win advertisers or, even better, to get away with charging them premium rates. A senior manager at one of Australia's major newspaper groups recently explained why his company is focusing on boosting AB readership rather than total circulation. "A good circulation result is one which attracts the readership we need and advertisers want," said Mark Scott, Editor-in-Chief of Fairfax's metropolitan newspapers, which include the respected broadsheet, *The Sydney Morning Herald*.

"Sure, *The Daily Telegraph* [a tabloid] sells many more copies than *The Sydney Morning Herald*," said Scott, "but their ad rates are lower because the *SMH [Sydney Morning Herald]* has that AB audience." Scott said Fairfax's Sunday title *The Sun-Herald* is significantly more profitable at its present circulation level of about 513,000 than it was when it was selling 600,000 copies. "We have held that AB audience so our advertising revenue is up and our costs are lower."

So what has this to do with the media report health? Scott explained that his newspapers do extensive market research so they know what the AB market wants to read and how they want its presentation. "We create our papers with those readers in mind and shape our marketing and promotions to reinforce their values and interests." In other words, the allocation of scarce resources in ever more stretched newsrooms is driven by what market researchers tell media managers about what AB audiences want to know about.

This has implications for how the media cover all the areas that affect peoples' health—politics, economics, and education, for example—as well as the coverage of health issues themselves. I haven't seen the market research, but it's not hard to guess what interests AB groups. They might want to know how to stay as healthy, smart, and good-looking as possible for as long as possible. They might want to know which biotech companies are good investments, and might be particularly interested in private health care. They are probably less interested in the needs of indigenous people, prisoners, the homeless, asylum seekers, or the poor, and it's probably a fair bet to say that they are also less interested in the ways in which disadvantaged groups have worse access to health care and prevention efforts.

Some might think this is overly cynical. Perhaps AB people are not all self-centred; perhaps they care about broader issues than those that directly affect their own lives and personal well-being. Nor can the compliance of journalists be assumed. In the chaotic and anarchic world of journalism, there are many who try to do far more with their jobs than to make their bosses wealthy—even if they have to try and "sell" their stories to their news managers on the grounds that the stories will be of interest to the ABs. Many other factors also shape and influence news production. And a truly compelling story is likely to get a run, even if not of direct relevance to the wealthy.

Nonetheless, it is important to remember the commercial imperative when examining media coverage of health. Many initiatives aimed at influencing health coverage, target journalists who are only one component of the media industry. Other powerful forces also shape the way for health coverage. An analogy can be drawn with efforts to improve the quality and safety of health care, another chaotic industry. Measures aimed at individual clinicians may be helpful in reducing medical errors, but it is also important to look at the broader system in which clinicians work.

Katherine A. Baverstock: The Media Can Play a Special Role in Providing a Voice for People to Express Their Experiences of Illness Top

A registered pharmacist for the last 15 years, I was trained in the biomedical model of health, to measure and note signs and symptoms, make assessments, and advise about treatments on the basis of available scientific evidence.

Becoming interested in the portrayal of medicines in the media whilst working in outback Australia (which is grossly underserved by health professionals), I began my doctoral project within this quantitative biomedical tradition. As I found during my literature review, research arising from this tradition assesses media writing about medicines for "quality." Such research focuses on certain categories of quantitative information about the medicine, such as the indication, associated risks and benefits, outcomes of treatment, contraindications, and cost, that would allow readers to analyse the evidence for themselves and decide whether they should use the medicine.

The research in this area seems to be advocating a position for the health journalist as an educator. Australia's Quality Use of Medicines Strategy has the objective of optimising the use of medicines within the Australian community. It lists the media as a partner in the strategy, together with consumers, health professionals, government, and the pharmaceutical industry. Similar to the other partners, the media have special responsibilities to ensure the quality use of medicines, as described in Box 2. Although many of these responsibilities sit comfortably within the codes of ethics observed by working journalists, some of these responsibilities made me uncomfortable as a health professional. Should journalists be viewed as de facto health educators with the same responsibilities as those of us in the registered health professions?

Box 2. Australia's National Strategy for Quality Use of Medicines: Responsibilities of the Media

The media are responsible for the following.

- Ethical and responsible reporting on health-care issues
- Reporting on medicines accurately and attempting to have errors corrected if they occur

- Being aware of the variety of available information sources on medicines and the limitations of each source
- Being aware of the impact of media reports on the use of medicines in the community
- Being aware of issues relevant to the broad context of medicine use, including risks of medicine use, non-drug alternatives, and the cost of medicine use to individuals and society
- Encouraging dissemination of messages that enhance the quality of medication.

As I progressed in this quantitative framework, I began to feel more and more uncomfortable with the narrow examination of the newspaper stories I had collected for my research. As my analysis continued, it became apparent that the newspaper stories contained themes far richer and more interesting than quantitative information about how drugs work. The stories were an intriguing insight into how the community viewed issues surrounding medicines and the use of medicines. Even more interesting were the narratives about experiences with medicines. I decided to transfer my research to a communications faculty, and explored a far different perspective of medicines in the media. One of my first realisations was that the media are much more than the newspapers, television, and radio focussed on by so many biomedical researchers. They also include new media (the Internet), other print media, and small-scale media, such as leaflets and posters, and even the messages on the pens given out by pharmaceutical representatives.

I would like to propose that rather than acting as educators, the media can play a special role in providing a voice for people to express their experiences of illness and their interactions with the technologies of health. The advent of the Internet has democratised the media because this medium is accessible to everyone. The Internet can cross national boundaries and counteract isolation—not only geographic isolation, but also the isolation that may be caused by the experience of chronic illness and not knowing anyone who has lived your experience. People who were unable to have their stories heard within the traditional medical consultation now have a forum where they can be heard and háve their stories validated.

There is much research published within the sociological and anthropological literature examining the narrative surrounding health and illness within various types of media. Research now needs to examine how patients use information they find within the media, and whether it does make a difference to the medical encounter. Will an informed and questioning client leave us feeling threatened?

Within the traditional health set up, lengthy communication between medical professionals and clients is often not possible. Many health professionals receive scant training in communication and counselling. The use of media technologies allows our clients to tell their story, a biography that may be ever-changing because of the experience of chronic illness. I would argue, that rather than being much maligned by health professionals, the media should be viewed as a tool that allows healing by facilitating the telling of stories.

ROLE OF MEDIA CONCLUSION

Televisions can come up with some advertisements and documentary related to the diseases. Some movies can be made like as Hollywood movie "THE BEAUTIFUL MIND" which can disemminate the relevant information about the disease to the society. A bollywood movie "TARE ZAMEEN PAR" is a good e.g. of it.

Radio channels can throw some advertisements on air about the disease which would be lot of beneficial to the society and specially to the rural population as they are more connected to the radio channels.

Newspapers can help a lot in disemminating the information about the disease. A separate columns can be published related to a disease revealing necessary information of the disease.

Through these means society can get aware about the disease and can know how to behave with the patient in that condition.

Hence media can play an outstanding role in awaring a society about the diseases.

References

1. Lantz JC, Lanier WL (2002) Observations from the Mayo Clinic national conference on medicine and the media. Mayo Clin Proc 77: 1306–1311. Available:http://www.mayoclinicproceedings.com/inside.asp?AID=227&UID=. Accessed 4 February 2005.
2. Schwitzer G (2003) How the media left the evidence out in the cold. BMJ 326: 1403–1404. Available: http://bmj.com/cgi/content/full/326/7403 /1403. Accessed 4 February 2005.
3. Kovach B, Rosensteil T (2001) The elements of journalism. New York: Three Rivers Press. 208 p.
4. Schwitzer G (2004) A statement of principles for health care journalists. Am J Bioeth 4: W9. Available: http://www.ajobonline.com/journal/j_articles.php?aid=663. Accessed 4 February 2005.

5. Schwitzer G (2000) The seven words you shouldn't use in medical news. Available:http://www.tc.umn.edu/%7Eschwitz/The7wor ds.htm. Accessed 4 February 2005.
6. Schwitzer G (2004) Ten troublesome trends in TV health news. BMJ 329: 1352.
7. Kaiser Health Poll Report (2004) Health care priorities. Menlo Park (California): Kaiser Family Foundation. Available: http://www.kff.org/HealthPollReport/dec 2004/Care/. Accessed 4 February 2005.
8. Coghan A (2004 October 9) Do you believe in miracles? New Scientist 2468.
9. Mudur GS (2004 December 27) Ethics blown to winds. The Telegraph—Calcutta. Available:http://www.telegraphindia.com/1041227/as p/knowhow/story 4139179.asp. Accessed 7 June 2005.
10. Moynihan R, Bero L, Ross Degnan D, Henry D, Lee K, et al. (2000) Coverage by the news media of the benefits and harms of medications. N Eng J Med 342: 1645–1650.
11. Cassels A, Hughes MA, Cole C, Mintzes B, Lexchin J, et al. (2003) Drugs in the news: An analysis of Canadian newspaper coverage of new prescription drugs. CMAJ 168: 1133–1137.
12. Smith D, Wilson A, Henry D (2005) Monitoring the quality of medical news reporting: Early experience with 'media doctor'. >Med J Aust. In press.
13. Australian Press Council (2001 April) Reporting guidelines. General press release No. 245. Available: www.presscouncil.org.au/pcsite/activitie s/guides/gpr245.html. Accessed 31 February 2005.
14. Woloshin S, Schwartz LM (2002) Press releases: Translating research into news. JAMA 287: 2856–2858.
15. Brown D (2005 May 15) Statin role weighed in cancer rate study: Women using drug had fewer cases. Washington Post; Sect A: 16.
16. Schwartz LM, Woloshin S, Welch HG (2005 May 10) Overstating aspirin's role in breast cancer prevention. Washington Post; Sect F: 1.
17. Kolata G (2004 July 12) Experts set lower levels for cholesterol. New York Times; Sect A: 1.
18. Kassirer J (2004 August 1) Why should we swallow what these studies say? Washington Post; Sect B: 3.
19. Okrent D (2004 October 31) Analysts say experts are hazardous to your newspaper. New York Times; Sect 4: 2.

20. Ebencamp B (1998 November 9) The Dateline doctor is 'in'. Brandweek 39(42): 20.
21. Eggener S (1998) The power of the pen: Medical journalism and public awareness. JAMA 279: 1400.
22. Day M (2005 March 24) Words of wisdom come up against marketing strategies. The Australian 26.
23. Australian Government Department of Heath and Aging (2002) The national strategy for quality use of medicines. Commonwealth of Australia. Available:http://www.health.gov.au/internet/wcms/p ublishing.nsf/Content/nmp-pdf-natstraten g-cnt.htm/$FILE/natstrateng.pdf Accessed 31 May 2005.

13

Power of Social Media in India

S.D. Livingston, P. Rajendran

Introduction

The power of Social Media in India mainly focuses on building and reflecting of social networks or social relations among the people India. Most social media provide means for users to interact over the internet such as email and instant messaging and videos. Social network service usually means an individual centered service. Social Media sites allow users to share ideas, activities, events, and interests within their individual networks. Facebook, Linkedin and Orkut are very popular in India.

Social networking sites began to develop more advanced features for users to find and manage friends. Social networking sites had tremendously grown and had gained popularity by 2005. MySpace was reportedly getting more page views than Google. Facebook which was launched in 2004 has become the largest social networking site in the world. Today it is estimated that there are now over 200 active sites using a wide variety of social networking models.

Background of the Study

The three main indicators of the power of social media are: 1. Socio-politico-cultural changes 2. Recruitment process and 3. Effects of advertising. Hence a questionnaire was designed to find out the effects of social media on youth, office goers and children with reference to the three indicators.

Sites like MySpace and Facebook emphasise the power of Social Media in India, by allowing their users to interact with each other by sharing pictures, joining groups, sending private messages. Networking sites are free, used by a lot of different people, and allow websites to market themselves or their product as they see fit.

Objectives

The objective of this paper is to find out the power of Social Media in

India. Social networking websites are designed to allow members to connect and communicate with one another. The features of these sites foster interaction, activity, and of course, community.

Hypothesis

This paper tries to identify the influence of Social Media in the Social, Political, Economical and Cultural aspects of a society. It also tries to identify the influences of Social Media in the recruitment process in corporates. This paper also tries to understand the advertisement pattern influenced by the Social Media in India.

Classifications

The power of Social Media in India can be analyzed under three major classifications. They are:

1. Power of Social Media in Indian Social, Political, Economical and Cultural aspects.
2. Power of Social media in Recruitment Process in India.
3. Influence of Advertisements of Social Media in India.

I. Power of Social Media in Indian Political, Social, Economical and Cultural aspects

The power of Social Media in India can be analysed under Social, Political, Economical and Cultural aspects.

(A) Power of Social Media in Indian Politics

The power of Social Media in India can be studied with the impact of the Social Media in Indian Politics.

Following is the response of the survey conducted among the youth, office goers and school children of our country.

A survey was conducted among 300 participants. Among them 100 were youth, 100 were office goers and 100 were school children.

	Youth	*Office Goers*	*School level*
High	28	21	18
Moderate	15	18	25
Low	30	35	22
Nil	27	26	35

The survey report says that the youth feel that the power of social media in Indian politics is high. 28% youth say that it is high. 15% say that the power of social media in Indian politics is moderate, 30% say it is low and 27% say that it has no influence. This indicates that the social media has not been able to make an impact on youth as far as politics is concerned.

Among the office goers 21% say that the power of Social Media in Indian politics is High whereas 18% say that it is Moderate, 35% say that it is Low and 26% says that it is Nil. In this case also, the social media has not been able to exert a powerful influence.

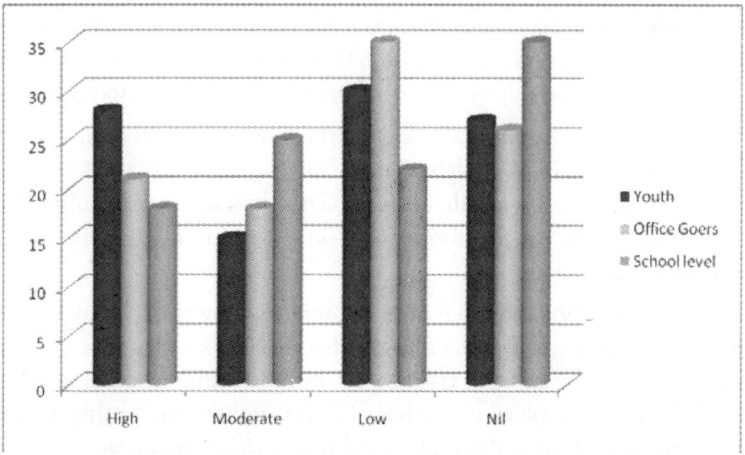

Among the school children 18% say that the power of Social Media in Indian politics is High whereas 25% say that it is Moderate, 22% say that it is Low and 35% say that it is Nil. Since children are more interested in play, it is not surprising that the results show that the social media lacks political influence on their lives. However, by comparing the results, the finding shows that the power of social media in Indian politics is high on youth compared with the office goers and children.

Anna Hazare, a 73-year-old social worker from Ahmednagar gave the people in power a run for their money. With more than 90000 'likes' on the 'India Against Corruption' Facebook page and thousands of others lending online support via twitter and their websites. Anna Hazare has taken the Internet by storm.

Narendra Modi, the chief minister of Gujarat, India is one of the seven finalists for "Must-Follow Politician on Social Media" in the Mashable Awards, and the only one from India.

(B) Social Media and Social Changes in India

The power of Social Media in India can be studied by observing its impact the Indian Society.

Following is the response of the survey conducted among the youth, office goers and school children of our country.

In the survey conducted to find out the influence of social media to bring about social changes in India, nearly 76 per cent of youth believe that social media empowers them to bring change in India.

Among the youth 76% say that the power of Social Media to bring in social changes in India is high whereas 11% say that it is moderate, 8% say that it is low and 5% says that it is nil. This shows that the youth with their ambitions and dreams rely on the social media as an agent of social change.

Among the office goers 52% say that the power of Social Media to bring in social changes in India is high whereas 30% says that it is moderate, 14% say that it is low and 4% say that it is nil. This indicates that the office goers with their cares and worries also depend on the social media for improving their position in society.

Among the school children 66% say that the power of Social Media to bring in social changes in India is high whereas 20% say that it is moderate, 9% say that it is low and 5% say that it is nil. Interestingly, though children like to run out and play with other children rather than sitting before a computer terminal, they also understand that social changes can be brought out by the social media.

Nevertheless, the finding shows that the power of social media to bring about social changes in India is high among youth compared with the office goers and children.

(C) Impact of Social Media on Indian Business

The power of Social Media in India can be studied with the impact of the Social Media in Indian Business.

Following is the response of the survey conducted among the youth, office goers and school children of our country.

	Youth	Office Goers	School level
High	67	61	44
Moderate	18	14	23
Low	11	18	30
Nil	4	7	3

In the survey conducted to find out the influence of social media in Indian Business, nearly 67 per cent of youth believe that social media impacts Indian Business Industry.

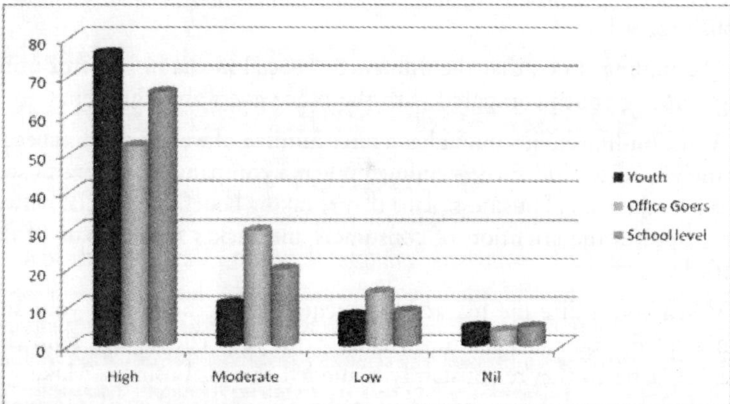

Among the youth 67% say that the influence of Social Media in Indian Business is high whereas 18% say that it is moderate, 11% say that it is low and 4% say that it is nil. Since youth are involved in buying the latest products online, they have found the social media highly influential referrals.

Among the Office goers 61% say that the influence of Social Media in Indian Business is high whereas 14% say that it is moderate, 18% say that it

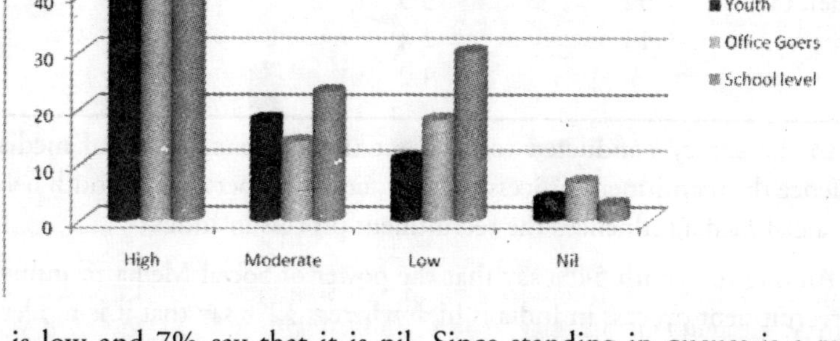

is low and 7% say that it is nil. Since standing in queues is a major problem for office goers, they find it highly useful to book train and film tickets online.

Among the school children 44% say that the influence of Social Media in Indian Business is high whereas 23% say that it is moderate, 30% say that it is low and 3% says that it is nil. Since children have no spending power, it is only natural that they think that the impact of the social media on business is less.

The finding shows that the influence of social media in Indian Business is high among youth compared with the office goers and children.

As the on-line environment has a huge number of websites, it has become extremely hard to find success online. When a company incorporates social media into their small business plans they're taking benefit of a social network which captures the attention of consumers and makes them a part of their client's lives.

When you utilize the marketing potential of Facebook into your small business plans you can become "friends" with your clients and send them regular updates so they're constantly reminded of your business. Making use of social networks such as twitter assists to keep a constant flow of information to clientele so that you could build brand recognition and customer attraction. However the regular updating and tweeting of these social networks and many more can prove overwhelming to the uniformed person.

II. Social Media for Recruitment

The power of Social Media in India can be studied with the impact of the Social Media in the recruitment process in India.

Following is the response of the survey conducted among the youth, office goers and school children of our country.

	Youth	*Office Goers*	*School Level*
High	54	41	51
Moderate	32	33.	29
Low	11	14	18
Nil	3	12	2

In the survey conducted to find out the influence of social media to influence the recruitment process in India, nearly 54 per cent of youth believe that social media influences the recruitment process in India.

Among the youth 54% say that the power of Social Media to influence the recruitment process in India is high whereas 32% say that it is moderate, 11% say that it is low and 3% say that it is nil. Since most of the youth visit job sites, this result is not surprising.

Among the office goers 41% say that the power of Social Media to influence the recruitment process in India is high whereas 33% say that it is moderate, 14% say that it is low and 12% say that it is nil. Though office goers already have a job, they may be using the social media for better job opportunities.

Among the school children 51% say that the power of Social Media to influence the recruitment process in India is high whereas 32% say that it is moderate, 11% say that it is low and 3% say that it is nil. Children hear a little about jobs from their working parents and teachers, so they do not really know about the recruitment process.

The finding shows that the influence of social media recruitment process in India is high among youth compared with the office goers and children.

Facebook added 100 million users in just about nine months. India currently has 48 million active Facebook users, which is considerable of the total users worldwide.

A *Social Recruiting Survey* conducted by US based firm by Jobvite shows that social media has become an important tool for recruiting top talent. According to the survey, which asked over 600 HR and recruiting professionals as to how they use social networking in their recruiting process, 73.3 per cent said they currently use social media to recruit candidates. The most commonly used medium is LinkedIn (78%), followed by Facebook (55%), Twitter (45%) and Blogs (19%). Jobvite also found that 46 percent of respondents are spending more on social recruiting in 2010 than they were in 2009.

Why Social Media Recruitment Required?

From the recruiter's perspective one of the reasons why social media has emerged as an important tool for recruitment is its power to offer them

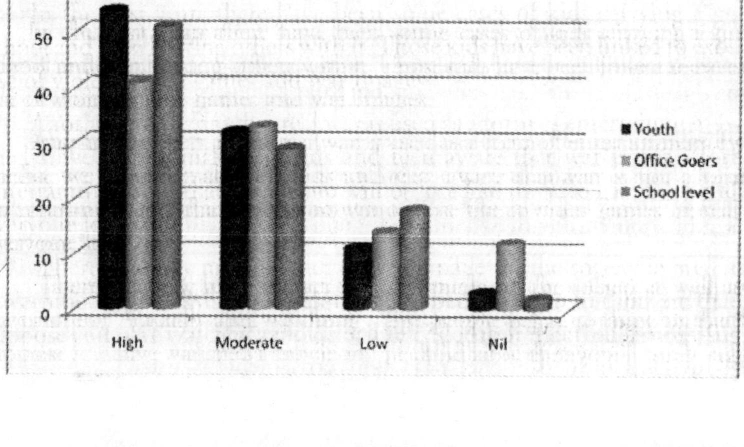

a broad perspective about the candidate. It tends to bring forth certain traits and personalities of a candidate which may not be reflected in their resume.

Secondly, social media recruitment widens the choice pool for the employers and also fastens the recruitment process.

Thirdly, it is a low cost tool with a good return on investment, thus saving both time and money costs. Additionally, social media increases the brand visibility of the recruiter.

From the applicant's perspective, social media helps applicants gain deeper insight into the company about certain facts and information which may not be readily available on the company website. They also get to know the openings available in various companies and apply accordingly, provided the companies are active on these social mediums.

II. Advertisements in Social Media

The power of Social Media in India can be studied with the impact of the Social Media in Indian Advertisements.

Following is the response of the survey conducted among the youth, office goers and school children of our country.

	Youth	*Office Goers*	*School Level*
High	45	36	59
Moderate	31	28	27
Low	16	17	7
Nil	8	19	7

In the survey conducted to find out the impact of social media advertisements in India, nearly 45 per cent of youth believe that social media advertisements influences the Indian Advertisement Industry.

Among the youth 54% say that the impact of social media advertisements in India is high whereas 31% say that it is moderate, 16% say that it is low

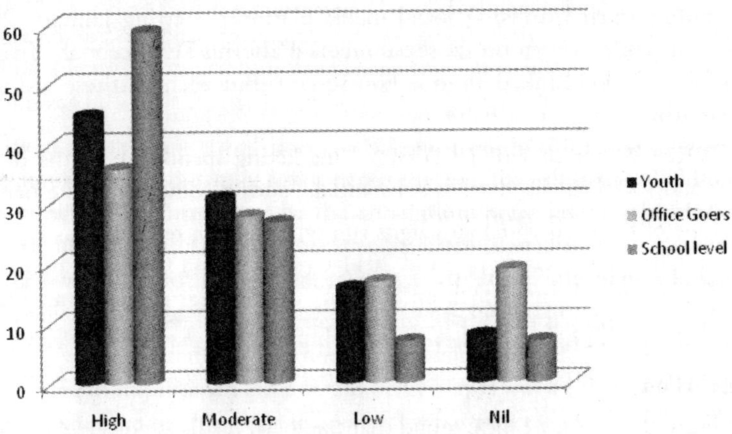

and 8% say that it is nil. Gone are the days when online advertising had no impact on people. But now with technological changes, the youth are swayed by advertising online.

Among the office goers 36% say that the impact of social media advertisements in India is high whereas 28% say that it is moderate, 16% say that it is low and 8% say that it is nil. Since most of the office goers are less curious than the youth in buying new products, they are less affected by advertising.

Among the school children 59% say that the impact of social media advertisements in India is high whereas 27% say that it is moderate, 7% say that it is low and 7% says that it is nil. Since children like to play online games and since they love to eat various food stuff, they find online advertisements very attractive.

The finding shows that the impact of social media advertisements in India is high among school children compared with the office goers and children.

Facebook, the world's largest social networking site, has just launched a new initiative under which advertisements will appear in the form of 'stories' or posts about a product in its news feed labelled as 'featured'.

Though the advertisements have generated a huge controversy abroad and are yet to be rolled out in India, many Indian companies using the social media platform as their marketing strategy are keenly watching.

The advertisements are displayed based on what users have 'liked' and actions made by their friends.

Jet Airways, recently crossed a milestone of 300,000 fans on Facebook. The airline started utilising social media platforms starting January, 2010 and is currently present on six social media platforms i.e. Facebook, Twitter, YouTube, Flickr, Linked in and Foursquare. But each of these are used differently.

"Over 80 per cent of Jet Airways' marketing spends are in the digital space and social media share is substantial," adds a company spokesperson.

One of the successful campaigns run on Facebook recently was PepsiCo India's 'Change the Game' around 2011 Cricket World Cup. PepsiCo India decided to run a Reach Block on February 11 last year to guarantee that it would reach 100 per cent of its target audience over a 24-hour period.

Conclusion

From the study, we have found that the social media is powerful medium for recruitment and advertising among youth, office goers and children though the percentage of influence may vary. But when it comes to socio-politico-economic changes, there is still a long way to go to make social media play a powerful role in society.

For many youngsters social networking sites are the main forum of interaction. As they spend more time online, they have less time actual interactions which in turn make them more isolated. In a self perpetuating cycle they turn again to the online world to quell their loneliness (The Hindu, dated 22.01.2012).

Social media has received great attention due to its rapid rise to the horizon. According to Vande Hatel, we have just seen the beginning of social networking and the participation of the networking sites are growing, there seems to be no limit to their size. Facebook was most visited website for the second year since its inception and accounted for 10.29 per cent of all US visits during the year 2011. Now Facebook has complete control over your online life.

Suggestions

To make social media more powerful in all aspects of society, the following points may be considered:

1. Teachers and parents should form relevant online groups which are children-oriented. For example, informative and knowledge-gaining inputs can be introduced in the group.

2. Schools should introduce recruitment awareness programmes for children so that they can be better equipped for their future. For example, counsellors can organise lectures and give information about the recruitment process in social media.

3. Advertisers must consider to advertise more children related products in social media to attract them.

4. Political campaigns and opinion polls must be conducted in social media in India. This will bring about a greater involvement among the people in politics.

5. Like IT companies, other companies too must give better Internet access so that it may create more awareness among the office goers about social media.

6. Inclusion of online marketing facility in social media will generate more business.

References

1. Acquisti, Alessandro, and Gross, Ralph. (2006). Imagined Communities: Awareness, Information Sharing, and Privacy on the Facebook.In Golle, P. and Danezis, G. (Eds.), *Proceedings of 6th Workshop on Privacy Enhancing Technologies*. (pp. 36-58). Cambridge, U.K. Robinson College. June 28-30. (conference paper)
2. Acquisti, Alessandro, and Gross, Ralph. (2009). Predicting Social Security numbers from public data. *Proceedings of the National Academy of Sciences*, 106 (27), 10975-10980. (journal article)
3. Adamic, Lada, Buyukkokten,Orkut, and Eytan Adar. (2003). A social network caught in the Web. *First Monday*, 8 (6). (journal article)
4. Agarwal, S., and Mital, M.. (2009). Focus on Business Practices: An Exploratory Study of Indian University Students' Use of Social Networking Web Sites: Implications for the Workplace. *Business Communication Quarterly*. (journal article)
5. Ahmed OH, Sullivan SJ, Schneiders AG, and McCrory P. (2010). iSupport: do social networking sites have a role to play in concussion awareness? . *Disability and Rehabilitation*, 32(22), 1877-1883. (journal article)
6. Ahn, Yong-Yeol, Han, S., Kwak, H., Moon, S., and Jeong, H.. (2007). Analysis of topological characteristics of huge online social networking services. *WWW '07: Proceedings of the 16th international conference on World Wide Web*. (pp. 835-844).New York, NY, USA (conference paper)

7. Ajith Sundaram. (2009). MR. (mastersthesis)
8. Ajith Sundaram. (2010). Evaluation of Social networking sites for business application. (mastersthesis)
9. Ajith Sundaram. (2011). Can Social Networking Keep Students In School A Proposal for an Ideal Social Networking Site for an Educational Institution.. *1*, 1. (journal article)
10. Albrechtslund, Anders. (2008). Online Social Networking as Participatory Surveillance. *First Monday*, 13 (3). (journal article)
11. Aleksandra Korolova, Rajeev Motwani, Shubha U. Nabar, and Ying Xu. (2008). Link privacy in social networks. *Proceedings of the 17th ACM conference on Information and Knowledge Management (CIKM\'08).* (pp. 289-298). ACM. (conference paper)
12. Ambrose, David. (2007). Virtual Interactive Communication: A Bicultural Survey Through the Lens of Web 2.0. Department of German (unpublished)
13. Andrejevic, Mark. (2005). The work of watching one another: Lateral surveillance, risk and governance. *Surveillance & Society*, 2 (4), 479-497. (journal article)
14. Athanasopoulos, E.A. Makridakis, Antonatos, S., Antoniades, D., Ioannidis, S., Anagnostakis, K.G., and Markatos, E.P.. (2008). Antisocial Networks: Turning a Social Network into a Botnet. (techreport)
15. Back, M. D., Stopfer, J. M., Vazire, S., Gaddis, S., Schmukle, S. C., Egloff, B., and Gosling, S. D. (2010). Facebook profiles reflect actual personality, not self-idealization.. *Psychological Science*, 21, 372-374. (journal article)
16. Backstrom, Lars, Dwork, C., and Kleinberg, Jon. (2007). Wherefore art thou r3579x? anonymized social networks, hidden patterns, and structural steganography. *Proceedings of the 16th international conference on World Wide Web.* (pp. 181-190). (conference paper)
17. Backstrom, Lars, Huttenlocher, Dan, Kleinberg, Jon, and Xiangyang Lan. (2006). Group Formation in Large Social Networks: Membership, Growth, and Evolution. *Proceedings of the 12th International Conference on Knowledge Discovery in Data Mining.* (pp. 44-54).New York ACM Press. (conference paper)
18. Baker, James R., and Moore, Susan M.. (2008). Distress, coping, and blogging: Comparing new Myspace users by their intention to blog. *CyberPsychology & Behavior*, 11 (1), 81-85. (journal article)

19. Barker, Valerie. (2009). Older Adolescents' Motivations for Social Network Site Use: The Influence of Gender, Group Identity, and Collective Self-Esteem. *Cyber Psychology and Behavior*. 1-5 (journal article)

20. Barnes, Susan. (2006). A privacy paradox: Social networking in the United States. *First Monday*, 11 (9). (journal article)

21. Baumgartner, J.C., and Morris, J.S. (2010). MyFaceTube Politics Social Networking Web Sites and Political Engagement of Young Adults. *Social Science Computer Review*, 28(1). (journal article)

22. Baym, Nancy. (2007). The new shape of online community: The example of Swedish independent music fandom. *First Monday*, 12 (8). (journal article)

23. Beer, David. (2008). Social network(ing) sites...revisiting the story so far: A response to danah boyd & Nicole Ellison. *Journal of Computer-Mediated Communication*, 13 (2), 516-529. (journal article)

24. Beer, David. (2008). Making Friends with Jarvis Cocker: Music Culture in the Context of Web 2.0. *Cultural Sociology*, 2 (2), 222-241. (journal article)

25. Bernd Ploderer, Steve Howard, and Peter Thomas. (in press). Collaboration on Social Network Sites: Amateurs, Professionals and Celebrities. *Computer Supported Cooperative Work (CSCW)*, online first. (journal article)13

14

Acceptability of Women - Can Media Play a Constructive Role?

Dewan, Anjali

Introduction

Communication is extremely important for women's development and mass media play significant role. In all spheres of life, such as the controlling of population growth, spread of literacy or improving the quality of life for vast masses, women have a crucial role to play. In this context, women have an important role to play to create awakening in them to achieve their potential as the prime movers of change in society. In today's world, print and electronic media play a vital role in effectively conveying effectively message that needs to be conveyed. It is true that media have brought to light, as never before, certain misdemeanors against women but in a very subtle manner, it also perpetuated the stereotyped image of women as a householder and an inconsequential entity in the traditional value system. By gradually shaping public opinion, personal beliefs and even people's self perceptions, media influences the process of socialization and shapes ideology and thinking. Indian society is full of diversified cultures, traditions and beliefs. Our mass media's role as a social constructor and representative of women has greater responsibility in binding these complexities of culture and processes with the people of the society.

The presence of women in media both in terms of numbers, whether absolute or in comparison with men and their status in terms of the position they occupy, is strongly influenced by the scene, not of their choice, but on account of the social and religious taboos which operated as legal sanctions, and even today operate as such, in many regions and communities, the constitution and laws not withstanding. Poverty, illiteracy, discrimination and male domination keep a vast majority of women away from the print media even as readers. As regards the electronic media, even where the community radio and television are available, either they are crowded out by the men, or on account of social inhibitions, women are unable to view or listen. Media has therefore largely come to be confined to the women in the middle and the higher classes, whether in the rural or urban areas and more particularly in the urban areas whether as passive consumers or as active players. The issue of women and the media can broadly be understood at two levels, both implicating and affecting each other:

- The participation of women in decision-making and expression in the media
- Representation or portrayal of women and gender relations in the media.

Participation and Expression

At the most basic level, women are under-represented in media institutions. Those who are within the field are often not in decision-making positions. Although women are increasingly entering into media, top management is still largely male dominated and the culture of patriarchy is perpetuated through this disparity. There is a gender division of labor that is evident through the way that stories are assigned. 'Soft' issues like fashion, culture, arts and lifestyle are often consigned to women media practitioners, whereas 'hard' and what is considered 'serious' issues like finance, economics and politics are often within the purview of their male counterparts. The criteria of newsworthiness are similarly and consequently understood through this gendered lens. Headline materials often constitute of 'hard issues' whilst 'soft issues' are shunted to 'special' and supplementary segments of the media. Gender stereotyped views and attitudes, such as the attachment of productive incapacity and women's reproductive roles can hinder women's opportunities to assume decision-making positions. Further, sexual harassment has been particularly cited as one of the methods to control and exclude women from these positions. As media is becoming increasingly privatized and concentrated on a few transnational media giants, this can be a serious cause of concern when individuals within the field are left with little legal recourse to ensure the protection of their right to equal gender status. Government intervention often focuses on licensing and ownership as opposed to structures and practices within the institutions that discriminates against women, or prevents their views from being expressed. This contributes to the continued marginalisation of women's themes in the media, their exclusion from socio-political institutions in the public sphere, and severely curtails media democratisation in the promotion of diverse cultural, social and political worldviews.

Women's Portrayal in the Media

Throughout Asia, women have been portrayed in the media as victims, subservient, nurturing, sacrificing and objectified sexualised beings. This not only inaccurately represents the diversity of women's lives, roles and experiences within this complex and rich region, women's contributions to the socio-political and economic development of society are often neglected. The perpetuation of stereotypes in images and representation solidifies women's traditional roles and unequal gender relations in multiple ways. Most visibly, women are seen as mourners at tragedies or as victims of violence. The Global Media Monitoring Project found that out of the small number of women who were interviewees in news stories (14%), 29% of them were as victims of accidents, crimes or other events. This does not only represent women as helpless subjects without agency, it also fails to emphasize men's role as perpetrators in instances of violence against women. Further, the dissemi-nation of these messages affects women's self-confidence, mobility and subsequently access and participation in public spaces for fear of assault. There are many more examples, such as women's portrayals in an increasingly consumer-driven culture and the commodification of women's bodies in advertising, pornography and conflict situations that can be cited and raised. These are two strategic objectives that have been outlined in the Beijing Platform for Action adopted by State governments at the Fourth World Conference for Women in 1995. They address broadly the two levels of discrimination which are to increase the participation and access of women to expression and decision-making in and through the media and new technologies of communication and promote a balanced and non-stereotyped portrayal of women in the media.

The various types of media are:

1. Electronic (Radio, Television etc.)
2. Print

Electronic Media

Radio and Television combined with satellite channels provide wide coverage on almost important aspects of life. Doordarshan and All India Radio have captured good audience size not only in cities but also even in semi-urban and rural areas. The program contents of both All India Radio (AIR) and Doordarshan give priority mainly to entertainment- based programmes. Women issues and their development programmes are reflected poorly in both the media. Lack of adequate planning and importance to women's programmes loses the target audience group. The Indian television programmes on women are generally based on the lives and cultures of urban society. In quantity there have been very few, in quality very poor programmes are concerned with the problems of women in rural areas. The main reason behind this is the commercial nature of Doordarshan, commercial sponsors and advertisers do not prefer women issue programmes, which they think are not very popular and or are liked by few audience. Television has been called the most real form of media. It is the real representation of women in TV and it affects the mindset of those who watch the television, specially the negative and debasing image of women as represented through money-spinning advertisements and serials. The systematic oppression of women by men is being projected by television. Many argue against the current trend of female TV characters opting to give up their career. Sex stereotype is also very much evident in television portrayal of men and women in their appointed roles. Various TV. channels show women characters dominating the serials and are either shown as silently suffering characters or as vindictive, revenge seeking, glamorous vamps.

Print Media

The print media which include newspapers, periodicals, newsletters and other channels are relied upon by the people as credible source of information, education and entertainment. The print media are known for fearless criticism and service. The media reflects events taking place in society and provides a platform for dialogue and debate on issues which can generate social changes. While electronic media carries more immediate weight on focusing attention on various issues, it is print media which has more persistent and lasting effect. It is felt that the way women are being projected in the print and electronic media is a reflection on the whole society. Though there is no authentic research done in this area, but it is estimated by those working in this field that print media, both daily and weekly, is on women's issues and about half of these are related to sex, prostitution, glamour, entertainment and crime. In the past few years, there has been an improved and increased reporting of issues related to women in the media particularly in the print. News related to women though still marginal have started to occasionally occupy important slots like the editorial, feature news, front-page news etc. However, women's visibility in the news is still dominated by sensational stories of glamour, sex, domestic violence and other forms of violence. Stories like women coping with adversity or building their lives are largely missing. Issues affecting women, their vast experiences and their lives, barely find their way into the mainstream media. Likewise, very few informative pieces or feature columns are published for women informing them about their legal rights, or about their potential for political activity. Many other studies have also established that when women appear in the news, they are mostly projected as passive victims or passive reactors to public events in news media. They hardly appear as speakers or participants in public event.

Newspapers

The lack of gender sensitivity in the media is evidenced in the failure to eliminate gender-based stereotyping. Generally, the media do not provide a balanced portrayal of women's diverse lives and their contributions to society in a changing world, often reinforcing stereotyped images of women and their roles in society. It is a common practice additionally to assess the professional success of a woman through questions and claims about her related to being a good mother and a wife. This is exactly the type of writing in the media that undermines the efforts of activists, who aim to establish gender equality in all areas of society. The prevailing portrayal of women in mainstream daily newspapers has the following characteristics:

- Positive images of women have a narrow scope and are based on new stereotypes of women's success like a pop star, a beauty queen, and a sport's woman with an outstanding result.
- There is an absence of the image of an active, assertive workingwoman, of a successful businesswoman, or a positive image of a woman politician.
- Average women are nearly always portrayed as victims of poverty, social injustice, domestic violence and organised crime.
- Misogyny in the form of rude jokes, mockery or open verbal aggression have become an accepted way of a systematic backlash against women activists working for women's political empowerment consisting of issues like freedom of abortion, freedom of sexual orientation, human rights.

It is the culture pages that help to round out the portrayal through the reviews of exhibitions by women artists, performances by female musicians, critiques of plays produced or acted by women, but here too are the seductive Swapna-sundaris and Mallika Shehrawats or the sexy silk Smithas and the razzle dazzle Kareena who the camera and the pen focus on. Only the Sports pages carry some positive news of the achievements of women athletes and players like Sania Mirza. Yet even here, when women achieve positive or even spectacular results, men find ways of undermining or ridiculing their success. The presence of women in media both in terms of numbers, whether absolute or in comparison with men, and their status in terms of the position they occupy is strongly influenced by the scene, not of their choice, but on account of the social and religious taboos which operated as legal sanctions, and even today operate as such, in many regions and communities. Even in those regions and communities where the social and religious taboos can no longer be enforced, poverty, illiteracy, discrimination and male domination keep a vast majority of women away from the print media even as readers. The positive side of women's progress and their contribution for national development has not been adequately discussed in the print media. The emphasis on stories about women, about their struggle for recognition is only the surface trimming. The actual message to audience still is that society opposes the liberation of women.

Magazines and Journals

Magazines differ markedly from newspapers in content, time element and methods of operation. In contrast to daily newspapers with its hurry-up headlines, magazines are published weekly, fortnightly, monthly or sometimes quarterly, because these publications usually deal with subjects in greater depth than newspapers do. Magazines fulfill four major purposes in our lives. They inform, guide and entertain the average reader. They also assist commerce through advertising. Information is imparted chiefly by printing news, while in depth articles and features help to give the reader the background necessary to understand intelligently current events and ideas. Entertainment is provided through numerous articles, jokes and cartoon strips. A newspaper is designed for family reading while magazines in most instances aim carefully at special interest audience. Indian Magazines contain primarily and predominantly volumes of advertisements and sexist writings. A vast majority of Indian Magazines are known for the portrayal of women as sex objects, consumers and slaves. Women journals are mostly elitist and sexist. They are not in a position to advocate the course of women and rejuvenate our socio-political economic and cultural orders. The targeted readerships of these magazines are the upper and lower middle classes living in cities. Most of women's journals consistently seek to direct women's energies into a narrow channel to define their concerns, pre-occupations and aspirations with an arbitrarily imposed feminine framework. The impression created is that the outside world belongs to men and the issues which arise there do not affect women except indirectly through the men related to them. Women's magazines confer status on women as a group and make womanly things a serious business. They provide a public platform and a symbolic social order which consistently offers a woman cheap and accessible source of positive evaluation alongside practical directions for fulfilling her potential as a consumer. They also preach the ideal of a woman's power of self determination by their overwhelming emphasis on self- help.

Indecent posters and boardings displayed everywhere are the crude reminders of distorted images and attitudes to women. Popular magazines with large circulations flash vulgar and obscene glossy photographs on their cover pages. The advertising world continues to use women to peddle its products and to present women as sexual objects. The image of the educated woman is typecast as insensitive, self-centered and uncaring. The economically independent woman is shown as domineering and ruthless. The woman is considered ideal only when she is in her nurturing roles and as a supportive supplement to man. The coverage of women issues in the English print media and in the Indian language press differs in a number of ways. This is quite expected due to the very difference of readership profiles and other characteristics. The regional language press has its compulsions to be biased, inflammatory, sensational, communal and partisan. This is so as it serves only a small segment of readers who are conservative and traditional and read such papers only to replenish and refresh their established beliefs.

There have been several studies of print media with regard to women which have found the print media guilty of sexism, distortion of image of women and propagation of sex stereotypes like mothers, housewives, dependant, passive, etc. The other side of such misinterpretation is that in most popular print media women are seldom shown as working women who are capable professionals, labourers, farmers. Rather the predominant image is that of the self-sacrificing housewife. The analysis done of the so-educational media like children's books, adult literacy primers for women shows that they are sexist and they perpetuate sex-stereotypes. The Print Media has also seen a growth spurt in the recent years particularly with regard to women and development magazines. The journals are mostly qualified for modern society and could be said to be positively harmful to the development of women as conscious individuals aware of themselves and aware of the society around them. If a woman wins a beauty contest, magazines or newspapers in particular give much importance to the news and even take her photographs on cover page but, at the same time if a woman gets the Nobel Prize she gets limited coverage. Here the difference of judgment in women's issues is quite marked in our media.

Information in the print reinforces the stereotype and traditional roles of women in society. In order to enhance the status and position of women in society the information messages should portray women in career oriented, lead roles and in a holistic image, which is truly representative of Indian culture and ethos. Media is an issue is related to all women's issues and it affects not only urban women but all women and all men. By reinforcing sex stereotypes and constantly glorifying motherhood and sub-servient wifehood the print media makes it difficult for women to break out of these prescribed roles, norms and behaviour patterns. Such conservative depictions reduce the few statements about sex equality and equal participation of women contained in the Constitution to mere window dressing. This is not a plea of literary writing for women to be scoured but to redress the enormous harm done by existing portrayals and images in print media. Women must resist being sold in this manner and it is time they took the power of this medium in their own hands to create truth in their idiom or the pressures of the mass market will make their struggle for change increasingly difficult. The status of women has not improved noticeably despite the government's and the media's claim about social justice towards women. What is needed is a wider change in the social outlook.

Clearly, the media does not provide a balanced picture of women's diverse lives and contributions to society in a changing world. Much remains to be done with regard to the participation, portrayal and access of women to the media and its impact on and use as an instrument for the advancement and empowerment of women. What our country needs in the present context are minimum regulation and more enablement. Media reinforces the conservative view of women and ignores their economic participation and contribution, especially that of rural women, over 50% of whom are directly involved in economic activities, in addition to housework and childcare. All this means that media, instead of challenging the view that women are inferior, subservient, unimportant, reinforces it and it establishes man as the active force, the doer, the one who matters. The needs and concerns, the problems they face are not articulated publicly, no public thinking and debates are initiated on their real concerns. Because their concerns and interests remain unarticulated in the print, women also remain neglected.

Conclusion

As media practitioners and institutions, independent code of ethics that specifically addresses gender issues within this field can be developed and implemented. These codes can be further modified to ensure that sexist and stereotyped coverage of women are considered ethically unacceptable within the industry. Self-regulatory mechanisms such as adoption of sexual harassment policies within media institutions can dismantle one of the real obstacles that hinder women's full participation in media. Consistent and sustained capacity building of all members within media institutions whether male or female, reporters, editors or producers on gender issues can not only raise awareness on the complexities and implications of gender dynamics and power relations within this field, but also broaden the base of experts that are able to work with these issues meaningfully. More airtime can be allocated to issues related to women that break away from the usual areas traditionally considered as women's issues. One concrete example would be to increase the portrayal of women as significant contributors to society as leaders, workers and thinkers, not just as carers, sex objects or victims. The development of appropriate alternative and community media can also enable the dissemination of diverse expressions and experiences, particularly from marginalized groups who are better able to own and manage them at the community level. Media has immense power in this process. It is one of the primary institutions which help shape the world. Taking accountability in this role and interrogating its own practices, perceptions, expectations and visions is crucial to imagine a society that is abundant in diversity, critical of inequality and resistant to marginalisation.

The issue of gender should be at the forefront of discussions concerning freedom of expression. International commitments such as the WSIS Declaration of Principles and a Plan of Action and the Beijing Platform for Action need to be aligned to understand women's rights and gender equality as a cross cutting principle. Particularly in light of the development of digital information and communication technologies in media that have the capacity to transcend national boundaries and enable proliferation of discourses at unprecedented breadth and speed, gender dimensions crucially need be to be surfaced and addressed. Otherwise, the move towards building Information Societies for economic, social and political development will be one that is substantively impoverished for want of principles in equality and non-discrimination. On the other hand, media can be utilized for projecting the true and positive image of women and to wipe out her traditional passive image that has been imprinted on the mind of the society as a whole, including the women. The potentiality of media as a powerful instrument of social change has first to be used to restore 50% of the humanity to its proper pedestal. Change has to be brought about not only in the status of women but in the attitude of the society towards them. Priority has therefore necessarily to be given to changing image of women, from a passive onlooker and recipient, to that of a positive doer and achiever.

However the scenario is not so depressing with the advent of women reporters and the presence of some senior women journalists in positions of responsibility. That has made a significant difference to the coverage of women's issues in the press. They have observed that in the past ten years, women's issues have increasingly, though sporadically begun to make news and to be considered worthy of comment. This is due to the growth of the contemporary, women's movement in India, with women's groups becoming steadily more active and vocal. The English press and the other language papers in India have been doing well as far as the coverage of women is concerned. Lead reports, articles, editorials, features and news analysis have been published on women's issues. For media to promote balanced and non-stereotype portrayal of women in their multiple roles, it is imperative that government, media,

NGOs and private sector should come together and forge joint strategies to promote gender equality and gender justice. In its new-found expansive role, media should foster a broad ethical content and moralizing impulse in the society so essential for the emergence of a civil society. Moreover for the society's abiding benefit media must nurture and transmit humane values of civilization. They must take upon themselves the proactive role of a protector and a promoter of human rights, gender justice and democratic order.

References

1. Agrawal, Bina, Bhasin, Kamla. Women and Media, Ch. 1, pp. 14-30. Vikas Publications, New Delhi.
2. Abraham, N. (1988). Women's Liberation and Indian Media, Vol. 25, No. 6, pp. 22-25. Vidura, New Delhi.
3. Allen, D., Rush, R. R., Kaufman, S.J. (1996). Women transforming communications- Global Intersections. Sage Publications, New Delhi.
4. Agrawal, Vinod, C. and Rai, Kumkum (1988). Women Television and Rural Development. pp. 56-64. National Publishing House.
5. Afsar Bano. (2003). Indian Women: The Changing Face, Kalaso Books, Delhi.
6. Bathla, Sonia (1998). Women, Democracy and the Media -Cultural and Political Representations in the Indian Press. pp. 77-113. Sage Publications, New Delhi.
7. Batra, P. & Grover, I. (1994) Magazine Circulation and Reading Habits of Rural Women', Media and Development, Har Anand Publication.
8. Chopra, Anshu (2008). Portrayal of Women in Print Media. Dissertation submitted to Women and Study Development Centre, Delhi University.
8. De, Utpal Kumar, Ghosh, Bholanath (2004). Issues on empowerment of women Monit Publications, New Delhi.
9. Jain, Devaki and Rajput, Ram (Ed.) (2003). Narratives from the Women's studies Family. Sage Publications, New Delhi.
10. Menon, Latika (1997). Gender Issues and Social Dynamics. Kanishka Publishers, New Delhi.
11. Mahapatra, Subhasini (2006). Status of women towards empowerment. Rajat Publications, New Delhi.
12. Nirmal J & Vardarajan Dhulasi B. (2005). Empowerment of women. Serials Publications, New Delhi.
13. Prasad Kiran (Ed.) (2005). Women and Media - Challenging Feminist Discourse. The Women's Press, Priyadarshini Vihar, New Delhi.
14. Reddy, P.A, Jayalakshmi, M. (2004). Exposure of women to mass media. pp. 50-56. Classical Publishing Company, New Delhi.

15

Innovation in Media Management

Masoumeh Shiri Aminlou, Maryam Taherian

Imagine the world of media in 2020: Will you still read your morning paper — on a tablet computer, on ePaper, which you can fold up and synchronise with the display in your electric car that takes you to work? Will you need any kind of device at all? And, at any rate: will the information you process have been edited the day before? The future of publishing, is a programme of events, designed to facilitate innovation and create transformational change within the publishing industry. The programme will raise the level of conversation around what is possible, looking beyond apps and e-books, and inspire people with 'show and tells' from innovators who are creating disruptive projects.

A panel of social media experts believe that in 2020, social media will be far more pervasive, interlinked, and location-aware than they are now. For today's people, rapid, constant change in the media, not only is accepted, it is expected. The anomaly is, that leaders of the traditional media companies too often see radical, revolutionary change as a threat to their personal and organisational futures. If a review of the programs of the major media conventions is a guide, these executives are remarkably risk-averse in creating new products, processes and services. They remain focused on marginally improving their current product offerings with the expectation that doing so, will shore up their declining or fragmenting audience—all within traditional business models. So there is a huge gap between what is and what must be, if media companies are going to avoid being replaced by true information and entertainment innovators, who are unbound by today's rules and unburdened by yesterday's successes. A bold approach to fostering and nurturing an innovation mindset is necessary for corporate survival in this transformational era. This article is your guide to nurturing that mindset, along with a detailed framework for managing innovation. It takes the lessons of leading-edge, innovative companies in other sectors and adapts them to media businesses. In short, this is a prescription for new product success. Will this prescription eliminates the risk of new product failure? Assuredly not. But it will lead to a far higher success rate.

What is Innovation?

Innovation is the creation of better or more effective products, processes, services, technologies, or ideas that are accepted by markets, governments, and society. Innovation differs from invention in that innovation refers to the use of a new idea or method, whereas invention refers more directly to the creation of the idea or method itself.

Power of the Innovation

The power of innovation is not in the thing, but in the process. Most of us think of innovation the way the dictionary defines it: a new idea, process or product. For highly innovative, Innovator Group (IG), innovation is a process that creates products that create new basis of competition. Indeed, (IG) values these new bases for competition to the degree that in 2001, nearly 35 per cent of sales came from products introduced within the last four years. Innovation consultant and author Thomas D. Kuczmarski sees innovation as "a mindset or way of thinking that focuses on creativity for the future"[1].

Innovation is a mindset or way of thinking that focuses on creativity for the future. As we enter this new era of storytelling, innovation will be the key to survival for media companies. That is not alarmist talk. It is a lesson from history. Failure to innovate is a prime source of business failure. During periods of revolutionary change, nearly all established competitors have failed. Does any media executive dispute that this is a revolutionary period? Business strategist's call a period of seismic changes such as this a strategic inflection point. That is a point at which a competitor introduces a new product, or customer preferences change, with the result that a company's product or service no longer is relevant. That is the point that traditional media are rapidly approaching. Here's an example from utter back: the gas lamp industry in the time of Thomas Edison's development of the incandescent bulb.

For most homes and businesses in America of the mid-1800s, the source of light was natural gas. In fact, residents of Baltimore had enjoyed gas street lamps since1816, but that was soon to change. In 1876, Thomas Edison opened his Menlo Park laboratory.[2] on the inventor's benches there were experiments to improve the "electric candle" that had been under development by several innovators for two decades.

Edison had the advantage of significant investor support and a mind attuned to innovation beyond even the innovations, his team was developing. So as his team of scientists perfected its version of the incandescent bulb, Edison was turning his creative skills to the incandescent bulb as a part of a system. That system would encompass the electrical generators to power the bulbs, the design of the sockets into which the bulbs would be placed, the fixtures, the wiring infrastructure in homes and cities and the devices for billing for power service. The leaders of the gas industry correctly saw this new technology as the threat it was. Their response? They sabotaged Edison's demonstration teams in the field. They heralded the benefits of gas service. They belittled the new technology. They used their contacts in local government to create a regulatory shield.

Most significantly, they dramatically improved their product. The new, improved gas lamp of the 1890s featured a mantle of cerium and thorium oxide that increased its candlepower fivefold while at the same time reducing the cost of service by two-thirds.

Did these improvements stop innovation and prevent the demise of the gas lamp industry? of course not. They merely delayed the widespread acceptance of Edison's innovative technology. The gas lamp industry was doomed from the day the new technology was introduced, but it was successful in putting off the inevitable for 12 years. Unlike the ice harvesters, however, the gas industry saved itself from extinction by developing a totally new use for its product—heating buildings. Thus, it was the coal industry that was the final victim of the light bulb.

Still, 12 years of extra business life isn't so bad; it would be nearly forever for the media industries of today. In 1986, fewer than half of American households had cable television (two-thirds do today) and cable revenue was less than one-fifth of what it is today. Three broadcast television networks dominated the home entertainment landscape. Direct broadcast satellite had not emerged as the consumer technology that most rapidly reached 1 million households. CNN and *USA today* were in their infancy. The *New York Times* was black-and white. Newspapers were seeing their last increases in circulation, and the internet was only a rudimentary defense department and research computer communications network.

So, the strategic question emerges: should leaders of media companies improve what they are doing or strike out boldly for innovation? If the past is our guide, improvement of successful products or services guarantees little. Innovation shapes the future and dooms the establishment, and real innovation usually comes from outside the establishment.[3]

Reacting to Challenge

Here's what happens when established industries reach a strategic inflection point at which innovation challenges their core business:

- They fight back by improving their old products and attempting to develop new products that use the new technology.

- The new field proves to be difficult, in part because the established businesses retain investment in their old technology.
- A host of new competitors enters the playing field.
- The established industries no longer can compete and cease to be dominant.

The Innovation Continuum

Fear not. The answer for sustained business success (and media industries are no exception) falls somewhere in between.

Innovation and incremental improvement are not mutually exclusive strategies. In fact NMC's review found that the road from improvement of existing products to true innovation is a continum.

Process improvement sits at the low end of the innovation continum. Better ways of producing products contribute to consumer benefits and increased margins. This comes from such changes as figuring out how to lower costs, expedite delivery and improve production processes. Technological innovation can contribute to process improvement as well. Witness the digital camera, direct-to-press platemaking and sales force automation, each of which has helped a major media industry.

When a company expands into new markets, it also climbs the innovation slope. Repositioning entail taking existing products into new geographic or demographic target niches. Aspirin, once a headache, fever and minor-pain analgesic, now is marketed as a preventative of stroke and heart disease. "Try our new, improved [fill in the blank]," shout the ads for products from laundry soap to newspapers. Product improvement sits at the midpoint of the continuum of better production quality to better content. Note that as media climb that slope, they move from improvement to innovation. As they move along that slope risk also increases, an issue we will examine in more detail when discussing why innovations fail.

Line extensions begin to test a company's willingness to truly experiment in new waters with new products. Without losing the umbilical cord to core products, the company extends what it does into new, but still related, ventures. Magazines publish niche, spinoff products, such as Country Living launching Country Living.

Gardens. Newspapers launch a Sunday magazine or a new daily section. ESPN adds ESPN2. Each of these is still in the realm of the familiar, however.

The next step is the scariest one; it requires the medium to go across the chasm into the unknown and truly new.

Risk of failure in new ventures nears its peak with the introduction of product lines that are absolutely new to the company. They may not be new to the industry or the world, but they are new to the organisation and they challenge the existing comfort levels, demanding the creation of new systems, processes and market knowledge. The most prevalent example today is the investment being made by traditional media in Web-based new media.

While nearly all print-based media, magazines and newspapers have made the investment leap into online products, they still are launching new-to-the-company products that are ink on paper. For example, many newspapers, such as Long Island Newsday, have ventured into magazine products. In October 1996, Newsday launched Distinction, a high-gloss, narrow-niche magazine aimed at households with incomes of more than $150,000. While the company could draw on its parent Times-Mirror's magazine management expertise and brand, the venture was truly new for the newspaper Another example of new-to-the-company ventures is Thomson's Target Media. Structured as an independent subsidiary of the giant Thomson media company, Target Media is a brash "skunkworks," an incubator of new product ideas. In 1997 the firm launched Curiocity for Kids, a free-circulation newsprint magazine aimed at middle-school-aged children. What made Curiocity unique was its business plan. It was conceived not as a stand-alone venture, but as a network of partnerships with both Thomson and non-Thomson newspapers in key markets. TTM provides content, packaging and national advertising support. The partner newspapers add local content and local advertising. To this mix is added a related Web site for kids, also developed in partnership.

At the apex of the new product continuum stands true innovation. It is the introduction of products or services that are new to the world. They can, and often do, create a strategic inflection point for competitors.

The "killer app"—computer shorthand for "killer application"—is a new good or service that establishes an entirely new category and, by being first, dominates it. " Risk is at its peak, but so is the opportunity for reward. Before a fledgling cable company, Home Box Office, introduced four hours of a polka contest in 1974, made-for-cable programming did not exist. That polka contest unleashed an entire industry. Billboard magazine revolutionized the record industry with its in-store sales tabulations.[4]

CNN reshaped television news and even foreign policy with its global 24-hour news programming. The personal computer, the disk operating system, word processing and spreadsheet software and now the Internet have forever changed human civilization. They are all killer apps. Remember Edison and the incandescent bulb?

Why Innovate?

Innovation in its many forms along the continuum is requisite for survival. Past success guarantees nothing. To succeed, media enterprises must see innovation as a necessary component of strategy. Strategic companies know where they are going. They envision the ends to be achieved. They conceive the strategies, tactics and critical success factors they will need to reach those ends. They apply the necessary resources to those ways. They know that innovation plays a role in that strategy.

In a study of 11,000 new product launches, Kuczmarski and Associates found that new products filled six distinct roles in the strategies of successful companies. The strategic roles of the new products were valued as "important" or "very important" by their companies in this order:

- Attract a new customer or market (93 per cent).
- Gain or maintain a competitive advantage (91 per cent).
- Retain customers (88 per cent).
- Fill a growth or profit gap (73 per cent).
- Arrest margin erosion (56 per cent).
- Utilize a new technology (31 per cent).

companies that link knowledge of their customers to their innovative efforts significantly enhance the success of their new products in the marketplace.

So, why don't more companies embrace innovation as a part of strategy? Aversion to risk is one reason. For many media companies, aversion to risk is embedded in corporate culture and reinforced by investors' appetite for profit growth quarter after quarter.

Another reason is that many executives just don't see either the threat or the opportunity that new products —their competitors' or their own—present. Innovation myopia, though, is nothing new.

Ever heard of IBM and the mainframe computer? IBM's chairman almost didn't.

"I think there is a world market for maybe five computers."

–Thomas Watson, chairman of IBM, in 1943. Having overcome that hurdle, IBM's engineering attention turned to microprocessors:

"But what is it good for?"

–Engineer at IBM's Advanced Systems Division commenting on the microchip in 1968

How's this for vision in the fledgling broadcast industry:

"The wireless music box has no imaginable commercial value.

Who would pay for a message sent to nobody in particular?"

–Investor's response to David Sarnoff's request for funding for development of the radio in the 1920s.

Then there is every business professor's nightmare:

Fred Smith, who was a Yale MBA student, proposed a company that would reliably deliver mail and packages by using a hubbed air transport network.

"The concept is interesting and well-formed, but in order to earn better than a 'C', the idea must somehow be feasible."

–Yale professor's critique of Fred Smith's paper on what Smith went on to develop into Fed Ex.

Innovation comes not from within established businesses, but from without. Established businesses have little apparent incentive for radical innovation.[5]

They retain a huge investment in infrastructure supporting the old products and the old ways of doing business. They have the turning radius of an aircraft carrier, not a speedboat. Their "rules" act as a governor on acceleration.

In contrast, new entrants to the market must innovate; otherwise they will be trampled by traditional businesses with enormous resources and profits. Also, they have no established rules at stake and no infrastructure to amortize.

Why Innovations are Stopped?

Aversion to risk is the key impediment to innovation and development of a new product portfolio in most companies.

Particularly in today's climate of investor pressure to widen margins, a company's proclivity to roll the dice on a new product can be easily dampened, and it often is. Even when given the go ahead for a new product project, many top executives often are stingy with resources. Equally limiting, the expectations of quick profits foreshorten the process of incubation.

Researchers have long studied new product success rates, the benchmark study being Booz, Allen & Hamilton's 1982 work, updated in 1991 by the Product Development and Management

Association, and again in 1993 by Robert G. Cooper for his thoughtful book, Wincing at New Products (1993, Addison-Wesley). In all of these studies across a rainbow of industries—and in the more recent work done in the field—the success rate for new products ranged from 55 to 65 per cent. In a 1991 survey of new product development, PDMA found that for every 11 serious ideas or concepts, three enter development,1.3 are launched and one succeeds. Now, we can look at this as disastrous news—a 1 to 11 success rate. There is, however, another more thoughtful interpretation. It is that these statistics describe a thorough process of disciplined creativity through which a success rate of 77 per cent can be achieved for new products that are actually launched. Viewed that way, this is an attrition curve or a risk-avoidance curve.[6]

This is an attrition curve or a risk-avoidance curve.

Whichever is the interpretation, the reality is that risk increases the closer a new product comes to launch.

Think of new product risk for a media company and its top executives as a poker game.

To sit at the table of new ideas costs the firm little if its executives play their cards smartly. Creation of those new ideas causes the company to make its first investment, an ante to play, usually small. In the case of a media company, what might that ante entail?

- Market research to really understand targeted segments of customers and their beliefs, lifestyles, needs and wants.
- The commitment of employees' time to think, brain-storm, create.
- The managerial expense of providing team leadership.

The player is dealt his cards and makes his first decision to bet or fold. In those early rounds, the stakes are low.

Similarly in the game of new media products, the early round investments are in the screening of ideas. Not until the idea has passed the hurdle of analysis and enters into development do the stakes increase. As the player raises the firm's investment in prototyping, field research, production retooling, creation of distribution channels and launch promotion, the amount on the table rises geometrically, reaching its peak when the firm launches the media product or service and goes into regular production and distribution.

The key to limiting risk is to weigh the firm's cards carefully early in the game when the stakes are low. The better the analysis and screening by the media company's executives of its new product "cards" in these early rounds, the better its chances of folding losing hands with minimal investment while riding potentially winning new products to launch and business success.

How to Achieve Success

Let's focus now on why new products often fail.

In his 1992 "NewProd III" research, Robert Cooper looked at 13 key activities in the process of developing and launching new products. They were:

1. **Initial screening.** The initial commitment of resources to the project.

2. **Preliminary market assessment.** A quick-and-dirty assessment of possible market acceptance of the new product.

3. **Preliminary technical assessment.** Answers the question, "Can the product be built?"

4. **Detailed market study.** Assesses customer needs and wants and position in the market

5. **Predevelopment business and financial analysis.**

Risk assessment, market attractiveness and competitive advantage.

6. **Product development.** The actual development of the physical product.

7. **In-house product tests.** Alpha testing in a controlled environment.

8. **Customer product tests.** Field trials with the customer, testing preferences. Also known as beta testing.

9. **Trial sell.** Test market of the product to a limited customer base.

10. **Trial production.** A limited production run.

11. **Final business analysis.** The last business and financial evaluation prior to launch.

12. **Production start-up.**

13. **Market launch.** Implementation of the marketing plan.

Cooper then looked at more than 200 projects across industries and found three common factors in the products that failed :

- Insufficient or faulty marketing research or homework. In 75 per cent of the failed new products, a detailed market study was not done or it was done poorly.
- Test marketing not done or done poorly. In 55 per cent of the failed products, no test marketing was done or it was done poorly.
- Detailed financial analysis omitted or inadequate. In50 per cent of the failed new products, inadequate or no financial analysis was performed prior to launch.

Having looked at the factors that contribute to new product failure, let's look at the flip side—the common traits of successful new products.

The consulting firm Booz, Allen & Hamilton did benchmark research in the early 1980s with analysis of 700 firms and their new products. Companies that were successful with their new products had a strategic plan that included a specific target for percentage growth from each new product. Additionally, their new products had these common characteristics:

- Product fit with market needs.
- Product fit with internal strengths.
- Technological superiority of the product.
- Top management support.
- Use of formal new product process.

Building on the Booz, Allen work a decade later in his NewProd III research, Cooper found that winning new products had 10 common traits. Ranked in ascending importance, they were:

10. Top management support.

9. Favorable competitive situation.

8. Market attractiveness.

7. Quality of execution of marketing activities.

6. Marketing synergy with firm's existing sales force and distribution system.

5. Quality of execution of pre-development activities

4. Synergy (fit) with firm's resources and core competencies (products).

3. Quality of execution of technical activities.

2. A well-defined product prior to the development phase.

And the Number 1 factor contributing to successful new products was a superior product that delivers unique benefit to the customer.

The winning new product starts with the customer (companies did extensive market research). The successful companies then translate customer need into viable product solutions. Finally, extensive customer tests verify that the product scores with the customer.

Of new products that were clearly superior and delivered unique benefit to customers, 98 per cent succeeded.

Motivation For Innovation

Where do all the good ideas come from? From what tree do the apples of new products fall?

What new product people call "ideation" is the process of idea creation toward the goal of innovation-based growth. It is one part perception, one part inspiration and one part organisation.

Perception

To conceive of new products that provide unique, relevant value to the customer, the media organisation must first know the customer—really well.

At NMC we teach the skill of hearing the voice of the customer through market research, segmentation and interpretation. This is not a process of just matching demographic or psychographic models to a media organisation's existing product lines. Rather, it is a process of scrutinising an organisation's customers' beliefs, lifestyles, needs, wants and time usage. From that process comes market perception, the first ingredient of ideation alchemy.

What was significant in new product ideation process is that they begin from outside-in, that is with concrete knowledge of the specifically targeted customer. Too often media companies work from inside-out, first looking at their existing products and trying to make them fit the customer. Finally, for this company, the ideas they created sprouted from the fertile ground of customer knowledge.

Research in 1998 of 1,100 U.S. software companies found that a firm's competence in gathering market knowledge is a key determinant of the success of its new products. The researchers found that the new products created by companies that had market knowledge competence had a distinct advantage and, as a result, performed better in the marketplace: This is disciplined creativity.

Creativity without process is like skydiving without a parachute. The challenge for executives is to foster an innovation culture that harnesses the power of creativity without stifling it.

Motivation

The second part of idea generation is the leadership art of motivation. Leaders can inspire creativity. Recent research into creative behaviour in corporations by Harvard Professor Theresa Amabile has identified three components of creativity. They are:

- *Creative thinking skills.* How flexibly and imaginatively people approach problems.
- *Expertise.* Knowledge, technical, procedural and intellect.
- *Motivation.* An inner passion to find creative solutions.

Media executives can influence all three components, although expertise and creative thinking skills are hardest. Creativity, in some form, is part of everyone. People just approach problems differently. Harvard's Amabile likens this to the scientific process.[7]

As if they were in a maze, some scientists sense, feel, intuitively know the most direct path to a solution. Others find reward in the thrill of exploration and discovery. They like the journey that takes them down blind alleys and wrong turns. Neither is wrong. To direct a path is.

Everyone is born with creative spark that is suppressed. The challenge is to motivate and unlock that spark. Motivation comes from within. It is an inner drive. Too often media executives equate motivation with external rewards and punishment exercised to elicit certain performance. A leader who does this is a transactional leader. This leader says, "If you, the employee, do this, you will receive this reward, but if you do not, you will be visited with that punishment." Transactional leadership does not spur motivation.

How then does an executive become not a transactional leader, but a transformational leader, one who can light the candle of motivation to create? Amabile, in her research, identified five tools of transformational leadership, ways for executives to unleash intrinsic motivation.

They are:

- Challenge
- Freedom
- Resources
- Teams
- Encouragement

To challenge employees, executives should match people to jobs that stretch their expertise and skills in creative, new thinking. An employee who has reached a level of comfortable competence is not challenged. Neither is one who is allowed to make a hole in a cocoon of security "Total security is vegetating," Hallmark's MacKenzie says. "Cocoons can be paralysing." The antidote is a combination of challenge and freedom. In the business setting, Amabile calls this "autonomy within limits." Let employees choose "how to climb a mountain," she suggests, "not which mountain to climb." MacKenzie calls this "orbiting the organisation." In orbit is where invention happens, not spinning off into space where innovation is of no use to the company.

Two resources available to executives in fostering motivation are time and money for a project. Organizations kill creativity with false deadlines or impossibly tight ones. Allow time, Amabile urges, for exploration of the "creativity maze." At (IG), a company that has a passion for innovation, people involved in the new product process are expected to spend 15 per cent of their work hours just thinking about new product opportunities. Think how far that is from the time allocation of most media executives.

The fit of resources to the task is likewise the executive's task and challenge. People, funding and time are examples of resources that a new product team needs. Knowing how much of those resources the company can afford, and apportioning them, falls to the executive. Resources are, after all, finite. Research shows there is a "threshold of sufficiency" beyond which application of more resources does not increase creativity. Below that threshold, the creative process can be starved. Again, it falls to the executive to determine that threshold and allocate resources accordingly. Teams are a key tool of creativity. Three components of a successful team are diversity of viewpoint, experience and skills; subordination of the individual to the team, and chemistry. Used well—and led well—in the new product process, teams can create a forum for buy-in. When team members are oriented to a goal, trust each other's technical competence and interact richly, they have an enhanced chance of creating new knowledge and, hence, new products."

Finally, an executive absolutely controls the flow of supervisory encouragement. Employees need cheerleading to sustain passion for the creative process. The transformational leader lends organisational support, fosters communication, diminishes the role of office politics and says, "Creativity is a top priority."

The result is what Kuczmarski calls an "innovation mindset."

Organisation

Institutionalising an innovation mindset is the third piece of ideation. A company with an innovation mindset understands that "failure is possible with new products and accepts the risk, knowing that innovation is the key to future success and that failure to innovate courts death.

A company with an innovative mindset also has a new product strategy as a component of its corporate strategy. New product initiatives are not flyers; rather they are anchored in corporate and new product strategy.

A company with an innovative mindset uses multi-functional teams that are dedicated to progress.

A company with an innovative mindset has a commitment by senior management to the new products strategy and process, and measures progress continually. It views its new products as part of an innovation portfolio, and it stays on top of the profit-and-loss picture of each product and the portfolio.

The innovation mindset:

- Supports the new product strategy
- Pervades the organization.
- Has the commitment of senior management.
- Is embraced by functional management
- Crosses functional divisions.
- Celebrates failure.
- Cultivates champions.

About those new product champions: These champions are passionate believers in an idea. They pursue acceptance of the idea through the decision-making maze, through development and into launch. These executives are as near fanatics as rational people can be. As a result they often are key to the success of the product.

Texas Instruments looked at 50 of its new product successes and failures and found that one factor marked every failure: The new product did not have a senior, volunteer champion. Tom Peters found the same thing at General Electric. Peters said that the role of the champion at GE was crucial in 24 new product histories he examined. Of the 15 successful new products, 14 had forceful product champions. Of the nine failures, only three had champions. At (IG), 25 per cent of revenues must be derived from products that did not exist five years ago. The company encourages product champions to keep their ideas alive and gives them incentives to do so.

The lesson is clear. Cultivate the new product champions. Encourage them to take risks. Don't let their passion for a new idea be dimmed by the naysayers of bureaucracy or the risk-averse supervisors. Reward their successes and celebrate their failures.[8]

Doing The Impossible

Institutions have a way of stifling innovation. Their culture, rules, history and even their past success form an impediment to changing "the way we do things here." Sir Francis Bacon, the philosopher, called these impediments "idols of the tribe." In the business setting, these idols become deeply imbedded practices. To innovate, executives must challenge the idols. In looking at institutional impediments to change, Joel Barker has popularised the concept of paradigms, the rules and filters through which everyone views their lives and commerce. Those paradigms, Barker asserts, too often blind people to innovation.

The exercise Barker recommends to break through the barriers of paradigms is toughminded brainstorming. Assemble a team (managerial or otherwise) and ask it to answer one question: What is impossible to do right now, but if you could do it, it would fundamentally change this business in crucially needed ways? In the team's answers can be found idol-smashing ideas and the seeds of true innovation.

Eight Characteristics of Creative People and Team

1. **Originality**: *As you probably know, originality attracts attention. When you do* something that no one else have done, people will start to be curious to

know how and where you want to end up with this original idea. Think of an idea, redesign it and make something new out of it.

2. Production: Learn to search for better ways to do tasks. Focus on what you do and you will find new possibilities and new ways of doing things.

3. Growth and Change: Creative people search for change constantly, so learn not to restrict yourself using the same old way of doing things. If you keep what you are doing, then you will get the same results. In life, you have to learn to change for the better, so you can grow and prosper.

4. Flexibility: Learn to be flexible and always learn the current inventions. People are challenged daily to be flexible in work, relationships, life and learning new things in general. If you have to learn something that could benefit you and benefit your business, then do so. As I mentioned in my book, "**the ultimate guide to achieve your goals** "you have to keep in your mind that you always **have to be flexible** in achieving your goals.

5. Independent thinking: Learn to become an observer and an analyst. Gather all the information you can and then analyse and come up with your own analysis. Always think for yourself.

6. Sensitivity: Observe the world around you. Observe the nature, flowers, and people. Pick a flower and see its colors, smell, etc... Your sensitivity to the world and to your environment will raise your creativity.

7. Innovation: You must have the courage to try new things and if you want to build something out of the ordinary, then do so. Innovation and having courage are necessary for creativity. Many criticize new ideas and innovations, but at the end, these new ideas will flourish.

8. Ask questions: Always ask questions and ask people to explain what they mean and the things you don't understand. Don't accept things as they are.

Always remember what Scott Adams said, "Creativity is allowing yourself to make mistakes. Art is knowing which ones to keep." only 3 per cent of the world's population manage to plan and reach their goals? The main goal for 2achieveyourgoals.com is to help you become from the top 3 per cent of the world's population who know how to achieve any goal they desire in all areas of life [9].

The New Product Process

The purpose of following a disciplined process in new product development is not to stifle creativity or impose bureaucratic hurdles on innovators. Rather, its aims are to link innovation to strategy, to increase customer focus, to reduce risk through analysis and to ensure excellence and success in the future. There is no magic one-size-fits-all process for creating new products. The best process is the one that fits each specific media company, its culture, its level of risk acceptance or avoidance, the competitive landscape and its capabilities in developing new products. What follows is a matrix that captures the best features of new product processes in companies. While these companies follow a process that results in high levels of success, remember that always overarching the entire process is a corporate strategy. The best process will fail in the absence of a well-developed strategy.

An Eight-Step Plan

Step 1. Develop a blueprint for innovation that is aligned with corporate strategy.

Step 2. Develop a formal process for generating ideas, also known as "Ideation."

Step 3. From each idea generated, develop a clear product description.

Step 4. Analyze the new product idea.

Step 5. Develop the product using a phased allocation of resources. (Remember risk increases over time.)

Step 6. Conduct two tests of each new product, an internal test and an external one. From those tests, improve the product (or kill it if warranted).

Step 7. Do a really great launch. (Benchmark the best launches that can be found. Then measurably beat them.)

Step 8. Re-examine the new product and its effect on the marketplace, then improve it.

Step 1. Align with strategy.

There are six key roles for new products in the most successful companies' strategies.

Those six roles are:

- Attract a new customer or market.
- Gain or maintain a competitive advantage.
- Retain customers.
- Fill a growth or profit gap.
- Arrest margin erosion.
- Utilize a new technology.

The important element to keep in mind is that alignment with strategy enhances corporate commitment to innovation. New product development should not be a wild "flier." In fact, innovation should begin with a plan, a blueprint. The blueprint for innovation starts with the company's vision, which usually looks out three to five years.

Step 2. Ideation

Having a means of capturing ideas from many sources is key to keeping the ideas flowing. Some ways to generate ideas that work are:

- Brainstorm. If you have fostered motivation for innovation in your organization, regular brainstorming sessions will be a fertile source of new product ideation. The rule holds: There are no bad ideas. Kill just one in its infancy and you will kill them all.
- Use focus groups of customers.
- Systematically attend trade shows (in and out of your industry). Too often media executives view the trade show as either a perk or an industry obligation. Too often only bosses attend, are exposed to new ideas, then return to the office with only an expense claim to show for it. Better to view trade shows, both within your industry and outside it.
- Survey customers. You don't need an advisory board to constantly turn up the volume of the voice of the customer through systematic survey research.

Remember, though, the key is finding the gaps in the lifestyles of your customers that you can fill with new products or services.

- Analyze the competition regularly. "Know your enemy. Know yourself," wrote the ancient Chinese military philosopher Sun Tzu. New ideas come from outside your established competitive environment, too.
- Solicit input from suppliers.
- Establish user panels or advisory boards of customers. Identify lead users. One very successful trade magazine company has developed a database of 5,000 "advisers," readers, advertisers and industry leaders.

They go so far as to send the advisers a letter of appointment and a certificate suitable for framing. When they embark on a new product initiative, they turn to the advisers first to test new ideas. And they regularly solicit new product ideas from that advisory board. It has paid off with new titles, new features and new line extensions.

Step 3. Describe the Product

Too many good ideas are lost for want of a solid product description. The goal here is to narrowly focus the attention of your company on a tangible new product idea. The temptation is to describe the product in terms of its physical attributes, not in terms of its unique, relevant value to the customer. One simple fill-in-the blank means of describing a new product idea challenges the new product champion to first put herself or himself in the position of the customer, next to consider gaps in customers' needs and wants and only then physically describe the new product.

Step 4. Analyse the Product

After clearly defining the product, the next actions involve "homework" and a rigorous analysis of the product. Studies show that insufficient or faulty market research or homework was a common characteristic of 75 per cent of failed new products. Omission of a detailed financial analysis was common to half the failures. If one goal of the innovation poker game is to minimise risk before significant investment is made in development of a new product idea, then new product managers need to know when to hold their cards and when to fold them. One successful means of filtering ideas is the use of two pre-development decision points or screens at which the choice is made to go with the product, hold it or kill it. In the first screen, you test the idea. In the second, you test the business case for the idea. Between the two tests is analytical homework, called the "investigation stage."

Screen One: A Gentle Test of the Idea. The initial screen is a "gentle test" of the idea against six must-meet criteria. That test is performed by managers across functions and can be accomplished swiftly without detailed analysis. The criteria against which the idea is measured are:

- Is the new product idea aligned with strategy?
- Can we do it?
- Does it produce unique, relevant value for the customer?
- Can we win?
- Does it have importance?
- Is it worth it?

Investigation Stage: The investigation stage is the preparatory work for a more rigorous test of the business case for the new product idea. In this stage the focus is on completion of :

- A thorough market analysis (the customer and the competition). Remember that failure to do adequate market research was a common factor in 75 per cent of failed new products studied.

- Detailed financial analysis. I had a boss once who believed that no idea was worth developing if it could not be expressed quantitatively. That firm guidance was valuable in giving needed analytical discipline to our efforts to start or acquire new newspapers. Analysis of a new product's cost projections, revenue potential and rate of return on investment provides the underpinning for making the decision on whether the venture is worth it.
- Internal capabilities. An examination of the product's compatibility with the company's ability to perform all of the distinct functions necessary to bring it from an idea to the delivered good, is simply a matter of asking the question, *"Can we do it?"*

Screen 2: Decision on Business Case. Now, having completed the investigative "homework" stage on the new product, you are ready to make your last development go/kill decision. To do so, with the more complete market, financial and capabilities information that you have gathered, more rigorously re-examine the six must-meet criteria that you gently tested before.

If the product passes this more rigorous examination, test the idea against "should-meet" criteria that you uniquely develop. Those criteria should fit with your company's strategy, your degree of willingness to accept risk and the role the new product will play in your strategy. Remember, this is your last chance to fold your hand before you begin to put serious money on the table. The risk curve climbs abruptly after this point. For that reason, this screen is your most critical test of the new product. Who decides to go ahead, hold or kill the idea? Again, the answer depends on your unique company structure, but minimally, senior managers should conduct the screen across functional areas. In most companies, where significant investment is anticipated, top level decision-makers will make the go/kill choice at this point

Step 5. Develop the Product

You have decided to go ahead with the new product. Development is progressing across functional boundaries and on parallel tracks. The temptation is to focus on the physical development of the product. Simultaneously, you need to be developing the supporting systems for the product to include such activities as accounting, advertising, sales support and training, customer service and distribution channels. It is best, too, to phase the development and allocation of resources to it. Risk rises in tandem with investment.

New product ventures frequently face the thorny question of whether to integrate or incubate the new product. Should a company leverage existing staff, production systems, and infrastructure or distribution channels? Or should it dedicate staff and physical resources to the new product? There is no simple answer. Each product and company presents a different model.

Step 6. Conduct two Tests

It's time now to prototype the new product. Prototyping need not be a lengthy process. In fact, the standard for prototype development and test marketing in the briskly competitive world of high tech is five *days* or less. Prototyping enables you to conduct two tests of the new product. The first is an internal test of your capabilities to refine, produce and distribute the product, and of the new product's fit with your core business. Ask yourself, does the developed product match or complement:

- Your strategy.
- The financial plan for the new product.
- Your position in the market.
- Your capabilities to manufacture, distribute, sell and service the new product.

The second is an external test in the marketplace using a prototype and, if possible, a test marketing. A test from the customer's perspective is the most valuable indicator you have of potential market reaction to your product. Does the product match:

- Your customer preferences.
- A unique and favorable competitive position.
- Your financial projections for sales.
- Your internal capabilities to sell it, distribute it and provide service.

A caveat about prototyping and research: Assure the validity of your test. Like most newspapers, the St. Louis Post-Dispatch faced declining readership and ad lineage in its Saturday paper. A robust Sunday paper and a modestly successful Friday product bracketed that edition. The challenge was to add readers and subscribers to a non-Sunday weekend product. *The paper made all the right new product development steps*, culminating in the prototyping and test of a tabloid Saturday edition that contained some of the most popular features of the Sunday and Friday broadsheets and was presented to potential subscribers and advertisers as a package buy.

Step 7. A Great Launch

A climatic launch can't make a success out of a bad product. But a bad launch can doom a good product. Here are some elements your launch campaign plan should include:

Determine if you will offer introductory pricing discounts. It's easy to lower the price of a product, but hard to raise it.

Create awareness. The tools of awareness-building are advertising, promotion, direct marketing, events and public relations. The key to success lies in integrating those tools well.

Make sure the new product delivers what you promise.

Step 8. Improve the Product

The last step in the new product process is constant improvement, which begins by listening to the customer. As mentioned earlier, one successful business-to-business magazine company has created an advisory board of 5,000 of its loyal readers and advertisers. The advisory board is constantly tapped for reaction to new titles, new features and new ventures of the company. That feedback is used to improve the products and is a great source of additional new product ideas. Internally, too, you'll learn how better to manufacture, deliver and service the new product. Improve those processes as well. The results will show in greater efficiency, quality and profit margin.[10]

Managing the Process

The preceding pages have examined the concepts of moti-vation for innovation and the new product process. It is time to summarize the managerial skills and activities necessary to win at new products. Managing innovation requires:

Awareness of how customers think and what they believe.

- Knowledge and awareness of what competitors and outsiders are doing and capable of doing.
- Managing culture ("The way we do things").
- Fitting innovation to core competencies.
- Managing the process of choosing projects.
- Managing individuals to nurture intrinsic motivation.
- Coordination of the work of multi-function teams.
- Expediting the process.
- Championing the product.

Conclusion

It might be tempting to tear out the chapter on the New Product Process, pass it on to your department heads and think you are on the way to innovative new products. While the ideas in that chapter certainly are core to developing new products, don't be seduced by checklists.

A process is just a process. To be effective it needs to be integrated into a new corporate culture that focuses on the customer in order to develop ideas from the outside-in, fosters creativity and celebrates rather than punishes failure. Executives have to learn how to motivate for innovation, cultivate product champions and above all instill throughout the company a sense of urgency about new product development.

Finally, your company has to be strategic. The new product process has to be linked to overarching company objectives. All your new products must provide your customers unique, relevant value.[11]

If you adopt the attitudes of innovation as well as the processes, you have a chance to succeed in the marketplace. The alternative is to see your company become the ice harvester of the new millennium. Look at change the way the Chinese do, as a Monster— the Monster of Change. There are three ways to respond to this Monster of Change. You can ignore the monster (or not even see it), but the monster will always be there. If you continue to ignore the monster, it will devour you.

You can try to resist the Monster of Change, to contort it or force it onto a path of your choosing. But the monster is powerful. You cannot control it. It will defeat your efforts to resist change, and ultimately it will devour you. Or you can leap on the back of the Monster of Change and ride it to where it leads. By riding it, you avoid its lethality. You survive and perhaps prosper. In the world of your media business, the Monster of Change is present. Innovative competitors, if ignored, will devour you. Resisting change, too, means corporate death. Only by riding the monster, by being an innovation organization that motivates to innovate and strategically harnesses the power of creativity, will you survive and prosper.

Notes

1. Thomas Kuczmarski, Innovation: Leadership Strategies for the Competitive.
2. James Utter back, Mastering the Dynamics of Innovation (Harvard Business School Press, 1996).
3. Douglas, North. Structure and Economic History North and Company, 1984.
4. Robert G. Cooper, Winning at New Products (Addison Wesley, 1993).
5. Kuczmarski, Innovation: Leadership Strategies for the Competitive Edge
6. Arnold Cooper and Daniel Schendel, "Strategic Responses to Technological.
7. Theresa Amabile, "How to Kill Creativity," Harvard Business Review (September-October 1998).

8. Tom Peters, The Circle of innovation (Knopf, 1997).
   Edge (NTC Business Books, 1996).
9. Robert G. Cooper, Winning at New Products (Addison Wesley, 1993).
10. Drew Davis, A guide to successful innovation for media executives. Management," American Marketing Association Journal of Marketing (Fall 1998).
11. Davis, W. 1991, The Innovators, In J. Henry and D. WalkerR (EDS) Managing Innovation, Sage Publications, London, pp. 142-149.

16

Socio–cultural Impact of Television on Children Against Regulations and Compliance of the Global Discourse

Maumita Chaudhuri

The 1990 Children's Television Act (CTA, 1990) requires broadcasters to provide educational and informational television programmes for children. A multi-method, multidisciplinary approach, utilising both cross-sectional and longitudinal designs, was used to investigate the degree to which the CTA has had an effect on children's viewing experiences and learning. Second-to sixth-grade children's preferences and comprehension of content from pro-social and academic programmes broadcast by the four major commercial networks (ABC, CBS, NBC, and FOX) were compared to those for similar programmes broadcast by PBS and Nickelodeon. Overall, girls and younger children liked educational and informational television programmes more than boys and older children did. Girls and older children understood the programmes best, particularly the pro-social ones. Over the course of 9 months, however, viewing educational and informational television programmes declined, particularly for older boys. Nevertheless, lessons were reported more often after viewing favorite educational than favorite entertainment-driven programmes. Results suggest beneficial effects of many commercial educational and informational children's television programs as well as the value of protections, such as requiring broadcasters to provide of educational and informational programmes each week, to ensure that educational television programmes survive in the competitive market place. Such policy decisions provide our children with access to quality television programmes that can improve their social, emotional, and cognitive well-being (Acuff, 1997).

Preschool children who view academically oriented television programmes are often better prepared for school and are often even better students when they attend high school. Similarly, children who view pro-social television programmes are often more altruistic. For example, children who viewed a pro-social episode of Lassie were later more likely to help an animal presumed to be in distress and in another study, children who saw a constructive compared to a destructive model from Mod Squad were more likely to help a peer who was working on a task in another room. In spite of these cognitive and social benefits, commercial broadcasters have overwhelmingly broadcast strictly entertainment programmes as their venue for children. Years of debate and attempts to implement voluntary compliance policies, by which broadcasters were expected to regulate themselves, led to little change in the quality of children's television programmes. This failure and 25 years of pressure by public advocacy groups led Congress to take action and pass the Children's Television Act of 1990 (CTA, 1990).

Children's Television Act

The Children's Television Act (CTA) linked the renewal of the local broadcaster's license to airing educational and informational children's television programmes. The FCC commissioners defined educational and informational programming as those that have content that "furthers the positive development of the child in any respect, including the child's cognitive/intellectual or social–emotional needs" (Federal Communications Commission [FCC], 1991). Broadcasters decided which of their television programmes were educational and informational, and indicated that identification on their license renewal forms. The flexibility of the FCC guidelines, in keeping with their dual obligation to enforce the law while protecting freedom of speech, immediately led to controversy about the quality of the programmes being broadcast to meet the requirements of the CTA. Researchers who examined broadcaster reports to the FCC often discovered distorted and inaccurate classifications of educational and informational television programs. For example, the license renewal form for WDIV-TV in Detroit, MI, listed GI Joe, a violent action–adventure cartoon, as an educational and informational television programme. This broadcaster described one episode as follows: "The Joes fight against an evil that has the capabilities of mass destruction of society. Issues of social consciousness and responsibility are show themes" (Center for Media Education and Institute of Public Representation, 1992). Such interpretations of educational and informational programming were inconsistent with the intent of the law. Because researchers repeatedly documented problems with local broadcaster compliance in meeting the requirements of the CTA, the FCC moved to strengthen the implementation of law. In 1997, the FCC introduced several new guidelines, which came to be known as the "Three-Hour Rule." Those who complied with these guidelines were rewarded with an expedited license renewal. Those who did not comply had to follow the usual but lengthier full license renewal procedure. Core educational programming is one provision that became required for an expedited license renewal under the 1997 guideline of the Three-Hour Rule. Core programmes must be (a) designed to meet the educational and informational needs of children aged 16 and under; (b) aired between 7:00 a.m. and 10:00 p.m.; (c) scheduled on a weekly basis; and (d) at least 30 min in length (FCC, 1996). Effective January 2, 1997, broadcasters also had to label educational and informational television programmes with an E/I (Educational and Informational) logo so that parents and children could find them.

Educational and informational programming before and after the Three-Hour Rule Content analyses conducted by the Annenberg Public Policy Center (APPC) on samples of Philadelphia, PA, programmess documented no change in the number of E/I programmes shown before and after implementation of the Three-Hour Rule. However, the Annenberg group did find that programmes broadcast after implementation of the Three-Hour Rule were more likely to be shown when children were awake and in the viewing audience. In particular, before the Three-Hour Rule, educational and informational programmes were broadcast at times when it was unlikely that any child would see them, such as 5 a.m. After the Three-Hour Rule, most E/I programmes were shown during the 7 a.m.–10 p.m. time period, when children are likely to be in the viewing audience. This meant that children were more likely to view E/I programs since the Three-Hour Rule was implemented. However, investi-gations of the educational strength of children's programmes, based on evaluations of the primary lessons of E/I programmes (e.g., lesson clarity, integration, involvement, and applicability) demonstrated that the educational value of the E/I shows actually declined from the 1996–1997 to the 1998–1999 sample of E/I programmes (Anderson, Huston, Schmitt, Linebarger & Wright, 2001).

Prior to the Three-Hour Rule, the 1996–1997 samples had a greater proportion of programmes that were rated highly educational (43%) rather than moderately educational (35%). The reverse was true in the year following the institution of the Three-Hour Rule. Only one third of the 1998–1999 sample of E/I shows were found to be highly educational and 46% were rated as moderately educational. In addition, 21–22% of programmes in both samples were minimally educational over time. The types of programmes that broadcasters chose to air to meet the Three-Hour Rule guidelines may have affected the overall educational strength of the shows. For example, Jordan et al. (2002) found that academically oriented programmes such as Bill Nye the Science Guy and Magic School Bus were generally rated higher on educational strength than were programmes with social and emotional themes, such as Disney's Doug and Disney's Recess. But broadcasters overwhelmingly chose to present pro-social programs rather than academically oriented shows to meet the Three-Hour Rule. Programs were also generally targeted at a middle-childhood audience. Although the in-depth content analyses of E/I programmes conducted by APPC group over several years revealed important information about what type of shows were available to children as a result of the Three-Hour Rule, 13 years after the passage of the CTA and 6 years after the institution of the Three-Hour Rule, we know very little about children's learning from E/I programmes mandated by the CTA (1990).

A child's learning from television programmes. In the new science of learning, comprehension and understanding play a more central role than does mere knowledge of explicit content. In the television area, learning with comprehension taps into comparatively abstract skills such as whether children can generalise programme lessons into their own lives, can understand important abstract content, including implicit as well as explicit content, and can remember important content over time. The developmental difference in children's comprehension of television content always varies. Many studies using a variety of methods demonstrate that children's comprehension of television programmes improves with development. The findings of this research also suggest that the format of such programmes, story versus magazine format for example, can affect children's interest in the television programmes that they view and their understanding of the content of those shows. Televised stories (e.g., Hey Arnold and Disney's Pepper Ann), which present content in an audiovisual narrative form with programme events woven together over time and space, typically convey social–emotional content such as helping others. By contrast, magazine formats, which most often present the content of the show in an expository format of discrete vignettes (e.g., Sesame Street and Bill Nye the Science Guy), are typically used to convey academic content (Anderson & Lorch, 1983).

For children to understand narrative plot lines, they must engage in specific cognitive activities. In particular, children must (1) separate the central, plot-relevant from the incidental, irrelevant programmes details; (2) order that content into a story scheme; and (3) draw inferences about the motivations and feelings of characters as well as connect and integrate cause–event sequences that are presented across the narrative structure. Experimental investigations document that the ability to remember more central plot relevant than incidental irrelevant details after viewing television programmes increases with age. Comprehension of the implicit central content, which involves inferences and understanding of character motivations, feelings, and abstract relations, improves by Grade 5, about age 10, whereas comprehension of the explicit central programme content occurs earlier, by about Grade 2 if the television presentations are clearly and sequentially organised. Preschool and young elementary school children do not remember implicit programme content that requires inferences well, even when studies assess memory immediately after viewing (Anderson & Lorch, 1983).

Visual and verbal measures of comprehension. Children's ability to display the content of television programmes that they understand also depends on the way they are required to demonstrate their knowledge. Children's comprehension of television programmes has been assessed with measures that vary along two major dimensions: (1) the amount of content children must produce versus recognise, and (2) the form of the assessment, such as the use of verbal versus visual measures. Free recall measures, in which the child has to tell someone else what happened without any reminders or hints being available, is far more difficult than answering a multiple-choice question or responding to a visual representation where the child only needs to recognize or identify some aspect of the show from several response alternatives. Both free recall and recognition measures are often verbal, though recognition tests, i.e., multiple-choice measures, are sometimes supplemented with a relevant picture taken from the television program (Bransford, Brown & Cocking, 1999).

The audiovisual nature of the television medium lends itself to assessment of children's visual memories. For example, picture-sequencing measures have been used to assess how well children can temporally integrate the visual events of a plot line. Regardless of the type of measure used, older children remember more information from televised material than younger children do. Even so, the use of multiple memory measures ensures that children have different ways to display what they know about televised material. For instance, young elementary school children, 7–8 years old, may better display their knowledge with a multiple-choice or picture-sequencing measure, where verbal and visual recognition skills are required, than with a verbal free recall measure, where verbal production skills are required (Anderson, et. al, 2001).

The value of programme choice in learning: Naturalistic versus experimental paradigms. Our knowledge of children's learning from television programs comes primarily from experimental studies in which children view specific television programs that have been selected and/or varied through the investigator's manipulation of the content, presentation format, and organization of the materials presented. Little study has been directed toward what children learn from programmes they choose to view. The latter naturalistic approach has the advantage of more closely approximating the everyday experience of children. The experimental focus of most television studies means that researchers have little information about what children learn from programmes that they like or do not like and that they choose to watch or not. The child's involvement with programmes may vary considerably based on whether the child chose to watch it or was simply shown that programme as part of a study. Cognitive research suggests that children learn material they are interested in better than material that they find to be boring, in part because interesting material maximizes their attention as they process the content (Calvert, 1999a).

Therefore, programmes that appeal to children, i.e., popular programmes, may well be processed more thoroughly than are unpopular programmes thereby maximising children's comprehension and learning of the content of appealing programmes. If this premise is true, programmes selected by children as favorites would be expected to be remembered better over time. The television programmes that children like may vary with specific characteristics of a child, such as age or gender. For instance, programmes that are age-appropriate—that are just about at the target age or slightly older than the viewer—seem to be better liked. Similarly, boys show a strong preference for television programmes that feature male casts and male interests, for example, programmes that feature action–adventure plots. Girls, by contrast, will view programmes that feature boys as well as girls. Girls, unlike boys, strongly prefer programmes that feature social and emotional themes. While educational television programmes often appear to be gender neutral, girls and younger children may find E/I programmes to be more appealing than boys and older children do. By contrast, boys prefer, and hence may learn more information from, programmes that are more strictly entertainment based, i.e., that are not designed to carry an educational message (Calvert, 1999b).

The Children's Television Act of 1990 requires broadcasters to provide educational and informational television programmes that are designed to improve the well-being of children. Well-designed educational television programmes have been found to have immediate and enduring academic and social benefits for child viewers. Research suggests that young preschool and elementary school children's social behavior benefits from viewing pro-social programmes, but they have difficulty remembering essential plot and relevant events in pro-social stories, even when retention is assessed immediately after viewing. This comprehension problem is particularly salient because the type of programme of choice to meet the requirements of the CTA is a pro-social story. Do young children understand the pro-social, social emotional messages embedded in these programmes?

The television programmes. In sum, there was no support for the hypothesis that children learned more social-emotional lessons from programmes broadcast on commercial stations than on Nickelodeon/ PBS. Instead, boys reported more social–emotional lessons from Nickelodeon/

PBS programmes and more informational lessons from commercial broadcast programmes. There were no differences in any of the types of lessons learned across the different types of broadcasters for girls. Put another way, boys learned different kinds of lessons from different broadcasters' programmes, but girls did not. Girls mainly reported social–emotional themes, regardless of broadcaster (Calvert, 1999a).

The relationship between type of lesson reported and educational strength was consistently strong for reports that contained social–emotional lessons. Although the partial correlation coefficients for educational strength were also significant for the other kinds of lessons, i.e., for informational, physical well-being, or cognitive lessons, the correlations were low, reaching toward a moderate degree of association in only a few cases, such as strength of clarity and relevance in learning reports taken from informational lessons and degree of engagement in lessons focused on cognitive skills. Overall, children's favorite programmes and most viewed programmes were the same, and those selections were consistent over time. The congruence between the children's reports of their favorite shows and reported viewing patterns provides some evidence of the reliability of the children's reports. Consistent with broadcaster beliefs, the reports of favorite shows, reports of viewing behaviors, and Nielsen assessments show that younger elementary school children watch educational and infor-mational programmeming more frequently than older children. The number of different educational and informational shows that the children reported watching varied with gender, period of the viewing season, and type of broadcaster as well as age. Girls watched more different educational programmes than boys. Thus, educational and informational television programmes lost much of their potential audience after the new fall season, which brought new programme offerings, had passed. During the course of the year, Nickelodeon began to drop some educational and informational programmes from their schedule. However, children did watch more different educational shows on Nickelodeon/PBS at the end of the season than they did at the beginning of the season (Calvert, 1999b).

Dropping these programmes seems to have increased the overall percentage of different Nickelodeon/PBS programmes that children viewed, perhaps as an artifact of having a smaller base of educational shows at the end of the season. By contrast, the commercial broadcasters added a couple of programmes to their schedule and did not drop any programmes. This kept their overall viewing rates of different programmes similar over time, though they could not beat the combined Nickelodeon/PBS lineup. This could have also been due to the tendency of commercial networks to run their educational lineups against one another on Saturday mornings and to broadcast their programmes less frequently than Nickelodeon/PBS did with their lineup, which enabled children to sample more programmes from the total lineup from Nickelodeon/PBS (Calvert, 2000, August).

Overall, children watched a greater number of educational programmes on Nickelodeon/PBS than on commercial television broadcasters. But this finding might be due to the behaviours of the younger viewers. It was also found that younger children watched more different educational shows on Nickelodeon than on the commercial networks, but the younger and older children did not differ from one another in their viewing of educational shows on the commercial networks. The low level of viewing Nickelodeon programmes by older children may have occurred because Nickelodeon dropped most of the programmes targeted at the preadolescent age group. Perhaps Nickelodeon and PBS have become branded as a station for younger children because they pull young children into their line-up early with Nickjr (for preschoolers) and PBS Kids (mainly for preschoolers), thereby contributing to their later loss of the oldest viewers by the end of the elementary age years who may then think of these broadcasters as being for younger viewers (Calvert, 2000, August).

The genre of programmes that children viewed was consistent with the kind of programmes available for them to view. Findings indicated that children preferred educational programmes that were animated more than live action shows, and preferred news/magazine formats the least. Within these categories, though, younger children watched expository news/magazine format shows than older children, and older children preferred live action shows more than younger children did. Social–emotional lessons were reported must often, followed by informational lessons, physical well-being lessons, and cognitive skills lessons. These findings are consistent with a prior assessment of children's learning from educational television programmes. The high incidence of social–emotional lessons might reflect the higher frequency of shows with socio-emotional themes. Within the types of lessons assessed, girls reported more social–emotional lessons than boys, who, in turn, reported more cognitive lessons (Calvert, 2000, August).

These findings are consistent with girls' preference for social–emotional programmes that have demonstrated positive effects of pro-social television, particularly altruism, on girls. The findings that boys in the present naturalistic study were more likely than girls to report cognitive lessons from their favorite educational and informational television programmes suggest important academic benefits might exist. Prior studies have shown, for instance, that boys who watched educational television programmes during the preschool years had better academic success when they were adolescents. When boys reported social–emotional lessons, they were more likely to be from shows broadcast by Nickelodeon/PBS than from commercial broadcasters; when the boys reported informational lessons, the lesson were more often from shows from commercial television than from Nickelodeon/PBS. Girls primarily reported social and emotional lessons, regardless of the broadcaster. This age difference was due to greater engagement during the beginning of the viewing and reporting season, perhaps because that is when the new fall schedule of programmes began: In addition, girls' reports were rated higher in strength than boys' reports in the areas of consistency and engagement. Over all reports, children scored highest in the area of generalise, followed by clarity, consistency, and engagement. All four components of report strength were strongly correlated for programmes that had social and emotional lessons, even when grade and gender were controlled. The decline in the number of programmes viewed, the number of lessons reported, and the educational strength of lessons paralleled the decrease in the number of different educational and informational children's programmes broadcast on Nickelodeon and PBS. Alternately, children may be watching the same shows repeatedly because Nickelodeon and PBS show the same series over the course of the week (Calvert, 2000, August).

Popular and unpopular educational programmes*: *Children's interest and learning. Findings also revealed that children in all grades might lose interest in educational and informational television programmes over the viewing season. Older boys in particular became least likely to view any educational programmes at the end of the season, from April–June. In sum, adult ratings of the episode content did not correspond to popularity of the shows with children. Moreover, adult ratings of the level of educational quality of programmes were unrelated to the educational strength of children's reports of the lessons in the programmes. Consistent with the findings from the naturalistic study of children's self-selected viewing patterns, girls and younger children liked the programmes more than boys and older children did. Overall, children liked pro-social programmes more than academic programmes, and they also understood pro-social programmes better. In contrast to the naturalistic patterns, children in the experimental study who were assigned to watch both popular and unpopular programmes showed a preference for popular pro-social programmes aired on commercial network television rather than those shown on Nickelodeon or PBS (Calvert, Huston, Watkins & Wright, 1982).

Comprehensibility may be a good predictor of children's visual attention in a laboratory setting, but it does not necessarily translate into higher levels of viewing in the natural environment. If a programme is too easy or boring, older children do not watch it during their free time. When children liked certain programmes, motivation, comprehension of explicit programme content, and understanding of the organisation of the programme (as assessed by picture sequencing) was higher. The findings suggest that programme popularity is the factor that pulls children into viewing experiences. It is notable that in the experimental study, the younger children liked the pro-social programmes more than the older children did. The particularly positive effects of popular over unpopular pro-social programmes on picture sequencing tasks suggest that children are processing popular pro-social programmes optimally. It is likely that motivational appeal translates into an investment of more attention resources and effort to understand them (Calvert, et. al, 1982).

Taken together, the results from the naturalistic and experimental studies suggest the importance of motivational variables for increasing children's comprehension of, and learning from, educational and informational television programmes. That is, even if older children can understand these programmes better than younger children as a result of their cognitive maturity and experiences, younger children are more likely to view those preferred shows, and hence, have more opportunity to learn from educational programmes. It appears that what expert adult raters view as educationally strong programmes bears little relation to what children choose to watch (and what is then available to be comprehended and learned as in the case of the naturalistic study), or to how well they can understand the programme content. Thus, APPC understood the multiple aspects of the value of these programmes, even if they might not be the strongest in terms of objective measures. With the implementation of the Three-Hour Rule, more educational programmes became available during times when children were in the viewing audience. Moreover, children are learning more social–emotional lessons from their favourite educational than from their favorite entertainment-based programmes. However, children are differentially interested in educational television programmes, and interest in these programmes diminishes over time, particularly for older boys (Calvert, Huston & Wright, 1987).

Developmental and gender differences in children's interest in educational programmes. The audience for educational and informational (E/I) television programmes was generally young elementary school children of both genders and older elementary school girls. Both Nickelodeon and ABC broadcast programmes attracted older girls. Beneficial effects of educational television for early grade school audiences is encouraging, suggesting that the preschool years are not the only ones where children will view and learn from educational programmes. Beneficial effects of educational programmes for girls also supplement longitudinal findings that boys are the primary beneficiaries of educational programmes. However, losing older boys from the audience, and having girls who focus almost exclusively on social–

emotional rather than academic lessons means that E/I television programmes are not living up to their potential. Although children did understand the abstract, implicit content well, it is questionable whether deep learning is occurring when children can understand 80% of the important content in a single viewing (Calvert et. al, 2002).

Part of the problem is linked to the age appropriateness of the programmes. Consistent with broadcaster beliefs, the programmes appear to be targeted toward the younger grade school years, with little challenging content for older grade school children known as teens. When E/I programmes featured actors who were early adolescents in social–emotional situations, as in the NBC line-up, older girls do appear to remain interested. However, similar age-appropriate programmeming directed at male interests was not apparent for older boys in any of the educational offerings of either type of broadcast network. Given that boys selectively search for male-directed content after they reach gender constancy in the grade school years, gender-neutral programmes may have more difficulty in pulling in teen boys. Children's interest in educational television programmes often is associated with better learning of programme lessons, suggesting that broadcasters could expand their impact if they create or distribute programmes that appeal to older as well as younger audiences and to boys as well as girls. Boys' traditional interest in fast-action, violent programmes coupled with reductions in violent content in E/I programmes may make it more difficult to pull older boys into the viewing audience of E/I shows. Even so, from the qualitative reports, it is clear that older boys can and do learn valuable social and academic lessons from their favorite educational programmes, and it is worth investing some creative effort to accomplish this goal for the older male children in the audience (Calvert et. al, 2002).

One important area for future research is to determine what takes many older children away from educational programmes—is it other kind of programmes, other activities that are seasonal in nature (e.g., exams or sports activities in the spring season), more academic work at school as the academic year comes to an end, or do they just outgrow educational programmes? Potential differences in interest for subgroups of children based on ethnicity and economic levels would also be useful.

Creating an audience is an important consideration for getting educational and informational television programmes to children. Nickelodeon broadcasts their programme series repeatedly. At times, they even broadcast programmes from the same series for several hours in a row. Nickelodeon also takes programmes that are not doing well off of the air, leaving the popular programmes for children to view. Perhaps this strategy also leads children to stay with the broadcaster, i.e., staying with the NICK brand. Another way to enhance brand loyalty is to broadcast the same programmes on different stations. Even if those specific episodes are not labeled E/I, repeated options to view a series and its characters may also create brand familiarity and loyalty, thereby increasing the market share of that broadcaster's E/I programmeming. This strategy has continued as Disney, who owns ABC from their cable station to their broadcast station. Similarly, CBS currently broadcasts Nickelodeon programmes, thereby increasing Nickelodeon's brand recognition and audience share (Calvert et. al, 2002).

The potential problem was that there was less diversity in programmes for each age group since broadcasters are only focusing on one age group. By fall season of 2002, CBS and NBC altered their programmeming strategies again, increasingly relying on outsourcing for E/I programmes. CBS expanded their use of popular Nickelodeon programmes designed for middle childhood. There is an unaddressed need for educational shows that appeal to older male children. This multimedia strategy may help the ratings of the CBS E/I and Nickelodeon programmes, as they are continuing to build on the Nickelodeon brand that is very popular with children. NBC also outsourced their children's E/I line-up to Discovery Kids with live programmes like The Crocodile Hunter entering their line-up. The Internet now allows children from diverse areas of the country, and the world, to bring their perspectives to questions that researchers ask. Such access ensured that the voices of many children were heard in the public debate about how to improve the quality of the television programmes they view (Calvert et. al, 2002).

This kind of methodology holds similar promise for other empirical and policy issues as well. However, there were problems in using this type of methodology with younger children. The most important was that children in early grade school do not have very effective keyboarding skills, thereby limiting their ability to spell correctly and perhaps augmenting the amount of time involved in their reporting. Keyboarding skills are an important avenue for writing on computers and one that still has not been adequately developed at the school level, in spite of its necessity for online literacy in the infor-mation age. Short cuts to spelling words such as "u" for "you" have become common and will increase if children cannot quickly write in a full grammatical structure. For those who are concerned about written literacy, basic keyboarding skills are important to consider for the curriculum. A second methodological contribution involves the importance of children's favorite television programmes as a way to index the overall popularity and impact of specific programmes on children. This consistency suggests that these two methods of collecting information from children are reliable. That is, one can ask children what programme they like the most, and thereby obtain information on what they view the most. This approach differs from showing children programmes in a laboratory setting and examining their comprehension, for they may never view these programmes in real-life.

Assessment of children's favorite programmes may provide an alternative quick and useful way to target the programmes that influence child viewers most (Cassell, 2002).

The CTA emerged, in part, because of grass roots pressures to improve the quality of children's television programmes. As this law moved from weak FCC guidelines, in which virtually any programme could be labeled as educational and informational, to one with stronger FCC guidelines, access to children's television has improved. More specifically, rules that require a minimum of 3 h of educational programmes per week (i.e., the Three-Hour Rule), that require educational broadcasts during times when children are likely to be awake and in the viewing audience, and that require broadcasters to label their educational and informational programme offerings, all work to improve the effectiveness of the CTA (Center for Media Education, 2001).

An interesting consequence of the CTA is that E/I programmes contain little violence, a sharp contrast from past examinations of children's commercial network programmes. This reduction may have occurred, in part, because broadcasters provide little time for their children's schedules because it is less profitable than adult programming. Broadcasting violent content may be too risky because it is not "FCC friendly." Consequently, violent children's programmes have been replaced on the entertainment broadcast networks with educational programmes that are of more value to children's development. Within children's television, quality programmes need not be a financial liability. Well designed programming that teaches social and emotional lessons can be profitable and draw large audiences, as demonstrated by Nickelodeon. Because of the potential for drawing a larger audience, thereby maximizing profits, most educational and informational programmes focus on pro-social rather than academic lessons (Center for Media Education, 2001).

Although the Three-Hour Rule may be particularly important in preserving educational television programmes and in diminishing the prevalence of violent programmes, educational television programs must still compete with strictly entertain-ment-driven programmes that are aired on other broadcast networks and that have sophisticated advertising campaigns. Pokemon is no longer as popular as it was in the 1999–2000 season, but other television programmes that are solely designed to entertain—and sell—have the same potential to pull children away from educational and informational programmes that are specifically designed to benefit their cognitive and social development. The implication is that the Three-Hour Rule does help to keep the playing field even and ensures that quality programmes for children can survive in the competitive arena. One remaining policy challenge is for the FCC to encourage broadcasters to create academically oriented programmes for children, particularly those that lead to deep learning. The high production cost and the limited age range for specific academic programmes are two likely reasons for the reluctance of broadcasters to invest in challenging programmes with an academic focus. Of the commercial networks, only ABC produced an original academically oriented educational programme, which was subsequently cancelled due to low viewership (Center for Media Education, 2001).

Although commercial networks rarely create academically oriented programmes, boys especially appear to learn important cognitive lessons from them. Moreover, adolescent males demonstrated long-term academic benefits from viewing educational programmes as children. Nonetheless, academically oriented programmes were not the top choices of programmes by children, making them less lucrative for the commercial networks to broadcast. But academically oriented programmes were not the most unpopular programmes either. Instead, they tended to fall in the middle of the viewing distribution. Another challenge is for the FCC to consider what the educational requirements of the CTA will be for digital television. Digital television will allow interactive television, bringing with it new opportunities for active engagement and learning. Decisions about what broadcasters must do for children with these new technological developments will frame the kinds of content available for our children to learn, the kinds of opportunities available for them to rehearse and learn key content messages through interaction, and ultimately, how our current generation of children will develop in the digital age (Center for Media Education and Institute for Public Representation, 1992).

In conclusion, the CTA has led commercial broadcasters to create and/or disseminate many educational and informational programmes that children enjoy and that lead to learning. The findings indicate that children are often learning social content, and to a lesser extent academically oriented content, from the educational television programmes they are viewing. Previous research has demonstrated that pro-social content has a beneficial impact on child viewers during the middle-childhood years. Popular educational programmes are particularly well liked and are most often well understood. To make an impact on a child audience, children must be willing to view educational programmes voluntarily during their leisure time, and pro-social programmes attract many viewers. The comparison of educational to non-educational favourite programmes revealed beneficial effects of educational programmes, particularly in the social and emotional area. That popularity may well reflect the careful depiction of science themes that are well integrated within stories in a comprehensible and engaging manner. We hope that such successes create a challenge and a sense of optimism for creative forces at commercial broadcast networks. Many children's futures can be affected by their ability to meet those challenges (Children Now, 2001).

The CTA has brought about a new era in children's programmes where beneficial educational and informational programmes can exist in the commercial arena, but protections such as the Three-Hour Rule are important for ensuring their survival. In a market place where educational programmes are competing against non-educational fare, commercial broadcasters may prefer pro-social rather than academic fare in meeting their CTA requirements because children like pro-social programmes more, understand them better and those programmes pull in a larger audience. A remaining challenge is to create more academically oriented programmes that attract a sufficiently large audience, including older boys, while delivering a comprehensible, interesting, yet challenging educational message.

Television Violence and the Legislative Response

Since 1954, the United States Senate Subcommittee on Juvenile Delinquency of the Committee on the Judiciary has conducted investigations on the impact that violence on television has on its viewers. Researchers found the television content extremely violent and half of the television hours monitored included violent programing. These programmes included crime, gunfire, fighting, and murder. The study concluded that under certain conditions some violent television could affect some children. In 1972, the Surgeon General issued a report concluding that violence in television had an adverse effect on certain members of society. Initially, President Reagan and Congress ignored the report. Eventually, however, both the House and Senate Committees on Appropriations directed the Federal Communications Commission ("FCC") to submit a report to the congressional committees on action the FCC planned to take in order to protect children from programming with excessive violence and obscenity. Ten years later, the Surgeon General issued an updated report, stating that the majority of observational or field surveys indicated that there is a positive correlation between television viewing and a variety of behavioural influences, including aggressive behaviour (Collins, 1970).

Furthermore, Liebert and Baron found that children who watch violence on, media that gets rewarded and not punished, are more prone to act violently. Liebert summarised the research from his own and other studies within the Surgeon General's Report, as well as 54 earlier experimental studies. For example, when television characters use aggressive means to reach benevolent ends, young children misinterpret the show's befuddled message(s) than when the characters behave consistently good or bad. Children also behave more aggressively after seeing a mixed pro-social/anti-social character (one who acts acceptable in a social context and then unacceptably) than when the character has behaved consistently in a totally pro-social way. Justifying the rational for aggressive actions does not appear to eliminate the influence exposure to aggressive acts has on very young children. Soon after this study, the National Association of Broadcasters ("NAB") required that broadcasters show sex or violence only as it relates to the plot and without unneeded emphasis (Collins, 1970).

(a) The Television Programme Improvement Act of 1990. Congress responded to the high rate of violence on television with the Television Programme Improvement Act of 1990 ("Improvement Act"). Former President George H.W. Bush signed the Improvement Act into law on December 1, 1990, which was "designed to encourage the networks, the cable industry, and independent stations to reduce the amount of violence currently shown on television." The main thrust of the Improvement Act was for the television industry to voluntarily establish standards on violence for a limited purpose and time. Former Illinois Senator Paul Simon originally introduced the Improvement Act, which gave the networks an exemption from antitrust laws in exchange for reducing television violence. In order to facilitate the reduction of violence in programming, a provision of the Improvement Act allowed the broadcasters and cable industry the opportunity to meet regularly during a three year period and focus on violence standards.

After persuasion from Senator Simon, the industry members met after two years in December of 1992. As a result of the meeting, the networks (ABC, NBC, and CBS) in a joint statement, created standards intended to "prohibit depicting violence as glamorous or using it to shock or stimulate the audience." The standards prohibit scenes showing "excessive gore, pain or physical suffering", and limit scenes that contain "gratuitous" or "excessive" violence, force inappropriate for home viewing, images that encourage imitation by or frighten children, and anything that abuses or encourages animal injury. The Improvement Act has some problems regarding the control over television content. First, only the networks apply and interpret the guidelines of the Improvement Act, not Congress, which results in the networks deciding on what content is explicitly violent or inappropriate for children. Secondly, the purported standards have not reduced the amount of violence on television because violent programs attract a larger audience and are more profitable to the stations. The networks merely put a caption at the beginning of a programme giving various ratings and warnings to parents for shows that may be sexually or violently inappropriate for youth.

(b) The Children's Television Act of 1990. On October 18, 1990, Congress enacted the Children's Television Act of 1990 ("Children's Act"). Similar to the Improvement Act, the Children's Act seeks to improve children's television through FCC regulation. The Children's Act serves the following three functions: (1) time restrictions on advertising; (2) airing programming beneficial for children and; (3) informing broad-casters at license renewal time that compliance with the above two factors is considered part of their duty to programme in the public interest. The Children's Act restricts advertising on children's television to twelve minutes per hour during the week and ten and one half minutes per hour on weekends. Further-more, the Children's Act educational programming requirement forces broadcasters to broadcast programmes specifically designed to "meet the educational and informational needs of the child audience" and established the National Endowment for Children's Educational Television. Children's television includes programmes originally produced and broadcast primarily for children ages twelve and under.

The Children's Act does not apply to programmes made for general audiences that may be viewed by children. The FCC assumes compliance with the educational requirement, unless a formal complaint is filed with the FCC challenging a station's compliance. Section 102(a) of the Children's Act requires the FCC to initiate a rule making proceeding to "prescribe standards applicable to commercial broadcast licensees with respect to time devoted to commercial matter in conjunction with children's television..." The FCC has conducted unsystematic reviews of ads being broadcast to check up on its licensees. For instance, a January 1992 audit found ten violations from more than the 160 television stations and cable systems that were inspected. Three stations cited as violators were levied fines of a maximum of $20,000, and three other stations received admonishments from the FCC. The Children's Act, like the Improvement Act, is not without problems. One issue is that broadcasters remain unclear as to what constitutes compliance. For instance, Atlanta's Superstation WTBS ("WTBS") challenged the FCC's finding that it went over the weekday advertising time limits. WTBS believed the ads promoting programming on other Ted Turner Broadcasting owned stations should not be considered "commercial matter." WTBS argued that the ads did not have to meet the FCC's standards because they were not sold for money to the broadcaster. The FCC, however, defined "sold" as any situation where the broadcaster receives valuable consideration from the advertiser, directly or indirectly, and WTBS received this type of consideration. They received an admonishment only, not a fine, because it agreed to monitor this practice more carefully in the future. Some broadcasters also argue that compliance with the Children's Act requires too much time and money. While some fear that broadcasters may give up on children's programming, the FCC's apparent leniency on network violators and the affirmative duty to broadcast for children, make it unlikely that stations will completely abandon children's television (FCC, 1996).

Censorship, Violence and the First Amendment

While Congress, the FCC and television networks have valid reasons to censor children's programming, what rights do adults have in the media? The First Amendment states that "Congress shall make no law respecting an establishment of religion, or prohibiting the free exercise thereof; or abridging the freedom of speech, or of the press; or the right of the people peaceably to assemble, and to petition the Government for a redress of grievances." Incidents of youth and school violence have created an opportunity for government involvement intc First Amendment rights. For instance, in December 1965, a group of adults and students in Des Moines, Iowa met at 16-year-old student Christopher Eckhardt's home and decided to wear black armbands and fast between December 16 and New Year's Eve to protest the Vietnam War and support a truce (Collins, Berndt & Hess, 1974).

On December 16, three students, including Eckhardt, wore the armbands to school even though the Des Moines principals' policy banned the armbands two days prior. Citing the student's First Amendment rights, the United States Supreme Court held in 1969 that students do not "shed their constitutional rights to freedom of speech or expression at the schoolhouse gate." Another example occurred in 1999 when an Allen High School (north of Dallas, Texas) 17-year-old honor student, Jennifer Boccia, wore a black armband to school to mourn the students killed in April 1999 at Columbine High School (Littleton, Colorado) and to protest against newly implemented school security policies. The school gave Boccia a three-day suspension and an order preventing her from speaking with members of the news media. The ACLU brought a lawsuit against Allen High School and its officials in order to protect Boccia's free speech rights, but an agreement was eventually reached and Boccia's transcripts were expunged of the incident (Collins, et. al, 1974).

Increased violent incidents, particularly, like the one at Columbine, have revived congressional attention towards violence on television, movies, music and video games, and the potential negative effects caused by those media (Collins & Getz, 1976). The Senate Commerce Committee on the marketing of violent entertainment to children held two hearings subsequent to the Columbine slayings. A safe harbor proposal was reintroduced in the Senate, and the Senate Commerce Committee approved the bill in 2000 (although it was not presented to the full Senate). The bill requires that violent programming be limited to hours when children are not likely to comprise a substantial portion of the audience. In 1999, two bills were introduced but no formal action has ever been taken. The first bill would have created a national youth violence commission to discover the causes of youth violence and report to Congress and the President. The second, the

Children's Protection Act of 1999, would have exempted agreements "relating to voluntary guidelines governing telecast material, movies, video games, Internet content, and music lyrics" from the antitrust laws. Other attempts to enact legislation dealing with media violence also failed, and Congress adjourned the session without the enactment of any legislation on the issue.

At former President Clinton's request, the Federal Trade Commission ("FTC") prepared and released a report in 2000 on the marketing of "adult-oriented" violent content to children. The FTC report found that the motion picture industry, the music industry and the computer gaming industry extensively advertised maturerated content in media predominantly viewed by children. The FTC found that these products' marketing plans specifically targeted children, and they were promoted and advertised in broadcasting most likely to reach children. After the report's release, the Senate Commerce Committee and the Senate Judiciary Committee held hearings on the marketing of violence to children and the FCC announced plans to examine the effects of "sexually explicit and violent" television programming on children. In late 2000, the FCC held a hearing on the "public interest obligations of TV broadcast licensees" and issued a report to Congress. The report included ways broadcasters could lower the violent programmes negative impact, such as limiting the inappropriate violence, language, or sexual content from child programmes, airing children programming (including ads) at appropriate times (not when a significant number of children are reasonably expected to be in the audience), and improving the existing programme ratings system and airing public service announcements to educate parents about the ratings system and the V-chip. "The FCC did not promulgate any regulations dealing with violent programming, however, nor did any legislative proposals on the issue clear Congress." The Media Marketing Accountability Act of 2001 would have prohibited "the targeted advertising or other marketing to minors of an adult-rated motion picture, music recording, or electronic game" as an unfair or deceptive practice. No formal action, however, has been taken on this bill (FCC, 1991, 1996).

(a) Opposition to Media Censorship as a Violation of First Amendment Rights. While Congress and the FCC have taken some action to marginalise violence on television, others are not convinced of the correlation between violence in the media and increased violence in children. Todd Gitlin, a high-profile veteran of the 1960's peace movement and a leading United States commentator and author on media and culture issues, argues that television violence does not cause violence, and that "the profiteers of television in the United States – the networks, the programme suppliers, and the advertisers - are essentially subsidized (e.g., via tax write-offs) to programme this formulaic stuff." Gitlin believes that "media violence isn't dangerous, it's just stupid." Gitlin further argues that Japan shows a greater amount of media violence and sex than the United States yet has a lower rate of violence. "Restrictions on the First Amendment are permitted when the speech constitutes fighting words, incites imminent lawless activity, is defamatory or is legally obscene." Individuals like Robert Peck, a lawyer and author, believe that "[a]s we continue to lose our First Amendment moorings as a people and think in terms of effects, we will see the bad tendency doctrine revived—even if under a new name. As a result, we will see increased authority to curb speech that supposedly leads people astray." Gitlin also gives his support of the V-chip, a device inside the television that parents can use to preclude their children from accessing certain television programming (Collins, Wellman, Keniston & Westby, 1978).

Under the V-Chip system, television programmes are rated similarly to the way movies are rated. Television ratings are sent electronically to the V-Chip, and parents can then set their televisions to block programmes with certain ratings. With or without the V-Chip, the television industry is often successful in using the First Amendment as a defense to their broadcasting of certain violent entertainment directed at children. For example, in *Olivia N. v. Nat'l Broad. Co.*, a damages action was brought on behalf of a nine-year old girl who was artificially raped with a bottle after her assailants watched the movie *Born Innocent*. The *Olivia N.* court found two problems with television censorship aimed at protecting children. First, regulating the television networks would "chill" speech and lead to self-censorship. In Helen Gerosthathos, television networks would be subject to liability because of their broadcasting choices thus dampening the variety of public debate. Secondly, the court was concerned that the adult population would have to watch only what is fit for children. In *Zamora v. Columbia Broadcasting System*, a father sued three broadcasting companies after his son killed an 83-year-old woman. The father alleged that television violence caused his son to become desensitized to violent behavior, thus leading to the murder. The *Zamora* court, as did the *Olivia N.* court, held for the broadcasting companies and found that the imposition of civil responsibility for damages would act as a restraint on the broadcasters' exercise of their asserted first amendment rights. The *Zamora* court also communicated the importance of giving viewers and the public access to social, political, esthetic or moral ideas (Children Now, 2001).

B. Support for Media Censorship. Unlike Gitlin, George Gerbner, the former dean of the Annenberg School of Communication at the University of Pennsylvania and founder of the Cultural Environment Movement, believes that media violence should be censored, and that violence in the media is not an absolute expression of free speech. Gerbner believes that "media violence is tantamount to censorship by media conglomerates that effectively shut out diverse points of view." Gerbner further attacks Gitlin's "case of Japan" argument as the "knee-jerk retort of apologists," which "assumes that media violence as the only, or major and always decisive, influence on human social behaviour." Gerbner further argues "heavy [television] viewers express a greater sense of insecurity and mistrust than comparable groups of light viewers. They are more likely to be dependent on authority and to support repression if it is presented as enhancing their security." Gerbner does not see the V-Chip as the solution and believes the technology protects the industry from the parents, and not the parents or children from the television industry. Gerbner sees antitrust as a better government regulation because it could create a level playing field, that is, antitrust regulation would admit new entries and there would be a greater diversity of ownership, employment, and representation as a means to reduce violence (Collins, et. al, 1978).

In 1997, the Motion Picture Association of America ("MPAA") president Jack Valenti submitted a system of voluntary parental guidelines to the FCC, called the TV Parental Guidelines ("Guidelines"). Under the Guidelines, television shows fall into one of six categories, which are age-based: TV-Y, TV-Y7, TV-G, TV-PG, TV-14, or TV-M. The Guidelines are applied to all television programs except for news and sports. While many advocates for censoring television violence agree with Gerbner, little has been done legally to force censorship of media violence. Courts often hold for defendants in First Amendment cases, making it difficult for plaintiffs to prevail. This is largely due to the *Brandenburg* test, which courts look to in analyzing media violence. In *Brandenburg v. Ohio*, the defendant was a former Ku Klux Klan member convicted of violating the Ohio Syndicalism Statute, which made it a crime to teach the doctrines of criminal syndicalism (FCC, 1996).

The defendant challenged the constitutionality of this statute on Free Speech grounds, and the United States Supreme Court held that "the constitutional guarantees of free speech and free press do not permit a State to forbid...the use of force [or of law violation] except where such advocacy is directed to inciting or producing imminent lawless action and is likely to incite or produce such action." Because the *Brandenburg* test requires plaintiffs to prove that listening to or watching violence caused or produced imminent lawless activity, the burden is often too high for plaintiffs to prevail and recover damages. For example, in *Davidson v. Time Warner*, the widow of slain state trooper Bill Davidson brought a suit against Tupac Shakur and

Time Warner, claiming that Shakur's rap album *2 Pacalypse Now* caused her husband's death. Ronald Howard was driving a stolen car, and Davidson pulled Howard over in an unrelated traffic stop. Howard pulled out a handgun and fatally shot Officer Davidson during the traffic stop. During the shooting, Howard was listening to *2 Pacalypse Now*, which contains at least one song advocating violence against police officers. Holding for the defendants, the United States District Court for the Southern District of Texas found that the *Brandenburg* test was not met because although the songs were insulting and outrageous, there was no proof that the artist intended to incite violence.

Proposed Solutions to Violence on Television

Properly addressing how to curtail media violence's impact on children without infringing on First Amendment rights is a multifaceted issue. The courts, the legislature and the entertainment industry struggle to find solutions. Many Americans believe that censorship alone is not the answer. Todd Gitlin stated that "the problem of TV goes far beyond violence…The money making machines that control as much of the culture as they can get their hands on, will make just as many moral reforms as they think they need to keep Congress and the FCC off their backs." His co-author George Gerbner agreed, saying, "The problem goes beyond violence, ratings, or any single factor, to the heart of the system…Citizens own the airways. We should demand that it be free and fair, and not just 'rated." Thus far, the remedies have been reliance on the industries to self regulate and provide parents with a means to help children pick suitable material for their age group. There are, however, a few alternate solutions that may provide the answer to balancing television violence with First Amendment rights (FCC, 1991).

A. Solution One: Replacing the Brandenburg Test with the Miller Test for Media Violence. By utilizing the *Miller v. California* test, courts could establish an exception to the Free Speech Clause for media violence that is similar to the obscenity standard. In *Miller*, the United States Supreme Court held that illegal obscenity could be determined by evaluating three factors. First, whether "the average person, applying contemporary community standards would find that the work, taken as a whole, appeals to the prurient interest." Second, whether the work "depicts or describes, in a patently offensive way, sexual conduct specifically defined by the applicable state law." The final factor is whether the work, "taken as a whole, lacks serious literary, artistic, political, or scientific value." Using the modified *Miller* test by substituting "violence" for "obscene sexual content" could satisfy the concern over freedom of expression versus harm to children. Advocates for the modified *Miller* test argue "that certain violent content, like pornography is obscene, and therefore entertainment companies should be held liable if they are producing and marketing obscene material." Furthermore, by holding that excessive media violence is obscene, courts and legislatures would have more autonomy to limit unwarranted violence on television. Broadcasters could still show violence, but violence that is classified as obscene would undergo stricter regulation. Opponents of the modified *Miller* test believe a chilling effect on the entertainment industry and the prevention of free speech would occur if the test were implemented. Opponents also assert that courts would have difficulty distinguishing good violence from bad violence. Advocates respond that the entertainment industry could adapt to strict standards for violent programming, just as they did with pornography (Cassell, 2002).

B. Solution Two: Media Awareness Programmes. Another proposed solution to deal with excessive violence on television is through education by creating media literacy awareness programs. The American Academy of Pediatricians suggests that parents become "media-literate" by "watching television with their children and teenagers, discussing the content with them, and initiating the process of selective viewing at an early age." Similarly, the Recording Industry Association of America ("RIAA") encourages parents to watch television with their children and discuss the content with them. The RIAA works with recording artists to develop public service materials in its "Talking with Kids about Tough Issues Campaign ("Talking Campaign")." The Talking Campaign helps parents to better communicate with their children about difficult issues facing their lives. For example, school media literacy programmes can help children interpret and analyse what they see and hear in the media. If parents and children became more educated and aware of violence in the media, neither Congress nor the FCC would get the level of pressure they do to impose regulations that prevent minors from accessing the explicit material in the media (Cassell, 2002).

C. Solution Three: Creating Universal Standards as a Means to Self-Regulate. A third proposed solution is for politicians and advocacy groups to work with the current system, allowing the media industry to regulate itself, and pushing those working in the industry to be more accountable for the material they produce. For example, Connecticut Senator Joseph Lieberman urged Hollywood to market its violent content to children more responsibly. Similarly, the FTC made three suggestions to the media industry in a report. First, the FTC suggested that the industry expand or establish codes that prohibit target marketing and impose sanctions for violations. Secondly, the FTC suggested improving self-regulatory system compliance at the retail level. Finally, the FTC suggested increasing parental awareness of ratings and labels. Likewise, the American Academy of Pediatrics urged producers and artists to exercise sensitivity and self-restraint in what they depict given the impact it has on children. Although some of the above attempts, like the FTC reports, have succeeded in bringing scrutiny to excessive media violence, each media industry (e.g. television, movies, and radio) has its own system of regulating violence. The various systems make it difficult for parents to choose appropriate materials for their children. Therefore, creating universal standards applicable to all the major media and entertainment industries could furnish parents and children with proper information so they can make educated decisions about a programme's content.

However, First Amendment rights are essential to the freedoms guaranteed by the United States Constitution, and the government cannot violate constitutional rights simply to protect children. While violence will always be a part of society, the government, parents, children, educators and the media must all work for the greater good. The broadcasting networks need to make a conscious effort not to air impressionable and inappropriate programming at hours when children will be watching. The government should work with parents and the media industry, instead of attempting to create legislation (often unconstitutionally) each time an issue with the media arises. Finally, parents must stop passing the torch of parental responsibility to the media for what it airs, and start taking responsibility in overseeing what programmes and media outlets their children are viewing.

References

Acuff, D.S. (1997). What kids buy and why: The psychology of marketing to kids. New York: Free Press.

Anderson, D.R., Huston, A.C., Schmitt, K.L., Linebarger, D.L., & Wright, J. C. (2001). Early childhood television viewing and adolescent behavior. Monographs of the Society for Research in Child Development.

Anderson, D.R., & Lorch, E.P. (1983). Looking at television: Action or reaction? In J. Bryant, & D.R. Anderson (Eds.), Children's understanding of television: Research on attention and comprehension. New York: Academic.

Bransford, J., Brown, A., & Cocking, R.R. (1999). How people learn: Brain, mind, experience, and school. Washington, DC: National Academy Press.

Calvert, S.L. (1999 a). Children's journeys through the information age. Boston: McGraw Hill.

Calvert, S.L. (1999 b). The form of thought. In I.E. Sigel (Ed.), Theoretical perspectives in the concept of representation. Hillsdale, NJ: Erlbaum.

Calvert, S.L. (2000, August). The Internet: Is cyber space for all girls? Paper presented at the American Psychological Association, Washington, DC.

Calvert, S.L., Huston, A.C., Watkins, B. A., & Wright, J.C. (1982). The relation between selective attention to television forms and children's comprehension of content. Child Development.

Calvert, S. L., Huston, A. C., & Wright, J. C. (1987). The effects of television pre-play formats on children's attention and story comprehension. Journal of Applied Developmental Psychology.

Calvert, S. L., Kotler, J., Murray, W., Gonzales, E., Savoye, K., Hammack, P., Weigert, S., Shockey, E., Paces, C., Friedman, M., & Hammar, M. (2002). Children's online reports about educational and informational television programmes. In S. L. Calvert, A. B. Jordan, & R. R. Cocking (Eds.), Children in the digital age: Influences of electronic media on development. Westport, CT: Praeger.

Cassell, J. (2002). "We have these rules inside:" The effects of exercising voice in a children's online forum. In S. L. Calvert, A. B. Jordan, & R. R. Cocking (Eds.), Children in the digital age: Influences of electronic media on development. Westport, CT: Praeger.

Center for Media Education (2001). Comments submitted as part of the Notice of Proposed Rulemaking on the obligations of digital television broadcasters to serve children.

Center for Media Education and Institute for Public Representation, Georgetown University (1992, September 29). A report on broadcaster compliance with the Children's Television Act. Washington, DC: Center for Media Education.

Children Now (2001). Comments submitted as part of the Notice of Proposed Rulemaking on the obligations of digital television broadcasters to serve children.

Children's Television Act of 1990 (1990). Publ. L. No. 101-437, 104 Stat. 996–1000, codified at 47 USC Sections 303a, 303b, 394.

Collins, W. A. (1970). Learning of media content: A developmental study. Child Development.

Collins, W. A., Berndt, T., & Hess, V. (1974). Observational learning of motives and consequences for television aggression: A developmental study. Child Development.

Collins, W. A., & Getz, S. K. (1976). Children's social responses following modeled reactions to provocation: Pro-social effects of a televised drama. Journal of Personality.

Collins, W. A., Wellman, H., Keniston, A., & Westby, S. (1978). Age-related aspects of comprehension and inference from a televised dramatic narrative. Child Development.

Federal Communications Commission (1991). Policies and rules concerning children's television programming. Federal Communications Commission Record.

Federal Communications Commission (1996). Policies and Rules Concerning Children's Television Programming: Revision of Programming Policies for Television Broadcast Broadcasters.

17

The Perennial Effect of Corruption on Communication on the Social and Professional Well-being: A Critical Analysis of the Role of Media in Moulding the Issues

Dr. Garima Sharma, Dr. Preeti Sharma,
Mr. Dauji Agarwal

Importance of Communication in Today's World

In an ever growing world, communication is the buzzword whether it is with our employer, customer, peer, subordinate or family. Part of the life-changing process encompasses working with the people and playing several communication roles. These roles, all have major impact on the change process in organisation and the life of individual. Yet, if a person is to learn about his/her world, the ability to communicate must exist. Even a baby learns to speak/to communicate through touch, vision and hearing. In India and in many other nations, good communication has become a symbol of people's status for quality in education and a tool for a total participation in national and international life. It is said that you can't judge a book by it's cover but how many of us judge people by the way they talk, or even by the way they answer. We form opinions about people the first time we see or hear them.

Objectives of Communication

Major part of our active life is spent in communicating with others. People need to communicate as they move from situation to situation, in family, organisation and other social groups for getting their work done and for relationships. The main objectives of communication are as follows:

(1) Exchange of information

(2) Advice and counseling

(3) Persuasion
(4) Suggestion
(5) Education
(6) Motivation
(7) Raising morale
(8) Warning
(9) Global business environment
(10) Technological advancement
(11) Need for better human and Public relations
(12) Gaining feedback

What is Corruption?

Corruption is one of India's main challenges whether it is political, bureaucratic, corporate or individual corruption. Corruption is a phenomenon that digs deep into peoples' everyday lives – and that the futures of many people are held hostage to while grand corruption has trapped generations in poverty; petty corruption has pulled out the roots of their potential for happiness. A basic perception is that, like the poor, corruption will always be with us: inevitable, immutable. It seems as if only the honest people are poor in India and want to get rid of their poverty by education, emigration to cities, and immigration, whereas all the corrupt ones, are getting rich through scams and crimes. It seems as if India is a rich country filled with poor people. Laws have been passed, committees and institutions have been set up, anti-corruption campaigns have been developed, but the problem still persists. Studies and public surveys have reinforced the public perception and have consistently shown that corruption still persists in India despite many efforts by the government. There are many things that can be blamed for this situation, which allows corruption to flourish?

1. The shortcomings of the system
2. Lack of proper circulation of messages
3. Convenience
4. Luxurious and Extravagant and sumptuous life style
5. Lack of generosity and being non-emotional
6. Acquisitive competitive feeling in every sphere of life by illegal means

Role of Media on Corruption and its Impact on Communication

Media has two faces; one is for removing corruption and the other for the menace of corruption in the society. Media plays an important role in our life. It has the power to speak boldly against wrong politicians. Media gives voices to the poor people. When nobody listens to a man only the media raises his voice. In my opinion, media plays a vital role in everyone's life. It solves their problems; It gives them choices as many new media and channels are coming up. Yes, sometimes it sensationalises the news items, but again I feel that media is something that is must for today. It helps and provides vital information to the people. Media is considered to be the 4th pillar of the society. The other three being legislative, executive and judiciary. It definitely plays an important role for the welfare of the society. Its duty is to inform, educate and entertain the people but nowadays we see that media is not doing its duty honestly. Instead of giving important information and educative programme, it is giving emphasis to sensationalise the public. They are only trying to attract people to increase their TRP rating. They raise the matter for 2 or 3 days then they forget that and never try to get the feedback of the cases.

Globally, there is a general consensus amongst most academicians and policy makers that the debilitating effects of corruption permeate through all aspects of public life. Several studies have shown that corruption not only stifles growth, it also perpetuates inequalities, deepens poverty, causes human suffering, dilutes the fight against terrorism and organised crime and tarnishes country's image globally. Definitely, the impact of corruption is multi fold, encompassing- economic, political, social, environmental and also the issues of national security. We have so many examples like- Anna Hazare's anti-corruption campaign got the popularity and support just because of media, it highlighted it and helped to reach it in the rural places also, the accused of Jessica Lal murder case have been apprehended just because of the positive role of media.

Who is Responsible?

Have we ever thought about as to who is responsible for this corruption? Of course not! Only we people are responsible for corruption. Because everything begins at our home, then reaches to society. Suppose, we are to go for vacation or somewhere else by railway and it is quite impossible to get the reservation, immediately, we will think of giving some extra money to the officials so that we could easily get the reservation. At public places, we make big noises against corruption, but on the reverse, we ourselves indulge in it easily. When our family members take illegal gratification, we keep mum. When someone else takes bribe, we again condemn him. When our daughter's marriage is to be settled, we suddenly go against Dowry system, we condemn it very much, but when we are going to the marriage of our son/brother, we virtually auction him in the market.

These are some of the examples which are responsible for the menace of corruption in a more extensive manner

1. **Mis-communication.** (Twisting and exaggerating and pushing behind the reality)
   A person wants to express something, but communicates something else to other person. The other person does not get the idea. This causses miscommunication and misinterpretation. The person who has received the wrong message (miscommunicated message), will surely misinterpret the message in society also. It will create confusion, doubts and sometimes a situation of dilemma.
2. **Mischief Mongering.** Really it creates a lot of panic in the mind of listener (society) i.e. Spreading the wrong information like rumours in social, professional, political scenario and economic front also like riots and war of words. Giving the shape of communal riots for a simple quarrel between two communities.
3. **Social Networking websites.** We all know very well that how much these websites like-Twitter, Face book, Orkut, Google and Blogging are giving us the benefit of being in touch with our friends and everyone living at a distant place. If we are unable to meet our old friends, we can search them through the above said websites. A few days back government has banned these websites due to the misuse of these sites by the people and exploiting their tender feelings. A case has been filed against these websites by the Supreme Court. But what will happen in future, nobody knows.
4. **Cyber Crime.** It is rightly said that,

"The modern thief can steal more with a computer than with a gun and today's terrorist may be able to do more damage with a keyboard than with a bomb".

The use of internet in India is growing rapidly. It has given rise to new opportunities in each and every field we can think of – be it business, entertainment, sports or education. There are two sides to a coin. Internet also has its own disadvantages. One of the major disadvantages is Cybercrime–illegal activity committed on the internet. Computers today are being misused for illegal activities like e-mail espionage, credit card fraud, spams, software piracy and spreading viruses on the computers and hacking the computers and websites, which invade our privacy and offend our senses. Basically, It is a criminal activity committed on the internet. Today, parents, teachers, govern-ment, and industry have been working hard to protect children online.

Cybercrimes can be basically divided into 3 major categories.

1. Cyber crimes against persons.
2. Cybercrimes against property.
3. Cybercrimes against government.

Effects of Corruption

1. Today the futures of many countries are held hostage to grand corruption that trap generations in poverty; petty corruption pulls out the roots of their potential for happiness.
2. The reality is that corruption permeates life, from the father who goes without shoes to pay a bribe so his child can attend a supposedly free school. Corruption is a cold hard fact of life in the 21st century.
3. Corruption eats away at the economies of poor countries. The perception of endemic corruption scares off foreign investors and has a knock-on effect on economic growth.
4. In some ways, changing the perception of corruption is changing the reality. A basic perception is that, like the poor, corruption will always be with us: inevitable, immutable.
5. But the reality is that aid is also a tool for reducing corruption, when targeted to improving governance and transparency - variables that are integrally linked to democratic development, equity and justice.
6. Corruption and poverty are related scourges, and intelligent aid is a powerful tool for reducing both. Reducing corruption can release economic potential for even greater gains against poverty. These are the messages we must be broadcasting.

Suggestions

- *First challenge:* bringing corruption into the *sunlight.* This is a function not just of communications, but of the entire anti-corruption infrastructure: investigative journalists and the media as a whole, effective freedom of information laws, awards and other forms of recognition, anti-corruption watchdogs and higher compliance standards in international institutions, among many other things.
- The second challenge is to persuade people to give up deeply ingrained and highly negative assumptions, that corruption is inevitable.
- When people live in fear, or resignation, they may be unable to see the possibility of change, and the idea of fighting back becomes more than they can cope with. Put simply, we need to offer hope.
- Six-Step Implementation Plan, to fight corruption-

1. Decide to adopt a no-bribes policy
2. Plan how to implement the policy
3. Develop anti-bribery programme
4. Implement the programme
5. Monitor the programme
6. Evaluate the performance

Conclusion

It is a fact that communication begins at birth with touch, then with vision, and finally with speech and hearing. Everyone needs to learn the "codes of his/her culture" because the language of each culture is different. Through the wonders of technology, we are more easily able to communicate whatever thoughts come to mind. Then there are the social networks—Friendster, MySpace, Facebook and Twitter—which allow for a continuous connection to friends and family, updated any minute of any day. Friendships should be able to blossom and families should grow closer with such unprecedented access. But there should not be any mis use of the tender feelings of anybody. In addition, people are now much better able to reach those of like mind and similar interests unlike any other time in history. No one is perfect in this world and so is the media. Media is like a watchdog in a democracy that keeps government active. From being just an informer it has become an integral part of our daily lives. With the passage of time it has become more matured and a more responsible entity. It is the time to uproot correption completely.

References

1. Ann Clay, Barbara (2006) The perception and reality of corruption. Canberra.
2. Babu, Maya, What Is Cybercrime?, October 11, 2004.
3. Centre for Media Studies, India Corruption Study 2005: To Improve Governance: Volume I – Key Highlights, New Delhi: Transparency International India, 30 June 2005.
4. cybercitizenship.org

18

Social Change Communication: A Study of Media Framing on HIV/AIDS News Stories

Uttam Kr Pegu

Introduction

HIV/AIDS which has become a global concern is no longer simply a health problem. It is one of the most challenging public health issues not only in India but elsewhere. The impact of AIDS is no less destructive than war itself and by some measures, far worse says United Nations Secretary General Kofi Annan (UNAIDS 2000). According to UNAIDS report on global AIDS epidemic (2011) at the end of 2010, an estimated 34 million people were living with HIV worldwide, up 17% from 2001 which means that the levels of new infections still continues despite efforts to mitigate HIV infection. In 2009, the number of people who got newly infected with HIV was estimated at 2.6 million. In most developing countries, HIV/AIDS infection is still considered as a stigma not to be discussed freely or even acknowledged. Given that societies most affected are not ready to accept its existence, it is difficult to assess its spread and impact in a holistic manner. Media, therefore, has the challenge of curbing this menace in the most effective manner. Because media plays an important role in everyone's lives it has enormous potential to educate and mould the general public. Yet in the response to AIDS only a small fraction of that potential has been tapped. Although there are examples of highly successful campaigns, by and large, media coverage of the epidemic is not sufficient to keep the public well informed. There are still millions of people who have never heard of AIDS, and many have serious misconceptions about the disease.

Communicating AIDS has been divisive because there are numerous constituents such as public health professionals, affected individuals, activists and journalists, each having their frame of reference toward this disease. Needless to mention that the media anywhere in the world whether print or audio-visual acts as a watchdog for the society. Although HIV/AIDS is of major concern to the world, it has remained under-reported or if covered at all, it is not presented with the full spectrum of facts, thus misleading those it is supposed to inform or educate. The news coverage of HIV/AIDS can be considered as some sort of risk reporting. An important and controversial dimension has been its manner of evaluating risk and communicating this information to the public (Covello, Winterfeldt & Slovic 1986). It is understood that evaluating risk and informing this to the public requires interpretive judgment in the face of technical uncertainty and scientific disagreement. Communicating HIV/AIDS, therefore, challenges the media to develop responsible reporting in the face of uncertain technical information and conflicting political goals (Nelkin 1987). The case of AIDS illustrates how such social factors converge with the constraints of journalism and the pressure from advocates to influence the style and content of the news stories (Kinsella 1989).

Media has a major role to play in containing the spread of HIV by disseminating knowledge to the public with the widest coverage. This task could be done in close cooperation with specialists, to avoid wrong, ineffective or counter-productive messages being disseminated. It can promote better awareness on (i) how the virus is transmitted and (ii) how its spread can be contained. It can also be used to promote better understanding and care for people with HIV positive. The media can move issues to the center stage or keep them out of public view. They serve as filters through which people receive news and interpret. The information they convey, their visual and verbal images, and the tone of their presentation can define the significance of events, shape public attitudes, and legitimate or call into question public policies (Gans & McQuail 1979). It is imperative that the media learn to refrain from blaming the infected persons, which, in turn, encourages the tendency to deny infection or ignore the risk of HIV infection even amongst the most vulnerable sections. Social and economic discrimination against the HIV positive is another area where media has to raise its voice clearly and conscientiously.

In the early 1960s, the dominant belief was that media messages would always be followed by the adoption of the communicated ideas as is posited in the 'magic bullet theory' (1930). There is a departure from this popular belief and that the media do not have such complete control over the social change process. DeFluer and Ball-Rokeach (1988) and many others have, however, noted that the mass media still play a major role in the social learning process and have enormous influence on how individuals acquire new ideas and change orientation in society. A purposeful and impact bearing information dissemination can only emerge after an assessment on the current practices of media coverage of HIV/AIDS so as to identify strengths, weaknesses and gaps in the dissemination of information on HIV/AIDS.

Media coverage of HIV/AIDS in Asia sparked off much debate in the United Nations report on the Fourth International Congress on HIV/AIDS in Asia (1997). Wolffers and Bevers (1997), highlights the media's negative reporting of HIV/AIDS especially in Southeast Asia and discusses how the discrimination of minority groups in the west, mainly gays and drug users are reflected in the Asian media. The status of drug users and sex workers in southeast Asia, who were among the first to be infected with HIV, is virtually the lowest in society and even the media personnel tend to look down on them or are indifferent to them. This is one of the reasons for the unsympathetic attitude of communities towards people with AIDS, and this emerges as a serious detriment in writing positively about HIV/AIDS.

Objectives and Methodology

This paper discourses on HIV/AIDS reporting and the transformative potential of media in raising its voice against social and economic discrimination inflicted on HIV positive persons. It also examines how social change communication models can inject fresh ideas and news angles among journalists in order to broaden the current scope and content of HIV/AIDS reporting. This paper is based on exploratory research technique which includes reviewing available literature on HIV/AIDS and the Media, in-depth interviews, analysis on government reports and publications and case studies. The perceptions of these methodologies have been given equal weightage as that would impart the much needed measure of validity, reliability and acceptability which is substantiated in the study.

Literature Review

Academic research on media coverage of HIV can be traced back to the 1980s when the disease peaked in the United States, Australia and many Western European countries. Research on media coverage of HIV/AIDS was focused primarily on the news media in the United States and Britain. Research on media coverage of HIV in Asia is limited to a few researchers and it still has to go a long way. Media has been severely criticized for not being systematic and comprehensive in their reporting of HIV/AIDS. It is also said that media has to shift from just awareness creation to public information and education with more localized reporting. Brown and Xenos (1994) discuss the causes and hidden nature of this epidemic in Asia which according to them is spread by the social invisibility of the infected. They argue that this makes it difficult to convince policy makers and the media that a problem existed and to persuade them to act.

The dominant paradigms in social research around HIV/AIDS have been psychological, focusing heavily on questions relating to individual behavior and how to change it. Although writings on HIV/AIDS in poor countries have tended to have a larger appreciation of the social and economic contexts, they tend to focus on the development of programs for behavior change, less care and support for those already infected. Since it was first recognised in 1981, AIDS has killed more than 25 million people, making it one of the most destructive epidemics in recorded history. One person is infected with HIV every six seconds that's 10 people infected each minute.

Despite efforts taken up by UNAIDS there are still 34 million people were living with HIV worldwide. This reflects the continued large number of new HIV infections and a significant expansion of access to antiretroviral therapy, which has helped reduce AIDS related deaths, especially in more recent years. The proportion of women living with HIV has remained stable at 50% globally, although women are more affected in Sub-Saharan Africa (59% of all people living with HIV and the Caribbean (53%). There were 2.7 million new HIV infections in 2010, including an estimated 3, 90, 000 among children. This was 15% less than in 2001, and 21% below the number of new infections at the peak of the epidemic in 1997. Sub-Saharan Africa remains the region most highly affected by HIV. In 2010, about 68% of all people living with HIV resided in Sub-Saharan Africa, a region with only 12% of the global population. The epidemic continues to be most severe in southern Africa, with South Africa having more people living with HIV/AIDS (an estimated 5.6 million) than any other country in the world (UNAIDS, 2011).

In Asia although the rate of HIV prevalence is substantially lower than in some other regions, the big size of Asian population makes it the second largest region of people living with HIV. In South-East Asia, the estimated 2, 70, 000 new HIV infections in 2010 were 40% less than the epidemic in 1996. In India, the country with the largest number of people living with HIV in the region, new HIV infections fell by 56% (UNAIDS report 2011). China and India both have seemingly low prevalence rates of 0.1 per cent and 0.9 per cent respectively. But while the prevalence rates are low, because of their massive populations, the actual number of HIV-affected people is huge.

According to Government of India, Ministry of Health and Family Welfare, Department of AIDS Control and National AIDS Control Organization press release (2010) the total number of people living with HIV/AIDS in India is estimated at 24 lakhs in 2009. Manipur has shown the highest estimated adult HIV prevalence of 1.40%, followed by Andhra Pradesh (0.90%), Mizoram (0.81%), Nagaland (0.78%), Karnataka (0.63%) and Maharashtra (0.55%). Besides these states, Goa, Chandigarh, Gujarat,

Punjab and Tamil Nadu have shown estimated adult HIV prevalence greater than national prevalence (0.31%), while Delhi, Orissa, West Bengal, Chhattisgarh and Puducherry have shown estimated adult HIV prevalence of 0.28-0.30%. All other states and Union Territories have lower levels of HIV. About 90% of people newly infected with HIV in India are believed to have acquired it during unprotected sex, but the common use of contaminated injecting equipment by two or more people on the same occasion is the main mode of HIV transmission in the north-eastern states.

Linge and Porter (1998), suggests that there is considerable uncertainty about the exact extent, course and impact of HIV/AIDS epidemic in Asia. They argue that this is primarily due to under-diagnosis which subsequently results in under-reporting. Other factors that prevent more accurate assessment of the extent of HIV/AIDS infection levels, according to them, include the high variation in the probability of transmission per sexual act; a long and variable period of clinical latency; and a limited knowledge of the political, social and economic consequences of the disease (Linge and Porter, 1998). The extended period between infection and death makes it harder, they infer, to persuade individuals, communities and governments to confront a problem that only has a hypothetical existence till the crucial moment of infection.

According to Teresita Marie P. Bagasao of the Asia Pacific Leadership Forum on HIV/AIDS and Development in the UNAIDS Regional Support Team based in Bangkok, less than half of young people know about AIDS and the way to protect themselves from getting infected. In spite of the fact that mass media have the potentiality to inform and educate the general public, HIV infections continue incrementally because appropriate messages and services have not reached those who are at risk. In surveys around the world, radio and television are cited as key sources of information about AIDS. However, it is also found that in spite of imaginative and highly successful campaigns, media coverage of the epidemic has not always been enough to keep the public meaningfully informed.

Media Coverage of HIV/AIDS: A Theoretical Perspective

HIV/AIDS gets media coverage and this could be due to the fact that AIDS is a disease which provides journalists all the ingredients of a sensational news story involving sex and death. It is argued that such a news story may not only be motivated by a desire to provide health education, but it may also be a negative force in this regard as journalists often report HIV/AIDS in a manner which reflects their own prejudices. In fact, media coverage of HIV/AIDS has been described as being erratic and distorted. Journalists have mystified the ways in which HIV can be spread, rather than concentrating on the modes of transmission. It is needless to say that the media have been recognised as a powerful tool to endorse awareness and education of public health issues.

However, there is a growing apprehension that the quantum of media coverage on AIDS is not sufficient to prevent this disease completely. It has been observed that there is a decline of coverage on HIV/AIDS news in the media. Journalists should treat HIV/AIDS as the most urgent health problem facing the world today as there is a mercurial rise in HIV cases despite commendable efforts by UNAIDS. One should come out of such a presumption that a health news story cannot sell and, therefore, it is trivial. There is a growing feeling that journalists lack discipline an commitment for it. Media, therefore, must first highlight the issues then gain public interest and not the other way round. In addressing some of the interventions that are required to improve coverage of public health issues, a well defined communication strategy is required for different stakeholders. Media practitioners, public health professionals, NGOs and government bodies all have a responsible role to play in this regard.

Social Change Communication theory intervenes that the media should extend the current framing of HIV/AIDS from primarily a health story to one that is linked to socio-economic, cultural and political factors. Journalists and journalism educators need to realise the complexity and interconnectedness of the web of issues into which HIV/AIDS is woven, especially if they want to engage in a meaningful discourse of this global crisis and its broad ramifications. Therefore, it is imperative that a broad range of strategies based on socio-psychological models of behavior are looked into from a theoretical perspective as this would help devise ways to communicate HIV prevention in a more effective manner. These communication theories tend to focus on behavior change at an individual level as seen in Behavioral Change Communication (BCC) and it assumes that it would lead to behavioral change by simply giving correct information about the transmission and prevention of HIV. Deane (2002) describes BCC as based on a belief that urgency of the epidemic necessitates a high degree of focus on behavior. It tries to encourage people to make informed choices. BCC theory involves the development of messages and approaches in order to promote and sustain individual behavioral change. These theories can inject fresh ideas and news angles among journalists so that it can broaden the current scope and content of HIV/AIDS reporting.

Concerns and Challenges of the Media Sector

- Journalists need to be trained to report HIV/AIDS in the most befitting manner. The electronic and print media houses should allow their journalists to specialise on different health matters. The media should allocate resources for capacity building that will enable reporters cover HIV/AIDS more extensively.

- It is felt that there is a need to allocate more time and space in the media for health information. The media houses should come together and develop a binding policy securing a column or a page meant exclusively for health issues. There should be a policy to encourage greater coverage of health issues particularly in the local media.
- Media organizations need to co-ordinate with NGOs and government functionaries so that they begin to think of the media as partners in the long run and integrated in their programmes health issues particularly HIV/AIDS.
- The media need to conduct regular research on how health information is being received and assess also its effectiveness. This will help them improve how they package such information. Feedback is an important aspect of this process as it will let them know whom they are reaching out to and with what effect.
- Media should organize interactive sessions between journalists and healthcare professional on public health. This will help create rapport to smart out strategies that can educate them on the issue. The stakeholders in the media need to interact among themselves to share experiences as far as health reporting is concerned.
- It is a known fact that the public look for news that has a bearing on their lives. The challenge is for the media to package health information messages in a more appealing manner to the public. They can do this through discussion with the experts on health issues.

Conclusion

Media has an important role to play in disseminating knowledge on HIV/AIDS to the public. This could be done in consultation with the concerned to avoid wrong or counter-productive messages being disseminated. Media can promote better awareness on the disease and foster a better understanding and care for people with HIV positive. It is felt that social and economic discrimination against the HIV positive is another area where the media has to raise its voice. It has been observed that in spite of highly successful campaigns worldwide, media coverage of the epidemic is not sufficient to keep the public meaningfully informed. Hence, increased HIV infections continue because appropriate messages and services have not reached those most at risk or people who are not well-informed about the disease. In our current era of entanglement, journalists must investigate and report HIV/AIDS in a way which reinforces people's attitude by correcting misinformation and thereby creating and maintaining an environment for AIDS prevention. Journalists need to keep themselves informed with the terminologies used in health communication. Vague terms such as cure, miracle and breakthrough may harm news consumers by misinforming them and, therefore, it should be avoided. It is generally accepted that education can change and render new attitudes which are more acceptable, more openly expressed and more likely acted upon. It is also believed that mass media campaigns on HIV/AIDS influence people to take actions they might otherwise not. The media, therefore, has to articulate its own understanding of HIV/AIDS reporting with greater sensitivity and transparency.

References

Altman, Dennis (1999). Globalisation, Political Economy, and HIV/AIDS. *Theory and Society*, Vol. 28, No. 4. http://www.jstor.org/stable/3108562. Accessed: 10/10/2011.

Bollinger Lori., Cooper-Arnold Katharine and Stover John (2004). Where Are the Gaps? The Effects of HIV-Prevention Interventions on Behavioral Change, *Studies in Family Planning*, Vol. 35, No. 1. http://www.jstor.org/stable/3181159. Accessed: 8/11/2011.

Brown, T., & Xenos, P. (1994). 'AIDS in Asia: The gathering storm,' *Asia Pacific issues,* 16: 15 -17.

Covello, V., D. von Winterfeldt, and P. Slovic. 1986. Risk Communication. Washington: Conservation Foundation.

Cullen, Trevor. Health Communication Theories: Implications for HIV Reporting in Asia and the Pacific, *Asia Pacific Media Educator*, Edith Cowan University, Western Australia. Accessed: 7/11/2011

Cullen, Trevor. 17th AMIC Annual Conference Under the section. '*Journalism Education' or 'Media and Development'*, Reporting HIV and HIV communication theories: What journalists and journalism educators in Asia and the Pacific need to know.

Deane, J. (2002). 'Approaches to HIV and AIDS Communication Strategies.' Retrieved December 10, 2011, from http://www.healthcomms.org/comms/hiv-aids/hiv02.html

Department of Communication Research, IIMC, New Delhi (2009). *HIV/AIDS Multimedia Campaign - an Evaluation Study* sponsored by National AIDS Control Organization (NACO).

Government of India Ministry of Health and Family Welfare Department of AIDS Control National AIDS Control Organization Press Release (2010). HIV declining in India; New infections reduced by 50% from 2000-2009; Sustained focus on prevention required.

Global Media AIDS Initiative. The Media and HIV/AIDS: Making a difference. *Joint United Nations Programme on HIV/AIDS (UNAIDS) UNAIDS* – 20 avenue Appia – 1211 Geneva 27 – Switzerland.

Gans, H. 1979. Deciding What's News. New York: Pantheon.

Kinsella, J. 1989. Covering the Plague: AIDS and the American Media. New Brunswick, NJ.: Rutgers University Press.

Linge, G., & Porter, D. (1998). No Place for Borders: *The HIV/AIDS epidemic and development in Asia and the Pacific*, New York: St Martin's Press.

McQuail, D. 1979. The Influence and Effects of Mass Media. In Mass Communication and Society, eds. J. Curran, M. Gurevich, J. Woolacott, chap. 3. Beverly Hills, Calif.: Sage.

Nelkin, D. 1987. Selling Science: How the Press Covers Science and Technology. New York: Freeman.

Ramasubban, Radhika (1998). HIV/AIDS in India: Gulf between Rhetoric and Reality. *Economic and Political Weekly*, Vol. 33, No. 45, http://www.jstor.org/stable/4407357. Accessed: 12/11/2011

UNESCO (2006). Final report, *Media and HIV/AIDS: Training of Trainers Workshop on Development of Multimedia Materials Dhaka*. Organized by UNESCO, New Delhi in collaboration with UNESCO, Dhaka.

UNAIDS (2010). *Report on global AIDS epidemic.*

Wolffers I., and Bevers M. (1997). *Sex work, mobility and AIDS in Kuala Lumpur, Malaysia*, CARAM-Asia/Vrije Universiteit, Kuala Lumpur/Amsterdam.

19

Ten Years of Private FM in India: Analysing Policy Perspective and Prospects

Dr. Ambrish Saxena and ***Susmita Bala***

FM broadcasting has changed the face of radio broadcasting in the country. FM as broadcast technology made a modest beginning in 1984 when the government decided to use it for local radio stations in 1984. Though local radio stations could not succeed as anticipated but the quality of FM broadcasting was noticed and accepted by broadcasting experts and policymakers. So, the government decided to use the FM technology also for city centric urban broadcasting.

When the first city centric channel of All India Radio based on FM technology was commissioned in Jalandhar in 1992, it came to be known as 'AIR FM Stereo' because of stereophonic sound quality of FM. When the second city based channel of AIR was launched on FM in 2001, the first channel became FM 1 and the new channel became FM 2. Thus, the identity of channels was linked to the technology which was being used for the purpose of broadcasting.

FM is considered the most suitable technology for broadcasting these days. FM technology is being used for all kind of channels, from AIR to private channels and from community radio stations to educational channels. AIR has shifted many of its Vividh Bharati channels and primary channels from MW to FM, and this process continues. The success of private FM channels is attributed to FM technology as the first decade of 21st century has witnessed the FM revolution.

1. Initial Steps Towards City Centric FM Broadcasting

The first ever city centric FM channel was commissioned at Jalandhar on October 2, 1992 and within a year's time FM channels came up in Delhi, Mumbai, Chennai, Panaji and Kolkata. The government decided to introduce partial privatization in FM broadcasting and accordingly AIR started leasing out time slots to private operators on its FM channels. Nine time slots were leased out on AIR FM channels (later named as Rainbow) of Delhi and Mumbai on August 15, 1993. Time slots were given to private operators in Chennai on September 1, 1993, Panaji on January 24, 1994, and Kolkata on July 25, 1994.

With innovate programming and aggressive marketing, efforts of private parties brought FM to the centre stage. However, they ceased to operate the slots with effect from June 26, 1998 as the government was contemplating full-fledged privatisation of FM broadcasting enabling private parties to set up and operate FM stations. At least this was on record though the confrontation between private programme producing companies and AIR programming heads was not a secret.

There was evidently a clash in the value system of AIR and that of private players. AIR was too possessive for its Broadcast Code and persistently asked the private production companies to adhere to the code while producing the programmes. Despite the agreement in that respect the private players were not too willing to follow the code. This created a mismatch between the programmes produced by AIR and those produced by private companies during the course cf broadcasting. Repeated controversies led to a legal tussle and finally the ties were broken between AIR and private players.

The formal beginning of privatisation of FM broadcasting was made in Ninth Five Year Plan (1997-2002) objective. In this plan, the policy objective for radio was improving the variety of contents and technical quality of broadcasting. It was during this plan period that the government allowed fully owned Indian companies to set up private FM radio stations on license fee basis. Though the government controlled broadcasting continued and Prasar Bharati Corporation was created subsequent to notification of the respective Act in 1997, the situation started changing in the beginning of the first decade of 21st century.

2. First Phase of Private FM Broadcasting

In May 2000, 108 frequencies in the FM spectrum (VHF 87-108 MHZ) were auctioned across 40 cities in the country. The government received 101 bids for an aggregate of Rs 425 crores as against the estimated amount of Rs 79.65 crores from bids for 37 frequencies as bidders for other frequencies defaulted. A total of 37 licenses were issues on city basis for a period of 10 years. The first private FM channel came up in July 2001.

Finally, only 22 licenses could become operational though one channel later closed down. Two licensees continued to pay license fees but they failed to float their channels. The deadline for operationalising the licenses was one year from signing the License Agreement i.e. December 29, 2001. However, ever after furnishing the bank guarantee and signing the License Agreement, 13 successful bidders could not operationalise their licenses within the required time frame and ultimately surrendered their licenses.

2.1 Failure of First Phase

The companies which were given license in the first phase started facing a rough weather since beginning. The private operators met the representatives of Information and Broadcasting Ministry in August 2001 to resolve the contentious issues, but the government was of little help. This led to delay in the launch of most of the private FM channels.

In August 2002, the tussle between Information and Broadcasting Ministry and radio operators came in open, the point of controversy being heavy license fee and other unjust conditions imposed on operators. In the wake of this, two companies Millennium Radio-Chennai and Midday Radio-New Delhi walked out of the contract. Other companies also threatened to pull out, while some got involved in litigation.

The result of the first phase of private FM broadcasting was disappointing as only 25 percent of the licenses could become operational. Most of the private operators were finding the projects commercially unviable primarily due to heavy license fee. The private players continued to suffer losses and to mount pressure on the government to amend the policy.

Meanwhile, a working group on Information and Broadcasting sector was set up under Tenth Five Year Plan (2002-2007). This group felt that treating private FM broadcasting services as source of revenue was counterproductive as that could hinder the growth causing delay in the roll out of private FM services. The group recommended that suitable corrective policy measures should be taken, so that future growth of these services could be accelerated and substantial private investment could be attracted to supplement the efforts and investment of All India Radio.

2.2 Radio Broadcast Policy Committee

Though the government failed to achieve the plan objective as stipulated in Ninth Five Year Plan (1997-2002), the Tenth Plan document identified the major thrust areas for expansion of FM broadcasting. The target was decided to increase the FM coverage from the then 30 per cent to 60 per cent of the population by the end of the Tenth Plan. The Plan document said that private operators should be encouraged to provide FM radio services in metros and small cities. And most importantly, it said that the system of bidding for license should be replaced by a revenue sharing mechanism.

Following this the government set up a committee named as Radio Broadcast Policy Committee headed by Dr Amit Mitra, then secretary general of FICCI, on July 24, 2003, to study the private FM broadcasting scenario and give recommendations for the second phase of licensing. The committee, in its report submitted in November 2003, recommended to introduce revenue sharing system between the government and the private players, and also to open up the broadcasting sector to FDI up to 26 per cent at par with other media sectors.

Mitra Committee recommended that the license fee structure should be revised and migration of the license terms from fixed license fee basis to one-time entry fee with an annual revenue sharing arrangement should be allowed. The entry fee should be determined by a competitive bid process that will reflect the true market value of the frequency. In addition, there should be an annual revenue share, which was recommended as 4 per cent of the gross revenue.

Mitra Committee also made two other important recommendations, *one-* to set up a Universal Service Obligation Fund to support non-commercial channels, and *two-* to use the scarce resource (frequency) rationally, efficiently and optimally.

3. Policy on Private FM Radio in Phase II

The recommendations of Radio Broadcast Policy Committee were substantial, also radical to some extent, but the government lacked political will to implement those recommendations. So, it decided to take some time for brainstorming. Finally, it was decided to send the Mitra Committee report for a second opinion.

3.1 Recommendations by Trai on Policy Change

In the light of the Supreme Court judgment on airwaves in 1995, the government was required to set up an independent authority to regulate airwaves. In 1996, Paswan Committee also advised the government to set up a regulatory body. Since the government failed to put a broadcast regulator in place, it decided to give the regulator's job to Telecom Regulatory Authority of India (TRAI) for the time being through a notification on January 18, 2004. Subsequently, Information and Broadcasting Ministry, on February 12, 2004, sent the report of the Mitra Committee to TRAI for its opinion and recommendations.

Based on the input received from Information and Broadcasting Ministry, Report of the Radio Broadcast Policy Committee and representations from private FM operators, TRAI prepared a consultation paper on April 14, 2004 and invited comments from all stakeholders. In its recommen- dations submitted in August 2004, TRAI recommended one-time entry fee and a revenue share (4 per cent of the gross revenue of the company) arrangement replacing the earlier licensing procedure. TRAI recommended multiple licenses at one centre, but added that one entity should not be allowed to hold more than three or one-third of the licenses in one city. TRAI refrained making clear recommendations about FDI, cross media ownership and news broadcast.

TRAI permitted no networking within the same city, no networking across licenses, but permitted the same between stations located in different cities belonging to the same broadcasting company. TRAI asked the government to make more frequencies available for big as well as small cities. However, it did not make any clear recommendation regarding non-commercial channels and niche channels.

3.2 Policy Document on Phase II Private FM Radio

In 2005, Information and Broadcasting Ministry formulated a policy on expansion of FM radio broadcasting services through private agencies (Phase II). The policy announced on July 13, 2005, incorporated major recommendations made by TRAI in respect of private FM radio broadcasting. The policy provided for granting license to enterprising broadcasters on the basis of One-Time Entry Fee (OTEF) quoted by the bidders (Closed Tender System). The policy also included provisions related to FDI, news broadcast, networking, and migration from Phase I to Phase II.

3.2.1 In Phase II, all the cities having population equal to or more than 3 lakh were considered.

3.2.2 The government changed the licensing procedure and the license fee calculation as compared to Phase I. In the new policy guidelines (mostly based on the recommendations of TRAI), two-stage selection process was adopted. Firstly, eligibility of bidders was determined, and subsequently financial bids were called from eligible bidders.

3.2.3 Reserve One-Time Entry Fee (OTEF) was fixed at 25 per cent of the highest bidding price in the city.

3.2.4 As per the revenue sharing formula, the permission holder was liable to pay an annual fee @ 4 per cent of the gross revenue of the company for each year or 10 percent of the OTEF, whichever is higher.

3.2.5 In Phase II policy, the license period continued to be ten years. The policy document prescribed no change in the FDI limit of 20 percent, and framed no rules with regard to cross media ownership.

3.2.6 The policy disapproved the recommendations of TRAI for multiple licenses (to one entity) at one centre. The government adopted the policy of one entity one channel in one city. It also provided for a cap of 15 per cent on the number of channels that an entity can own at the national level.

3.2.7 In Phase II, ban on the broadcast of news and current affairs programme continued. The policy document endorsed the Phase I policy of making adherence to AIR Broadcast Code and Commercial Code compulsory to private broadcasters.

3.2.8 TRAI recommendation of permitting networking across cities (between channels of the same entity) was not accepted by the government. The policy guidelines permitted an entity to network its channels in C and D category cities within a region only but did not permit networking by two entities of their channel in any category of cities.

3.2.9 The policy guidelines permitted migration of Phase licenses to Phase II regime subject to fulfillment of certain conditions.

4. Fresh Efforts for Revamping Private FM Radio

The government initiated the bidding process for Phase II of private FM radio on June 8, 2007. By the end of 2007, 136 channels (including Phase I channels) became operational.

The cities covered in Phase II were having population of more than three lakh, and so a need was felt to cover the cities with lesser population in the next phase.

4.1 Recommendations of Sub Group on I and B

The Sub-Group on Information and Broadcasting under Eleventh Five Year Plan (2007-2012) noted that the FM coverage remained at the level of 40 per cent by population as against the Tenth Plan target of 60 per cent. The Sub-Group emphasised on border area coverage through FM and laid the responsibility of doing this on Prasar Bharati. It said that in urban areas private sector can take a lead role.

The Sub-Group recommended that the AIR should go in for digital broadcasting in a big way commencing with the Eleventh Plan using the Digital Radio Modulation (DRM) technology for Short Wave and Medium Wave as well as FM transmitters compatible with DRM+ technology. The proposal was to increase the coverage from 40 per cent to 75 per cent by population using DRM+ compatible transmitters for FM. This provided an option of leasing out transmitters to private operators.

4.2 Trai Consultations for Phase III

In view of recommendations by the Sub-Group on Information and Broadcasting, the government decided to initiate steps for further revision in private FM radio broadcasting policy. On November 13, 2007, the government made a formal request to TRAI to suggest measures for the third phase of private FM broadcasting. On January 8, 2008, TRAI released a consultation papers and conducted discussions with all stakeholders and experts including FICCI and BECIL for about 10 days. The consultations proved significant in view of finding consensus on issues where opinions were sharply divided.

Through the consultation process TRAI mainly tried to resolve regulatory issues particularly the issues which remained unanswered or untouched in Phase II policy. It may be noted that TRAI, while making recommendations for Phase II, took a deliberate decision of leaving certain issues for consideration under Phase III so that implementation on Phase II could not delay. One major task before TRAI in the third phase was to recommend measures for expansion of FM radio broadcasting to major parts of the country.

4.3 Recommendations by Trai for Phase III

On the basis of comments of stakeholders, internal analysis and available best international practices, TRAI finalised the recommendations on February 22, 2008. Vital issues covered by TRAI in its recommendations included additional FM channels in a district, FDI limits, networking of programmes and news and current affairs programmes on FM radio. A summary of recommendations follow.

4.3.1 The geographical basis for bidding should be changed from city to district. In the new system, OTEF should be re-fixed based on the maximum bidding price through the auction for the district. Annual fee is to be determined considering revised reserve OTEF.

4.3.2 After following the basis of district the availability of frequency will increase. This can help in providing additional channels in A+, A, B and C category cities, as envisaged in Phase II. In D category cities (now changed to district basis) the number of channels may be reduced to three to five.

4.3.3 Since city basis was not acceptable to the government, TRAI later accepted the viewpoint of the government and agreed to continue the city level licensing in the larger interest of expediting the process.

4.3.4 At least three channels in any district/city should be given to three different entities. After this any existing operator may bid for other channels with the condition that maximum number of channels to a permission holder in the district/city will not be more than 50 per cent of total channels in the district/ city.

4.3.5 FDI limit should be increased from 20 to 26 per cent in the case of news channels and to 49 percent in the case of non-news channels.

4.3.6 FM channels should be allowed to broadcast news but with the condition that they have to take contents from authorised sources.

On the recommendations of TRAI, Ministry of Information and Broadcasting sought some clarifications on November 18, 2008. TRAI responded back with its comments on November 28, 2008.

5. Phase III Policy on Expansion of Private FM Radio

In the light of recommendations and clarifications made by TRAI, the government could have launched Phase III policy on expansion of private FM radio in 2009 only but it took too long. A Group of Ministers (GOM) was formed with Finance Minister Pranab Mukherjee in the chair to finalise the policy. The GOM in its meeting on January 22, 2011 approved the policy.

The GOM sent the policy draft to the cabinet which approved the 'Policy Guidelines on Expansion of FM Radio Broadcasting Services through Private Agencies (Phase Ill)' in its meeting held on July 8, 2011. The meeting decided in favour of online bidding of licenses instead of conventional open bidding process. The government also announced that it may issue approximately 700 licenses in Phase III.

5.1 Policy Guidelines on Expansion of FM Radio Broadcasting

FM Phase Ill Policy will cover FM radio services to about 227 new cities, in addition to the present 86 cities, with a total of 839 new FM radio Channels in 294 cities. All cities with a population of one lakh and above will get private FM radio channels under this policy. The highlights of this policy may be discussed below.

5.1.1 The long pending demand of the broadcast of news by private FM radio channels has been accepted by the government in Phase III but with a rider. The private FM channels have been permitted carriage of news bulletins of All India Radio.

5.1.2 The line between news and non-news was blurred in Phase I and Phase II policies, but Phase III policy has clarified this issue. Now, the broadcast pertaining to certain categories like information related to sporting events, traffic and weather, coverage of cultural events, festivals, coverage of topics concerning examinations, results, admissions, career counselling, availability of employment opportunities, public announcements pertaining to civic amenities like electricity, water supply, natural calamities, health alerts etc. as provided by the local administration will be treated as non-news and current affairs broadcast, and will therefore be permissible.

5.1.3 The limit on the ownership of channels, at the national level, allocated to an entity has been retained at 15 per cent in the third phase, similar to the cap prescribed in Phase II. However, channels allotted in Jammu and Kashmir, North Eastern States and island territories will be allowed over and above the 15% national limit to incentivise the bidding for channels in such areas.

5.1.4 The city wise limit of owning the channels has also been modified. Private operators have been allowed to own more than one channel but not more than 40 per cent of the total channels in a city subject to a minimum of three different operators in the city.

5.1.5 In Phase III, one significant departure from the earlier stand taken by the government is on the FDI limit. Now, the FDI+FII limit in a private FM radio broadcasting company stands increased from 20 per cent to 26 per cent.

5.1.6 Phase III has also rationalised rules with regard to networking of channels. As per the new policy, networking of channels will be permissible within a private FM broadcaster's own network across the country instead of in 'C' and 'D' category cities only of a region allowed at present.

5.1.7 A choice is proposed to be given to the private FM broadcasters to choose any agency other than BECIL for construction of CTI within a period of 3 months of issuance of LOI failing which BECIL will automatically become the system integrator and set up co-location facilities and CTI.

5.1.8 The government has finally taken initiative of providing special incentives for North East (NE) Region and Jammu & Kashmir (J&K) and Island territories.

- Private FM radio operators in North East (NE) Region and Jammu & Kashmir (J&K) and Island territories will be required to pay half the rate of annual license fee for an initial period of three years from the date from which the annual license fee becomes payable and the permission period of fifteen (15) years begins.
- The revised fee structure has also been made applicable for a period

of three years, from the date of issuance of guidelines, to the existing operators in these states to enable them to effectively compete with the new operators.

- Apart from the fee relaxation, it is further proposed that Prasar Bharati infrastructure would be made available at half the lease rentals for similar category cities in such areas.

5.2 Review of Phase III Policy

The Phase III policy on private FM radio broadcasting is a step in the right direction, though taken by the government with a delay of three to four years. The new policy has brought cheers to Phase II operators as well, as the benefits of policy modifications in Phase III will also be available to them.

5.2.1 The incentives provided in Phase III policy with regard to J&K, North Eastern states and Island territories will make the operations viable in these areas and are expected to result in better off take of channels. The steps taken in the new policy will bring down operational costs and improve viability in general.

5.2.2 To improve the viability further as against a maximum of 4 channels in D category cities permitted in FM Phase II, the new policy proposes only 3 FM channels in D category cities so that there are lesser operators to share the advertisement pie.

5.2.3 In Phase III, the lockin period of shareholding of promoters/majority shareholders has been reduced from the present 5 years to 3 years. This will give the operators greater freedom to change the shareholding pattern.

5.2.4 Phase III policy will allow operators to distinguish themselves from others to be able to cater to niche audiences. This will happen because of content diversification in view of news content, and also because of the provision of multiple ownership of channels in a city,with the exception of D category cities. This will also increase the overall listenership base and the listening time.

In Phase III, e-auction for the channels will be conducted in batches. The number of batches will be decided by Information and Broadcasting Ministry, depending upon the response from the bidders after auction of first batch. The Ministry of l & B will appoint an independent expert agency, through a transparent selection process, following established procedure, to conduct e-auction. The Ministry will separately issue a detailed Information Memorandum, in due course, enabling the prospective bidders to participate, and also indicating the cities, reserve prices city-wise, number of channels to be taken up in each batch and other procedures for e-auction. A Notice Inviting Applications (NIA) for participation in the Auction(s) will also be issued in due course of time.

But, the final question remains i.e. how much time the government would take in executing the Phase III policy. The government started working on policy modifications in 2007 but could announce the policy in 2011. Yet, the bids have not been invited. Going by the experience of government functioning inviting bids, issuing licenses and ensuring the operation of channels may further take one to two years. It may also be noted that the success rate of Phase I and Phase II policies has been 25 to 35 per cent in terms of the number of channels launched as against the number for which the bids were opened. Also, there are apprehensions that not many private operators will be coming forward for bidding for setting up channels in smaller cities. So, broadcasting experts are keeping the fingers crossed on the success of Phase III policy.

References

1. Saxena, Ambrish, Radio in New Avatar : AM to FM, Kanishka Publishers, Distributors, New Delhi.
2. http://info.shine.com/Article/Industries/FM-phase-III-policy-a-reason-to-cheer/5249/cid1.aspx
3. http://www.rediff.com/business/report/phase-3-for-fm-radio-cleared-and-air-news-allowed-on-pvt-channels/20110707.htm
4. http://www.bestmediainfo.com/2011/07/radio-industry-welcomes-fm-phase-iii-at-large/
5. www.idstonline.com [Article by Abhijit Mukhopadhyay, CEO, IDSTPR]
6. www.indiantelevision.com

20

Mass Communication Paradigm in Conflicted Society

Md. Nawaz Khan

Introduction

Communication refers to any interaction in which meanings are shared, messages are exchanged and actions are provoked. In the absence of communication society cannot survive as its patterns and systems are the products of socio-culture, socio-political and socio-economic environments existing in it. Communication takes place at the individual level as well as at the social level and is vital for human existence and progress of humanity. Mass communication is communication that reaches a large audience through channels comprising mass media which include newspapers, magazines, radio, television, advertising, movies, the internet etc.

When a society is grappled with conflict, communication is a remedy. It encourages conflicting groups to hold dialogues to express their feelings. Mass media with their power of appealing to the mind and capability of moving hearts can change the attitude of the people and help reduce conflict. While the communication has a positive role in the amelioration of conflict, there is a complex interplay between communication and conflict.

With a total geographical area of 22,327 sq. km. inhabited by a population of 27,21,756 (Census of India-2011) belonging to 33 ethnic communities speaking 29 different dialects, Manipur is a mini India showing wide scale diversity of cultural mosaic. Besides the four major ethnic groups-the Meiteis, the Meitei Pangals, the Nagas, and the Chin-Kuki-there are Nepalis, Bengalis, Marwaris and other Indian communities settled in the valley. The five hill districts are inhabited mainly by ethnic tribal communities including the Nagas, the Kukis, the Paites etc. Comprising about 60 per cent of the total population of the state, the majority Meiteis are distributed throughout the valley. The Naga comprises Zeliangrong, Tangkhul, Mao, Maram, Maring and Tarao. Zeliangrong consists of three sub-groups including Rongmei, Liangmei and Zemei. The Chin-Kuki group consists of Gangte, Hmar, Paite, Thadou, Vaiphei, Zou, Aimol, Chiru, Koireng, Kom, Anal, Chothe, Lamgang, Koirao, Thangal, Moyon and Monsang.

Despite being rich in ethnic plurality, Manipur has been grappling with ever-increasing ethnic conflicts besides violent assertions made from time to time by over 28 insurgent outfits organised on ethnic lines. While insurgency in quest for ethnic and regional identities has cost peace and progress of the state, major clashes between the Meiteis and the Pangals in the valley and between the Nagas and the Kukis in the hills in the early 1990s showed vulnerability of being a multi-ethnic society. Besides, the issue of Manipur's territorial integrity and the demand for Greater Nagaland are causing uneasiness on the relationship between the Meiteis and the Nagas while the demand for Kuki homeland is compounding the complex political issuefomenting a climate of insecurity and mistrust in the state.

Nevertheless, the ethnic plurality in Manipur is both inescapable and desirable for all the groups in the region. This calls for an early resolution of the conflict. By addressing the issue of ethnic equations in Manipur, mass media can contribute to the peaceful co-existence of the different ethnic groups through encouraging dialogues. This is where the paradigm of mass communication becomes significant.

Mass Media in Manipur

As in other socio-political settings, the media in Manipur reflect the social, economic and political relations of the state. Manipur has about 30 dailies and journals. English dailies published at Imphal include the Imphal Free Press, the Sangai Express, the Manipur Mail and Hueyen Lanpao. The Hueyen Lanpao and the Sangai Express have Manipuri editions also. Poknapham, Sanaleibak, Ireibak and Naharolgi Thoudang are vernacular dailies published from Imphal. A few dailies in tribal dialects are also published from different hill district headquarters of the state. Some of the other existing newspapers are Kangleipakki Meira, Gosem (Thadou/Kuki Language Daily), Zalen Banner (Thadou/Kuki Language Weekly News), AJA (Tangkhul Daily), Manipur Express (Paite Language Daily), Lamka Post (Paite Language Daily) etc. Besides, national newspapers published in other cities of the country also have their limited circulation in the state. These include the Telegraph, the Times of India, the Hindustan Times, the Statesmen etc. Besides, there are some correspondents and stringers for various national and international news agencies, newspapers, magazines and electronic media houses.

Electronic media in Manipur include the All India Radio, Imphal, AIR Imphal FM and AIR Churachandpur FM. Manipur has only one television service- Doordarshan Kendra, Imphal while there exist some local cable television networks such as Information Service Television (ISTV), Image Cable TV, Hornbill Cable Network, Laizan Cable Network and Tribal Cable Network. Satellite television connectivity is available in almost every household of the urban areas in Imphal.

Even as the relationship between the mass media and various segments of society is very important, mass media professionals play a crucial role in a culturally diverse society like Manipur. In the absence of coverage by national mainstream media the increasing conflict in Manipur proposes a big challenge for local journalism. Though media are considered a sort of mirror of society they provide images through which a large part of the social world is interpreted. Minority communities frequently complain about biasedand partial reporting which is one-sided and often discriminatory. News coverage is often described as favouring majority groups over ethnic minorities. Journalism is blamed for presenting minority as "others" using the division of "us" and "them" which can reinforce prejudice among public. If the prejudice is widespread in society and among journalists then media are likely to reflect the prejudice. As various groups do not interact daily their knowledge about the other are shaped by media. While journalism seems to have an ambivalent role in ethnic relations, biased news and opinion widen gaps.As a result the disadvantaged position of minorities and ethnic prejudices are attributed to media while journalists defend their objectivity.

Voices against the local media bias would make one wonder if the ethnic divide and prejudice would creep in local media and if the local journalists would succumb to inherent sentiments of "us" and "them". If it is so, this local media tendency would be problematic for the conflict-torn Manipuri society. One of the reasons for stereotyped media portrayal of ethnic minority may be the low representation of working journalists from the ethnically minority communities in the composition of media houses and newsrooms besides their being in non-directive roles.

Mass Media and Conflict Resolution Initiatives

In conflicted society many stakeholders including the government and citizenry make efforts for conflict resolution. Manipur saw various conflict resolution initiatives to promote the idea of diversity of cultures for peaceful co-existence among communities sharing politico-cultural space. However, not all institutions have contributed equally to the conflict resolution initiatives.As such discrepancies between rhetoric and exclusion of minorities continue to exist. Civil society organisations have been making efforts to address the hill-valley divide. Organising even public feasts for members of various communities on occasions of festivals, efforts are made to foster communal harmony in Manipur. But media has not kept pace.

To address the issues a process of dialogue between different groupseither through the intervention of the state or the civil society is urgently called for. In this direction media can play a key role through encouraging members of various communities to integrate into their society and take an active part in its social, cultural, economic and political affairs. Mass media, being pervasive in the society, can play a potential role in conflict resolution through promotion of cultural practices of constituent groups in the society. But media do not see everyone equally. The dominant and influential constituents get more attention while others get little attention that too often negative and demeaning. At times journalists commit mistakes of negative stereotyping and broad generalisation of minority communities due to lack of background information on their part. This would lead to increased gap among conflicting groups. As such, the increasing conflict in Manipur poses a great challenge for mass communication in playing a meaningful role in conflict resolution. Reporting on events in conflict-torn society should be sensitive and responsible thereby assisting citizens to rebuild their society and to reduce tensions or at least not exacerbate existing divisions. Such conflict-resolution mass communication helps citizens live peacefully and move toward democratic institutions.

Though mass communicationcan play a part in rebuilding societies, it cannot end conflict. Journalists can be a community of peace and confidence builders among the conflicting communities. Since journalistic writing has the power to perform the role of mediation, media can act as mediator between conflicting groups. The problem of prejudice and discrimination within media houses should be addressed. Journalists should be trained to understand the conflict, and make them aware of the deeper responsibilities and constructive possibilities in reporting on conflict in societywhich in turn should reflect through their writing. Journalists can be educated on the dynamics of conflict and the importance of looking beyond the superficial facts through workshops, externshipsand publications. A responsible press should be established through regular media training programmes. Conflict-reduction mediamust be linked with the work of governmental and non-governmental agencies in conflicted societies.The government and civil society organisations should take initiatives to form journalist-mediators who might catalyse a paradigm shift in their profession of journalism. As journalists intervene to report on conflicts, deepeningof their self-awareness is crucial for looking at the practical ways in which journalism can promote conflict resolution.

Conclusion

Owing to the varied ethnic composition of Manipuri society, cultural plurality in the state is in escapable. More than mere toleration is needed to address the problem of conflict in Manipur. There is a need to make the paradigm of mass communication fit into the reality of Manipur as interactions among the ethnic groups are called for. Dialogue allows different groups to address their differences leading to conflict resolution. Hence, in Manipur there is an urgent need to initiate a dialogue on issues related to conflict. With media as mediator between conflicting ethnic groups is the right response in addressing the conflict situation in Manipur for ushering in peace and ensuring development. For achieving this goal, journalists through mass communication should perform the role of mediation by catalysing a paradigm shift in the profession.

References

1. Berger, Guy. (2000). Grave New World? Democratic journalism enters the global twenty-first century, Journalism Studies, 1(1) (2000): 81-99.
2. Coman, M. (2000). Developments in Journalism Theory about Media "Transition" in Central and Eastern Europe 1990-99. Journalism Studies, 1(1) (2000): 35-56.
3. Gandy, O (2000). 'Race, Ethnicity and the Segmentation of Media Markets' in Curran, James and Gurevitch Michael (eds) Mass Media and Society, Third Edition, Hodder Headline Group, London.
4. Gillespie, M (1995). Television, Ethnicity and Cultural Change, Routledge, London.
5. Howard, Ross. (2002). An Operational Framework for Media and Peacebuilding. Vancouver: IMPACS.
6. Jakubowicz, K (1999). 'Public Service Broadcasting in the Information Society' in Media Development 2/1999.
7. Keane, J. (1991) The Media and Democracy. Cambridge: Polity Press.
8. McQuail, Denis (1994). Mass Communication Theory: An Introduction, Third Edition, SAGE Publications Ltd, London, California and New Delhi.
9. Morley, D (2000). Home Territories: Media, Mobility and Identity, SAGE, London.
10. Price Monroe E. & Thompson, M. (Eds.) (2002). Forging Peace: Intervention, human rights and the management of media space. Edinburgh: Edinburgh University Press.
11. Robins, K (2003). 'Beyond Imagined Communities? Transnational Media and Turkish Immigrants in Europe' in Hjarvard (ed) Media in a Globalised Society, Museum Tusculanum Press, Copenhagen.

12. Scannell, P (1989). 'Public Service Broadcasting and Modern Life', Media Culture and Society, 1989. Vol. 11 (2) pp. 135-166.
13. Servaes, J. (1986). Communication and Development Paradigms, An Overview. Media Asia 13.
14. Sreberny, A (1999). Include Me In: Rethinking Ethnicity on Television, Broadcasting Standards Council, London.
15. Ward, S. J. A. (2004). The Invention of Journalism Ethics: The long path to objectivity and beyond. Montreal: McGill-Queen's University Press.
16. Watson, James (1998) Media Communication: An Introduction to Theory and Processes, Macmillan Press Ltd. London.
17. Will Kymlicka (1995). Multicultural Citizenship: A Liberal Theory of Minority Rights, Oxford: Oxford University Press.

21

Creative Use of Media (Print Media) For Development: Some Less Known Stories

Pramoda Kumar Jena

Introduction

Communication has always played the role of either an agent of development or obstacle to development. In either way when it is to perform an extraordinary job, it needs to be creative.

The role of communication in development continues to be part of a wider debate about the nature of development itself. Several experiments conducted so far have proved the importance of communication in the process of development. However, social, economic, political and cultural factors over-shadow the importance of communication as a component of development. Development communication in order to be effective metamorphoses itself to meet the new challenges and adopts different roles in order to win the heart of the target audience, a prerequisite for the development process. Communi-cation supports the process of development in its own way, depending upon its effectiveness, reach and contextual relevance. True media cannot build roads, it can only tell that a road link can solve many ills. Media cannot supply hybrid seeds, it can only explain the high yielding capacity of the hybrid seed.

When a metal coil rotates around a magnet electricity is produced. This basic principle of motor has been creatively utilized in so many gadgets today. On a similar footing potentiality of different medium has been utilized for achieving different goals.

Media Potentialitys

Every medium has the potentiality to support development in its own way depending upon its effectiveness, reach and contextual relevance.

Accordingly no medium is a substitute to the other, but can be supplementary, for the effectiveness of the medium depends upon the local conditions.

The video in Taparana and Manekchowk could effectively bridge the gap between the common people and the decisionmakers. The power of publicity can achieve many things. The chhatera experiment of the Hindustan Times, and the experiment of Identifying Backward Village by the Udayavani have shown the publicity power. Yes, newspapers can also become leaders of a target audience, as the Adike Pathrike and the Gramya vani have demonstrated. Nevertheless interpersonal communication is the best. At least Albert Mayer and S K Dey believed thus. Radio has contributed a lot in the process of agricultural innovations. With proper co-ordination, the audio-visual medium of television can do wonders. The Kheda television experiment illustrates the point. A computer (data processing unit) could elevate the status of a district from 17th spot to 5th spot in the ladder of 'successful implementation of government schemes'. A telephone link to a village could transform the economic status of the village. Of course in all these experiments, the commitment of the development agents or the coordinators played a very important role. Mass Media are not the cause, but only the facilitators.

This paper documents the creative use of newspapers in the process of development.

The Udayavani

The power of publicity and the fear of publicity can make a newspaper do wonders. The power of publicity of a newspaper encourages people to participate in the development process. Chhatera experiment of the Hindustan Times is an example. When the Hindustan Times adopted village Chhatera all the agencies—All India Institute of Medical Sciences New Delhi, Indian Agricultural Reaserch Institute Pusa New Delhi, Haryana Agriculture University Hissar, Rotary, Lions and many other NGO's rushed to the village.

Similarly the fear of publicity has done wonders. As monsoon approached the Udayavani a daily published from coastal Karnatak published an advertisement. "The person who would report the biggest pit on the road will be suitably rewarded". The moment this advertisement appeared in the newspaper Municipality people swung into action and repair work started. This small but creative approach of the newspaper solved the problem of the common man with ease. Here the newspaper did make use of the character of the newspaper fear of publicity.

In an another attempt 'the power of publicity' was creatively used by the newspaper. The news coverage of a bridge construction in September,1979, set in motion a series of local initiatives, co-operations and use of appropriate technology in the neighbouring area. Students of Regional Engineering college at Surathkal, as part of the national Cadet Crops activity, built a 165-feet suspension bridge across a river in a nearby village at a very low cost of Rs. 65,000.

The first news story of the bridge construction with its picture motivated the people of other villages in the district to seek a permanent solution on their own to overcome their difficulties. Soon stories of similar bridge construction even in the far-flung

Villages started pouring in. An agriculturist who had very little education built a rope bridge with the help of local people. An engineer designed a rope–trolly to cross a river, and a group of youngsters used a canoe to log a cable across another stream. Thus, the spirit of self–help started spreading. At least 20 such bridges were constructed in various villages by local initiatives within six years since the first story appeared (Daithota, 1990).

Identifying the Backward Village Experiment of the Udayavani is also a pointer in this. Similarly the fear of publicity not only has a preventive effect on the corrupt officials but also expedites the work which otherwise would never had seen the light of the day.

The Adike Pathrike

Adike Pathrike, a farm journal publishing from the same district since November 1988 is a classic example of media creativity. This journal is unique in the sense that it is not only the first journal of its kind but also the only journal of its kind. This newspaper is of the farmers, for the farmers and by the farmers. The journal was started by a group of farmers to meet their information needs. All the members of the Board of Directors, all the editorial staff are practicing farmers.

The journal functions on the principles self help. It encourages lateral communication very aggressively. The pathrike publishes the problems of farmers and seeks solutions from other farmers based on their personal experiences. Over the period the farmers could realise that they could be the masters of their own destiny. Yet in another column it has introduced a novel plan of plant friendship. A farmer with surplus seeds, seedlings and medicinal plants shares them with fellow farmers through its columns. Besides the other columns are also so tailored that it facilitates farmers participation. It also organises discussions on different subjects of farming in which both experts and farmers take part.

To produce 'farmer writers' Adike Pathrike conducted a series of workshops to train the farmers in writing.

Adike pathrike has many achievements. Lot of farm related issues raised by the journal were picked up by the state media and forced the government to act promptly.

The Gramyavani

The author has experimented with a newspaper as tool of rural development. This newspaper the Gramyavani was part of the Ph.D project. The newspaper was designed after a careful analysis of different instances of media contributing positively to development. The following observations were considered while the newspaper was launched.

1. Success of any project depands considerably on the commitment of the persons involved. Kheda television, Albert Mayer's Etawah project, Adike Pathrike and others were the illustrations.

2. People cannot be developed. They can only develop themselves. So unless the spirit of self help is cultivated all development efforts prove short-lived.

3. Information alone is not enough to motivate the people. If someone is genuinely interested to bring some change he must take initiatives.

Paul Hartman et al, in their study, The Mass Media and Village Life, have also observed:

There is clearly a need for more small scale activity. Those outside government and the officially bureaucracy who seek to promote change in favour of the poor by supporting small-scale organised activity and communication seem more likely to have a lasting impact.

4. "A person involved in the problem of his own community can instinctively present it in a better way as he gets to the heart of the matter while outsiders fumble around"(srivastava, 1980).

5. Communication gap not only exists between ruralites and urbanites but among ruralites themselves. If there is a revolutionary development of growing cabbages without chemicals on the other side of one's village he does not even get to know about it (Sripadre,1994).

The problem of local news flow is of great concern. Communication by the local people at the grassroots level is a must to solve problems with local know-how to the extent possible. Only when the local media are strengthened it can compliment the national media to reach the grassroots (vilanilam.1980).

So to ensure participation of the local people a sort of small-scale local initiatives that involve the people concerned essential. This helps the integrations of the medium with the people over a period of time. And more it integrates, people identify themselves more with it and the medium transforms itself into a social institution.

This observation was also made by Wilbur Schramm (1977) Only when communication can build itself into a social structure, it is going to show any real hope of extensive results.

In consonance, the medium which builds itself into a social institution is termed as a rural medium of communication by the researcher. This is built over a period of time with the hopes and confidence of the people. The Gramya was experimented as a rural medium of communication.

The Approach

When Gramyavani was launched, the approach was something like the supply of information input and coordinating with the government agencies. But more stress was on cultivating the spirit of self-help and mutual help. Therefore, factors such as participation, mobilisation of government machinery, integrated approach, grassroots level activities and commitment to the cause in addition to the available rural medium of communication were taken into account.

The experimental newspaper was devised thus:

The whole newspaper was conceived as a tree. Its roots were the KNOWLEDGE GENERATING SYSTEM (Media reports, Information of government plans, policies, programmes and schemes), Its stem which was carrying three branches was the KNOWLEDGE DISSEMINATING SYSTEM (editorial staff who worked like activists) and its branches which were representing three segments of the society was the KNOWLEDGE PRACTICING SYSTEM. Families were the basic units that constituted the society in its entirety. Each family had three levels namely, the father, the mother and children. The newspaper planned different packages for all the three segments in its integrated approach to the family. The father in a rural family was a farmer, and the focal of development thrust. The newspaper would provide him articles on different subjects like horticulture, psciculture, poultry, dairying, new farm techniques and other aspects of rural life. However, it was decided that the newspaper's job should not confine to the mere publishing of an article. Instead, it should have a follow up action.

For example, an article on banana cultivation was planned, the detailed information on the advantages of horticulture in general and banana cultivation in particular, expected profit vis-à-vis paddy, input per acre, favourable soil and climatic conditions, market trends, government incentives etc., were ascertained from the district horticulture officer. Then a progressive farmer who had own 'the best horticulturist' award for his banana cultivation was interviewed to incorporate his experiences.

The article proposed a workshop at the farm of the progressive farmer. Interested farmers were advised to contact the newspaper. Four farmers did respond to the article. A workshop was organised in which the district horticulturist, the interested farmers and the progressive farmer participated. The participating farmers got practical demonstrations and the practical tips were re-enforced by the horticulturist. Hence the newspaper could make the scientist and the farmers face to face.

The message spread through Mass Communication (The Newspaper) and the interested farmers responded and the same was re-enforced through interpersonal communication. So the communication approach was a hybrid of Mass communication and Interpersonal communication, mass communication reach and inter personal impact.

The package for the village women included:

(i) A readers forum for the educated women to help them pursue their academic activities.

(ii) Stitching leave plates was introduced as a vocation to earn some extra money.

(iii) Food processing training camps were orginised.

(iv) In additions, during such camps discussions on topics like household management, sanitation, environment protection, alternative source of energy, first aid, child-care etc. could also be arranged.

Rural students are also a deprived section compared to their urban counterparts. In order to improve the situation, a comprehensive plan was chalked out for them.

(i) Publication of a regular column on general knowledge, general English, science, social studies and other subjects.

(ii) Regular literary competitions for the students of the rural schools. Apart from this, workshops were conducted to give shape to their talent.

The objective of the newspaper was to prove itself as an effective tool of rural development. As one looks at the process of rural development on finds an external (mostly) input inter-venes in a social system to manipulate certain age old practices, conventions, traditions and attempts to dislodge a monolith feudal structure etc. to achieve some change which he believes is beneficial for the target audience. So for this complex process the development agent (an individual, an organisation, or a media institution needs to develop oneness with the target audience to ensure their active participation, a prerequisite in any development process. To ensure participation of the target audience the newspaper the GRAMYA VANI carried all these activities. By this the newspaper first developed oneness with the target audience. Slowly but steadily the newspaper could become a rural medium of communication. And the newspaper's objective to prove itself as an effective tool of rural development was fulfilled.

References

1. Daithota Iswar and B P Sanjay,1990. The eighteenth Elephant. Manipal: Udayavani.
2. Hartmann paul, B. R. patil and Anita Dighe 1989. The mass Media and Village life: An Indian Study, New Delhi :Sage.
3. Jena P K (1992) Cowdung Journalism: Story of a Wall Newspaper', Interaction10(2), Varanasi.
4. Jena P K (1996) Effective Use of Media for Rural Development: A Study of Communication Patterns in Orissa. Ph.D Thesis Submitted To Mysore University.
5. Jena P K (2003) Gramyavani: An Experimental Newspaper. A True Story in Purposive Rural Communication.
6. Macbride, Sean, 1982. Many Voices One World: UNESCO, New Delhi: Oxford.
7. Mayer Albert and Associates, 1958. Pilot Project, Berkeley: Indian University of Calfornia Press.
8. Melkote, Srinivas R 1991. Communication for Development in the Third World: Theory and Practice.
9. Schramm,Wilbur.1964. Mass Media and National Development. Paris;Unesco.
10. Schramm, Wilbur.1977. Communication and Development: A Revaluation. Communicator. April.1977.
11. Singhal Aravind and E M Rogers 1989. India's Information revolution, Newdelhi: Sage.
12. Sridharan, Sumi 1975. 'Village Chhatera' in Mehra Masani (Ed.). Communication and Rural Progress. Bombay: Leslie programme of training for democracy.
13. Sripadre 1990. Editorial. Adike pathrike. Nov.1988.

22

Film Studies and Society

Saloni Saxena

In today's scenario films are playing a critical role in our life because now most of the films were making on the reality. When we watch any movie most of the people must relate that particular movie with their life. The film gives them a lesson that how to avoid the problems of life insist in the film.

The word, Society, came from the word "Social" which refers to a characteristic of living organisms. It always refers to the interaction of them to their collective coexistence. Now come on the film studies means that deals with various theoretical, historical and critical approaches to the film.

I chose this topic because I think in this time films are a major part of our society. Now a days film are making on such a topic like social issues, education, politics, domestic violence, crime etc. These topics are related to us on anypoint of our life that's why we so attached with these films. In these times there is a very big issue regarding the titling of films, there are films named FASHION, DELHI BELLY, RAAZNEETI, ARAKSHAN, 3 IDIOTS, PAGE 3, TAARE ZAMEEN PAR, FALTU etc. All these films are based on a theme like education, reservation, reality of cinema, and situation of metro cities. So the people have started to think like that what his son or daughters want to be, they does not force them to be according to him. This is the impact of films on our society. Now if we take the example of the movie 3 idiots there is a dialogue in this film is "AAl IS WELL" so the people started to say these words when they are in some problem or nervous. Government also made some milestone like some time ago in up board the ratio of failed students are at a very huge level but now the ratio is less there are more passed students right now. So today's films are theme based on such topics where people must have to think. Films are giving a platform to perform We have changed our living life style according to the films, the way of talking and dealing with the other person that all are changed because of the films. Even the most little thing like saying bye bye, cut the cake on birthday, have adopted by us, it was not in our tradition.

My research is based on applied research and in my research I have select questionnaire as a tool, researched over 200 people age limit between 15- 30 and the findings which I have concluded that 60 per cent of people still watch the films for only entertainment and the rest of the people actually influenced by the films or they began to think like the film said.

Introduction

Film studies and society this is the topic of my research paper. In this I have covered the social and physical impact of films on the society as well as on the government. First of all when we are talked about the films then we find that in these times there are a lot of movies were produced on such topics like Education, any current issues like child labor, Women exploitation in their married lives, reservation system, corruptions etc.

When man comes home after day's work, he needs some sort of entertainment and relaxation. Cinema has proved to be a wonderful and forceful means of entertainment and amusement. A young man of today can do without food but not without a film. The cinema is the cheapest and the most popular form of amusement. Laborers can afford to miss their evening meal, not their evening show.

Students prefer films to reading books. Thus, cinema exercises a very powerful effect on society.

Cinema is a universal teacher. It educates the people in different branches of learning. Our film producers have made very purposeful films to collect public opinion against some of the social evils as dowry system, the labour exploitation. It can teach us natural history, geography, botany, chemistry etc. These films increase our knowledge, broaden our outlook. Social pictures throw light on social evils as untouchability, casteism, unemployment and the curse of widowhood, etc. These films ripen our eyes and create in us an urge for improvement.

Before some time ago films were not made who covered the topics like the above are but now a days films were highlighting on these topics like 3 Idiots, Aarakshan, Raajneeti, Gali Gali me chorhai, Taarezameen par etc. so the trend has been changed of Bollywood movies which inspire a common men to the government.

Governments have changed the education system. In this time a student can not be failed by the school till 8th class and after that in high school there are grading system in this there are very few chances of failing the students. But if we take a look before some time ago near about 2 to 3 years in UP boards there were a huge number of failed students in 10th as well as 12thin fact the result of passing students was went only 30 % or 40%. In that conditions many students attempt suicide every year there are 30 students were committed suicide due to the results. That's why government has to think on this and then he passed a law regarding the education system. But we did not capt our mind on how did it happen? This was done through the help of films. A lot of films have been made on this topic like I AM KALAAM, TAARE ZAMEEN PAR etc. These films have changed the thinking of society as well as of the government.

The cinema is a powerful and effective means of communication. Because of its audio-visual character it has a great mass appeal. Such a powerful and effective means of communication can be gainfully utilized in a variety of ways. This most popular source of entertainment for millions of people can be used as an instrument for creating public awakening. It can help to a great extent in enlisting public co-operation in the task of nation building.

The cinema exercises a great influence on the mind of the people. It has a great educative value. It can achieve splendid results in the field of expansion of education. There are certain subjects, such as science and geography, which can be more effectively taught with the help of talkies. Lessons on road sense, rules of hygiene and civic sense can be taught to the students and the 'public as well in a very effective manner with the help of cinema pictures. Many successful experiments have been made in various countries on the utility of films as a means of education. Feature films have been produced for school and college students and students are being benefitted by them.

Cinema films have the power to influence the thinking of the people. They have changed the society and social trends. They have introduced new fashions in society. They may be described as pace-setters. They can create a direct impact on our social life. Films can go a long way towards arousing national consciousness and also in utilising the energies of the youth in social reconstruction and nation-building by a skillful adaption of good moral, social and educative themes, and by introduction of popular sentiments, films can, to a great extent, formulate and guide public opinion.

Titling of films

In today's scenario which is called the youth scenario, we are the second largest country in the world in the context of youth. So there are a lots of movies specially made for them but there titles are very different which creates enthusiasm on the society. If we think about the film according to the title we can never aspect what the film is in real like Kamine, 3 Idiots, Band Baaja Barat, Faaltu etc. these are some various films choosen from different fields who's title create a type of enthusiasm. The main reasons for such type of topics are that people want something new which is unknown to everyone, there must be some uniqueness in that because, this is not the time where people only watch the movies for entertainment but in this time society think about the reality behind the reel life and the real life.

There is a director named Madhur Bhandaarkar who is specially famous for presenting the real life on to the silver screen. His films, such as **Page 3** based on the reality behind the camera means the social life of the celebrities, The other film is **Traffic-Signal** based on the beggars who live their life on the side of the road and how can a traffic signal be a most important part of their lives, **Corporate**, this film relates with the field of corporate sector the business field, **Fashion**, which highlighted the condition of fashion world and after all these films he decided to make a film on the life of an actress film name **Heroine.**

Impact of Films on the Society

Man has instincts, different thoughts flows which leave an effect on the minds. The social impact of the cinema in India is also seen in the nationwide popularity of film-based programs on various television channels. It's mostly the young generation that has been caught up by the film-song programs. Popular film song has gone very deep into the Indian collective memory and conscience. The person laughs with the films and tears with them. Scenes of 'Shaheed Bhagat Singh', a film by Raj Kumar Santoshi and Manoj Goswami makes people national-minded and sentimentally involved in the film show. The film dialogues are occupying places in our real life. Dialogues of Mugle Azam found place in the normal interaction of people for a long time. People talked and walked like Prithvi Raj, the great king Akbar. In the same way, plays by Agha Hashat and Devdas by Sharat Chandra left a deep impact on the masses. In the same way, film 'Sholey' created an emending effect on so many.

It is always good and well groomed to see good subjects on cinema. They have a very positive and long-lasting effect on the minds whereas cheap and shabby movies affect the tender minds of audience very badly. There is general feeling that present day crimes are all due to effects of cinema by the common man but as well as a coin have two faces this films also have two faces on negative and the other is positive. It depends upon what would you like to choose?

Movies are created to provide refreshment and recreation to people. Not only for recreation, they create awareness about happenings in our surrounfdings. But now a days movies had a great impact on not only youth but also on children. Impact mainly depends on us, any movie will have bad and good and it is ourselves should able to distinguish between them. If we take positive things in a movie become completely commercial, nobody is thinking of the society they thinking only about money. There are also some movies that make us to wake up. On the other hand film industry is giving livelihood to many artists, technicians etc. coming to the point of youth, Youth is a part of life where we get much to enjoy. In any stage of life, we do not have that much power and enthusiasm and also time to watch movies. Youth as grownups, They should make themselves to grasp good things in a movie. Movies has a power to make the world and break the world.

Fashion movies and music industries impact society. For instance, a teenager may choose to cut her hair for a short curly hairstyle or highlight it simply because her favourite star looks the same in a particular movie, or her favorite rock star wears the same. These fashion trends have all happened at different times where people can simply copy their favorite celebrities after watching them on TV or going out to the movies. Media influence is an all important factor in today's society.

In India, Bollywood celebrities greatly influenced the latest fashion among young boys and girls because it uses glamorous look and standout fashion trends. From time to time, film makers create new exclusive designs and styles feature in the movies, which are accepted in everyday's lifestyle. Fashion movies generally took advantage of the inherent theatrics of fashion. In Hollywood, on the other hand, several fashion movies greatly affect the viewers' preference because of its standout and beautiful clothes and styles.

When we watch TV or a movie we usually see many images of violence and people hurting others. The problem with this is that it can become traumatic especially in our children as we see it more and more. Our kids that are starting to grow and are shaping their personality values and beliefs can become aggressive or they can lose a sense of reality and fiction of what they are seeing.

In the past years there have been some cases of kids carrying a gun at school and even hurting others with it. Those kids have been linked to excessive use of violent video games and war images.

Another problem is that real war is used as a form of entertainment by the media, we should make our kids and teen aware that war is not a form of entertainment and that there is no win or lose like in video games, in real war everyone lose.

There is a very huge impact of films made on the society as well as on government. Actually after watching a film people began to think on that like suppose you have watched a movie on the child labor then you'll surely suggest the guy who have a child labor or you will take any action for stopping this. There is some other Movies like **Munna Bhai MBBS, Lage Raho Munna Bhai and Swadesh** etc. which inspire the society and the youth very much.

If we take the example of Munnabhai Mbbs, after watching this film many people started to help others in a different manner like the film's character Munna. Like this the other film named Lage raho munna bhai in this film The character dreamed about GANDHI JEE actually he is a gangster but he changed his life by choosing the way of Gandhigiri, he solves every problem in the Gandhi jee's way and finally he got his love. This film create a huge impact on the society people also started to solve their problems in Gandhigiri most of the youth changed their life. 'Swadesh' movie is one of such movies where one can get inspiration from the character 'Mohan' to do small small projects using available sources for the benefit of the society.

There is another film named "SLUMDOG MILLIONAIRE", This film is also baesd on children living their life in slums. In this film a child named Jamaal used to live in the casuals area or can be called slums where he spent his childhood and after that the whole story between the slums and till to be millionaire is all about the film Slumdog Millionair. This film also nominated for the Oscars and got 7 oscars in various fields of film. It was a milestone for the Bollywood. If we go further then a film's name struck in our mind that is "No One Killed Jessica" based on the real killing accident whose suspect have released by the court because of money and political power. This film made a very powerfull expressions to the people and let them to think is really our police system reliable and the political system is it really not corrupt? There are many questions of these types have struck in our mind after watching these films. So it is very clear that films make a huge impact on the society.

Movies are inspired of what happening in society and this movies then inspired mass.For example lets take film nagaarjun starrer shiva its was youth based film subjected to voilence in the society, this film impacts message of violence in minds of youth there was a very fashion among the youth, at that time everybody takes cycle chain in hand wrapped on wrist and move in style. Movies affect our lifestyle maybe in positive or in negative sense.

It is all about the social impact of films on the youth but films have also changed our life style from morning to the night; everything has been changed by the films. In present era people adopt fashion trends films.

Conclusion

After this research based on th topic "THE FILM STUDIES AND SOCIETY" I have found that the films have the graet influence on the mass as well as on the society. Films are the best way to describe or to inform what would you think about any particular topic. In this times most of the films were made by capturing the audience in Centre because films are made on such a topic like Crime, Dowry, Child labor, Women exploitation, corruption, Education, Honor killing etc. this are some topics which are mostly covered by the film makers. In this era Films are totally Infotainment means information with entertainment. Any message which have to give to the mass was given in this fashion like the Film "GALI GALI ME CHOR HAI" in this film they covered the most hot topic of corruption in our country but they presented this topic in funny style with lots of comic characters. These types of films are called infotainment.

Last but not the Least I Would like to say that Films have both the aspect Positive as well as Negative if youth inspire by the films then surely some youths also got negative sense of the films like Smoking, Behaving in violence way, jumping from high level, performing stunts with byckor with four wheeler or without these things. So these are some negative aspects of the films But in my opinion avery coin has two faces so that is not a big deal its upon you that how would you take it? In my research method that is questionnaire I Found that 75 to 85 per cent of the people have influence by the films and rest of the people does not agree with this statement. In this method I have also find that 10 per cent of the do not watch the films and rest of the mass used to watch the film.

23

Schizophrenia: Health Issues, Social Changes and Responsibilities of Media

Chhavi Bartaria, Shashank Bharadwaj, Prashanta Kumar Pal

Introduction

Schizophrenia, also sometimes colloquially called split personality disorder, is a chronic, severe, debilitating mental illness that affects about 1per cent of the population. Other statistics about schizophrenia include that it affects men about one and a half times more commonly than women. It is one of the psychotic mental disorders and is characterized by symptoms of thought, behaviour, and social problems. The thought problems associated with schisophrenia are described as psychosis, in that the person's thinking is completely out of touch with reality at times. For example, the sufferer may hear voices or see people that are in no way present or feel like bugs are crawling on their skin when there are none. The individual with this disorder may also have disorganised speech, disorganized behaviour, physically rigid or lax behaviour (catatonia), significantly decreased behaviours or feelings, as well as delusions, which are ideas about themselves or others that have no basis in reality.

There are five types of schizophrenia, each based on the kind of symptoms the person has at the time of assessment.

(i) *Schizoaffective Disorder*. This type of schizophrenia is characterized by a combination of schizophrenia and mood (affective) disorder symptoms.

(ii) *Catatonic Schizophrenia*. This type of schizophrenia includes extremes of behaviour, including:

- Catatonic excitement - overexcitement or hyperactivity, in which the patient may mimic sounds (echolalia) or movements (achopraxia) around them.

- Catatonic stupor - a dramatic reduction in activity in which the patient cannot speak, move or respond. Virtually all movements stops.

(iii) *Childhood Schizophrenia.* Also known as childhood-onset schizophrenia or early-onset schisophrenia. This is basically the same as schizophrenia, but onset takes place earlier in life. Onset means the first appearance of the signs or symptoms of an illness.

(iv) *Disorganized Schizophrenia (Hebephrenia).* Also known as hebephrenia (hebephrenic schizophrenia), disorganised schizophrenia is thought to be an extreme expression of disorganisation syndrome. It is characterised by incoherent and illogical thoughts and behaviors; i.e., disinhibited, agitated, and purposeless behaviour.

(v) *Paranoid Schizophrenia.* In this type of schizophrenia the patient has false beliefs (delusions) that an individual or group of people are conspiring to harm them or members of their family.

Causes of Schizophrenia

Schizophrenia is not directly passed from one generation to another, and there is no single cause for this illness. Genetically, schizophrenia and bipolar disorder are very much similar, these two disorders share a number of the same genes risk. However, the fact is that both illnesses also have some genetic factors that are unique. There are some genetic com-monalities with schizophrenia and epilepsy as well.

- Environmentally, the risks of developing schizophrenia can even occur before birth. Difficult life circumstances during childhood, like the early loss of a parent, parental poverty, bullying, witnessing parental violence; being the victim of emotional, sexual, or physical abuse or of physical or emotional neglect; and insecure attachment have been associated with the development of this illness.
- Factors like how well represented an ethnic group is in a neighbourhood can be a risk or protective factor for developing schizophrenia.

Schizophrenic Symptoms and Signs

According to the *Diagnostic and Statistical Manual of Mental Disorders* (*DSM*), symptoms of schizophrenia include the following:

Positive, More Overtly Psychotic Symptoms

- Beliefs that have no basis in reality (delusions)
- Hearing, seeing, feeling, smelling, or tasting things that have no basis in reality (hallucinations)

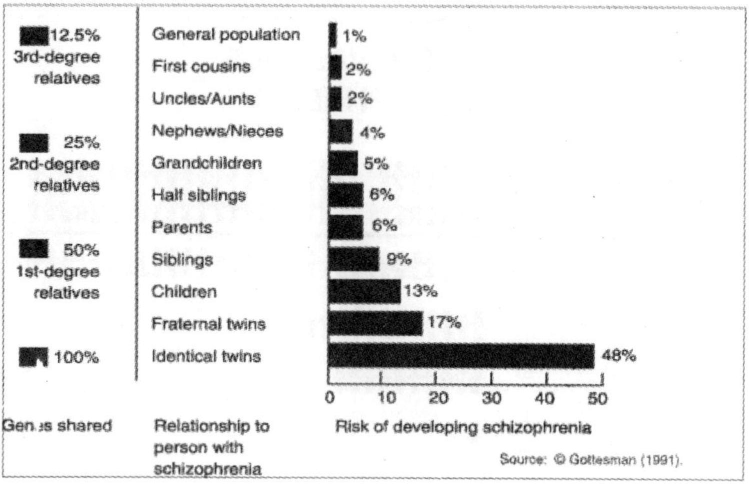

- Disorganised speech
- Disorganised behaviours
- Catatonic behaviours

Negative, Potentially less Overtly Psychotic Symptoms

- Inhibition of facial expressions
- Lack of speech
- Lack of motivation

Diagnosis of Schizophrenia

Not a single medical test is available to diagnose schizophrenia in someone. Therefore, health-care specialists diagnose this disorder by gathering medical, family, and mental-health information, Schizophrenia is a serious disorder of the mind and brain but it is treatable. The earlier someone with schizophrenia is diagnosed and stabilized on treatment, better the long-term prognosis for illness. Teen suicide is a growing problem regarding this disease. And in some rare cases, children who are as young as five can develop schizophrenia.

Although there was no cure for schizophrenia till 2007 but the treatment success rate with antipsychotic medications and psycho-social therapies were high and it was estimated that a cure for schizophrenia could be found within 10 years i.e. by year 2013.

The Risks of Getting Schizophrenia

After a person has been diagnosed with schizophrenia in a family, the chance for a sibling to also be diagnosed with schizophrenia is 7 to 9 per

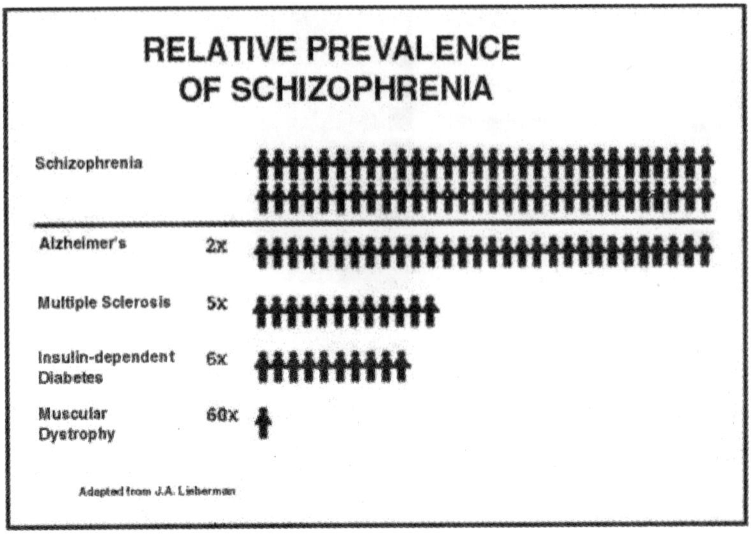

cent. If a parent has schizophrenia, the chance for a child to have the disorder is 10 to 15 per cent. Risks increase with multiple affected family members.

Prognosis for Schizophrenia

Individuals with schizophrenia have more than twice rate as compared to healthy ones. Research shows that people with schizophrenia or schizoaffective disorder have a better quality of life if their family members tend to be more supportive and less critical of them.

Occurrence of Schizophrenia Compared to other well-known Diseases

Therefore, the approximate number of people is suffering from:

- Schizophrenia: Over 2.2 million people
- Multiple Sclerosis: 400,000 people
- Insulin-dependent Diabetes: 350,000 people
- Muscular Dystrophy: 35,000 people

Suicide Risk in Schizophrenia

- People with the condition have a higher risk of attempting suicide than the general population. Suicide is the number one cause of premature death among people with schizophrenia.

Schizophrenia and Violence

- People with schizophrenia are far more likely to harm themselves than to be violent toward the public, but violence is not a symptom of schizophrenia. Most people with schizophrenia, however, are not violent toward others but are withdrawn and prefer to be left alone.

Schizophrenia and Jail

- The vast majority of people with schizophrenia who are in jail have been charged with misdemeanors such as trespassing or murders etc. Many individuals with schizophrenia revolve between hospitals, jails and shelters.

Management Aspect Regarding Schizophrenia

In terms of weight management, more research is needed to explore how to best help people with schizophrenia retain the weight loss they achieve and even to prevent weight gain in the first place.

I am form IBM department and growing as a responsible citizen and in the corporate system if I am a part of HR system, I make less stressful work for my employees and if we are in job then we may able to work shorter hours but in a more flexible way as Under the Disability Discrimination Ac 1995, all employers must make "reasonable adjustment" to facilitate the employment of disabled people including those with a diagnosis of mental ill health.

Awareness Activities

SAA has organised numerous public awareness programmes and lectures, of local, national and international experts. SAA regularly organizes programmes on the occasion of World mental Health Day, 10th October and *Schizophrenia Day on May 24th*. SAA has produced a movie – "Devrai" which narrates story of a person suffering from mental illness. SAA publishes newsletter and has published several books on mental illness and its management.

The Government has a different approach and perspective in dealing with people having HIV/AIDS as compared to those having Mental Illness in India.

Myths Regarding Schizophrenia

It is even good to say that no mental disorder is more a mystery, misunderstanding and fear than schizophrenia, in spite from ignorance, images of the aggressive, sadistic "schizophrenic" are existing in the media.

So, the schizophrenic patient also has to deal with the confusion, fear and disgust of others, regarding this following are some myths:

- All schizophrenic patients have same symptoms.
- People with schizophrenia are dangerous, unpredictable and out of control.

- Schizophrenia is a character flaw.
- Cognitive decline is a major symptom of schizophrenia.
- There are psychotic and non-psychotic people.
- Schizophrenia develops quickly.
- Schizophrenia is purely genetic.
- Schizophrenia is untreatable.
- Sufferers need to be hospitalized.
- People with schizophrenia can't lead productive lives.
- Medications make sufferers zombies.
- Antipsychotic medications are worse than the illness itself.
- Individuals with schizophrenia can never regain normal functioning.

Possible Media Responsibilities Relevant to Schizophrenia

Up till now numerous myths and misconceptions has been grown in our society from generations in respect of persons diagnosed with mental illness. Till 1997 in Pune, India, professional treatment was the only solution available for persons with mental illness.

Schizophrenia Awareness Association (SAA) was established as a Public Charitable Trust in 1998 for increasing number of families who were in need of a solution to their problems.

Though in the beginning the major focus area of Schizophrenia Awareness Association was people suffering from schizophrenia. Three major areas of focus of SAA are:

1. Creating public awareness about mental disorders using various media.
2. Empowering afflicted families through training, SHSG, talks of experts and formal training.
3. Networking with other similar NGOs at the national and international levels for exchange of information, for creating a common platform for advocacy and for capacity building.

In the global level Canada play major role in creating the awareness. The emblem of Schizophrenia society of Canada's is Iris Flower. This flower represents 'Faith, Hope and Courage'. Personally, I feels that the newly establish commission will make faith, hope and courage a reality and make a major changes in the mental illness situation.

Movies, Documentaries about schizophrenia are also play a key role in creating the awareness among peoples.

- The movie, "A Beautiful Mind", tells the story of Nobel Prize winner John Nash's struggle with schizophrenia. It follows his journey from the point where he is not even aware he has schizophrenia to the point where Nash and his wife find a way to manage his condition. The paper shows that the movie provides a lot of information and insight into the psychological condition of schizophrenia, including information on the symptoms, the treatment and cures, the life for the individual, and for the individual's family.

- *People Say I'm Crazy* is the only film about schizophrenia ever made by someone with schizophrenia. This film tells the story of a young man, John Cadigan, who develops schizophrenia at age 21 while studying art at Carnegie Mellon University in Pittsburgh, Pennsylvania. This conclusion shows that, John rejoins his family and community, fulfills his dream of launching his career as an artist, and moves into his own apartment to begin living an independent life. John filmed his life for over 10 years from when he had his first psychotic episode at age 21 until he was well into recovery a decade later.
- In bollywood, Aparna Sen's 15 Park Avenue is just the sort of film that will receive much critical acclaim, but will stop short of popular acclaim, it's an Aparna Sen film, and second, it deals with a difficult subject like Schizophrenia.

But news and entertainment media tend to link mental illnesses including schizophrenia to criminal violence.

Following are the name of famous people who have been diagnosed with schizophrenia, or are highly suspected of suffering from schizophrenia.

- Tom Harrell (Jazz Musician)
- John Nash (Mathematician/Nobel Prize Winner)
- Albert Einstein's son-Eduard Einstein
- Dr. James Watson's son (Dr. Watson is co-discover of DNA and Nobel Prize winner)
- Alan Alda's Mother (Alan Alda is the famous TV actor from the series MASH)
- Andy Goram (Scottish Soccer Player/Goal Keeper)
- Lionel Aldridge (Superbowl-winning Football Player)
- Charles "Buddy" Bolden (Jazz Musician)
- Antoin Artaud (Dramatist, Artist)
- Mary Todd Lincoln, wife of Abraham Lincoln (past-President of the United States)

  Vaclav Nijinsky (Famous Russian Dancer)
- Jack Kerouac, Author, was diagnosed with Schizophrenia

References

Drake, R.E., McHugo, G.J., Xie, H., Fox, M., Packard, J., & Helmstetter, B. (2006). Ten-Year Recovery Outcomes for Clients with Co-occurring Schizophrenia and Substance Use Disorders>. *Schizophrenia Bulletin*, 32, 464-473.

Penn, D.L., Chamberlin, C., & Mueser, K.T. (2003). *The effects of a documentary film about schizophrenia on psychiatric stigma.* Schizophrenia Bulletin, 29, 383-391.

M.C. Angermeyer, S. Dietrich, D. Pott, H. Matschinger. *Media consumption and desire for social distance towards people with schizophrenia European Psychiatry*, 20, 3, 246-250.

Patricia A. Stout, Jorge ViUegas, and Nancy A. Jennings. (2004). *Images of Mental Illness in the Media: Identifying Gaps in the Research, Schizophrenia Bulletin*, 30, 3, 543- 561.

Net Sources

- Everyday Health
- BBC Health
- Psychiatry online
- Medicine net
- Schizophrenia.com

24

Coverage of MGNREGA in Two National Dailies: Comparative Study of The Hindu and The Times of India

Shah Alam

Introduction

At present, most of the leading newspapers are paying attention to the rural coverage as government is taking several steps for the development of rural India. With the launch of MGNREGA by UPA government in 2005, rural journalism got an opportunity to come in mainstream journalism.

The Mahatma Gandhi National Rural Employment Guarantee Act (MGNREGA), an Indian job guarantee scheme, enacted by legislation on August 25, 2005. The scheme provides a legal guarantee for one hundred days of employment in every financial year to adult members of any rural household willing to do public work-related unskilled manual work at the statutory minimum wage of Rs.100 per day. The Central government outlay for scheme is Rs. 39,100 crores ($8 billion) in FY 2009-10.

This act was introduced with an aim of improving the purchasing power of the rural people, primarily semi or unskilled work to people living in rural India, whether or not they are below the poverty line. Around one-third of the stipulated work force is women. The government is planning to open a call center, which upon becoming operational can be approached on the toll-free number, 1800-345-22-44. It was initially called the National Rural Employment Guarantee Act (NREGA) but was renamed on 2 October 2009.

Findings

A: Classification of MGNREGA news in three broad categories:

MGNREGA related stories which appear in two newspapers are broadly classified into the following three categories;

1. News
2. Articles
3. Editorials

News

By the definition, news is the information about recent events or happenings specially as covered by newspapers, periodicals, radio or television. In this dissertation study MGNREGA related news which appears in both the newspapers are studied. MGNREGA news stories are written keeping in mind the news value factor such as timeliness, currency, prominence, proximity and novelty etc.

March, 1-31, 2010

Newspaper	*Number of News*	*Area Covered (sq. cm)*
The Hindu	14	2240.78
The Times of India	09	1413.86

April, 1-30, 2010

Newspaper	*Number of News*	*Area Covered (sq. cm)*
The Hindu	11	2079.53
The Times of India	08	1188.24

Articles

An article is a stand-alone section of a larger written work. These non-fictional proses, compositions appear in magazines, newspapers, academic journals, the internet or any other type of publication.

The article offers the opportunity for providing more breadth or depth, context of history or other explanatory material on current or recent news of either general interest or on a specific topic. Like here articles published on a specific issue, MGNREGA, are studied and analyzed.

A news article can include account of eye witnesses to the event happenings. It can contain photographs, statistics, graph, recollections, interview, polls, debates etc. An article includes headline, lead, body and conclusion.

March, 1-31, 2010

Newspaper	*Number of Articles*	*Area Covered (sq. cm)*
The Hindu	00	00
The Times of Indi	01	395.08

April, 1-30, 2010

Newspaper	*Number of Articles*	*Area Covered (sq. cm)*
The Hind	01	814.58
The Times of India	02	872.96

Editorial/ Op-ed

An editorial in a newspaper or magazine expresses the opinion of the editor, editorial board or publisher.

An op-ed, abbreviated from opposite editorial, due to the traditions of newspapers placing such materials on page opposite to the editorial page. It similar in form and content to an editorial but represents the opinion of an individual writer, who may sometimes but not always is affiliated with the publication.

We refer to the editorials to get a detailed account on an issue as it clears the doubts surrounding the events/issues. They are different form news and articles as opinions are expressed here, whereas news is more detached kind of writing where a third person narrative is used.

The editorial board comprises of a group of editors usually at print publications to dictate the tone and direction that the publication's editorials will take. In this dissertation study editorials and op-ed are analyzed which gave a more focused and detailed analysis on MGNREGA news.

March, 1-31, 2010

Newspaper	*Number of Editorials/* Op-ed	*Area Covered (sq. cm)*
The Hindu	01	291.6
The Times of India	02	330.82

April, 1-30, 2010

Newspaper	*Number of Editorials/ Op-ed*	*Area Covered (sq. cm)*
The Hindu	01	350.26
The Times of India	00	00

Comparison and Conclusion

March 1 to April 30, 2010

Categories	*Times of India*	*The Hindu*
No. of News/Area (sq. cm)	17 (2602.10)	25 (4320.31)
No. of Articles/Area (sq. cm)	02 (784.04)	01 (814.58)
No. of Editorials/Area (sq. cm)	02 (330.82)	02 (641.86)
Total	21 (3716.96)	28 (5776.75)

Inference

The content analysis of the section reveals that "The Hindu" was ahead than "The Times of India" in publishing MGNREGA related stories, as "The Hindu" published 28 stories (including news, article and editorial type) and "The Times of India" published 21 stories (including news, article and editorial type) in the same period (from March 1 to April 30, 2010). So the area covered by MGNREGA related stories in "The Hindu" and "TOI" was 5776.75 and 3716.92 cm sq. respectively.

Whereas, "The Hindu" leads in publishing news as it published 25 while The Times of India published 17 news related to MGNREGA.

"Times of India" leads in publishing "Articles" as it published 2 articles while "The Hindu" published just 1 article related to MGNREGA.

Both newspapers published 2 editorials but the area covered by "The Hindu" was more than that of "The Times of India".

The conclusion drawn through this section shows that "The Hindu" gave more attention in publishing day to day MGNREGA news where as the "The Times of India" focus more on the analysis part that is articles.

All in all the total study can be summed by saying that both the newspapers treated the MGNREGA news content in quite different ways where The Hindu paid more attention to day to day coverage while The Times of India published the stories in more attractive manner as it published more photographs in comparison to The Hindu.

References

Krippendorff, Klaus. Content Analysis: An Introduction to its Methodology. New Delhi: Sage Publication India Pvt.Ltd.

Neuendorf, Kimberly A. Content analysis: Guidebook. New Delhi: Sage Publication India Pvt.Ltd.

Joseph, T. M. (2008) New Governance Paradigm: Issues in Development. Delhi: Kalpaz Publications.

Rajan, Nalini. 21st Century Journalism in India. New Delhi: Sage Publication India Pvt.Ltd.

Aggarwal S. K. (1990) Investigative Journalism in India. New Delhi: K.M. Raj. Mittal Publications. http://nrega.nic.in

The Times of India. New Delhi: Bennett Coleman & Co. Ltd

The Hindu. New Delhi: Kasturi & Sons Ltd.

25

Green Growth – Environmentally Sustainable Economic Growth

Dr Ahsanuddin Haider

Introduction

Green Growth is a policy focus for the Asia and Pacific region that emphasizes environmentally sustainable economic progress foster low-carbon, socially inclusive development. UNESCAP's Green Growth Programme has evolved to emphasise the Sustainable Livelihoods Approach (SLA), a rights-based approach that recognises the poor as a key stakeholder in the development process. Green Growth encourages the use of participatory assessments which identify the main constraints, opportunities and concerns faced by the poor and to include them into the policy planning and implementation cycle. The SLA supports vulnerable communities by providing pro-poor social services and by creating an enabling environment for sustainable development. The concept of sustainable livelihoods is used by some as a replacement term for sustainable employment and work in the formal and informal economies with reference to a person's capacity to maintain and enhance their capability and assets both now and in the future, while not undermining the natural resource base. Adopting this approach allows Green Growth to work towards win-win solutions: addressing the environment in ways which enhance opportunities for the poor to participate more fully in society and thus improving their quality of life.

The Need for Sustainable Consumption and Production

Whenever a product or service is produced or consumed, natural resources are used (water, energy, material, etc.) and pollutants or emissions are dumped in the biosphere. However, ecosystems can only absorb a certain amount of pollutants before they break down. Therefore, there are natural limits to how much each person can consume and produce. Humankind's current ecological footprint exceeds the carrying capacity of the Earth by

1.3 times! Moreover, with an expected world population of about 9 billion in 2050, our allocation of resources will be even more constrained in the future. It is with this in mind that there is a clear and very crucial need for more sustainable patterns of consumption and production.

In 1987, the World Commission on Environment and Development (Brundtland Commission) of the United Nations defined sustainable development as "*meeting the needs of the present without compromising the ability of future generations to meet their own needs.*" Most definitions of sustainable consumption and production (SCP) are now going beyond this understanding and also include aspects of economic and social development. Sustainability in consumption and production activities means to use natural resources and the absorption capacity of the biosphere at a rate at which replenishment and restoration is possible. Given that there are limits to the capacity of the Earth's ecosystems to absorb pollution and provide natural resources, the only way to maintain economic progress in the long term without approaching these limits is to decouple economic growth from environmental degradation.

The United Nations Economic and Social Commission for Asia and the Pacific (ESCAP) promotes the concept of eco-efficiency in production and consumption cycles because there is a need to expand the scope of the SCP debate beyond products to encompass infrastructure and services as well conventional economic development planning has primarily focused on the supply side of the economy: emphasising the building of more power plants, dams and highways to increase the supply capacity for energy, water and roads as opposed to improving the efficiency of energy and water consumption. The promotion of eco-efficiency, however, requires policy options for demand-side management, such as expanding public transportation and railroads, licensing the right to purchase private passenger cars, and regulating water and energy prices to improve society's efficiency of consumption. This is all the more pressing in view of the limited ecological carrying capacity of the region and the prospect of continued rapid economic growth in the Asia and the Pacific.

In line with this, ESCAP pushes for public policy that provides for improved, eco-efficient infrastructure with increased access to resources in order to improve the eco-efficiency of consumption. While eco-efficiency can be implemented on a business level to improve the triple bottom line, the concept can also be adapted to the whole economy, in order to address rebound effects. As the progress obtained in production processes of individual products can easily be outstripped by the absolute increase of the social demand for goods and resources, it is important to apply the eco-efficiency concept to the economy-wide levels. In this context ESCAP is developing a framework for eco-efficiency indicators (EEI) to assess the macro-level environmental impacts on society and identify policy measures that can improve the eco-efficiency of the economy to achieve greater ecological, economic and social benefits. EEIs will also help to measure the eco-efficiency of economic growth of different countries which can be used for performance comparison to enhance regional and/or sectoral eco-efficiency.

The underlying principle of SCP is the need to reduce the ecological impact of consumer patterns, rather than reduce the well-being that consumption is intended to produce; in other words, to improve the quality of consumption, by reducing the quantity of resources used in production. Making the "business case" for a sustainable consumption ethic is a great challenge and requires courageous political and cultural leaders. Compelling arguments for sustainable consumption must appeal to both the humanity (that is, "it is the right thing to do") and the collective desire to remain globally competitive on all fronts. Farsighted leaders will recognise the innate competitive advantages presented by cultural values and traditional resource management practices, and engage them for building greener, more competitive economies.

Material vs. Spiritual Wealth

The 'traditional' resource intensive and inefficient approach to consumption and production in the Asia-Pacific region is detrimental to the environment and to economic growth in the long run. Other negative side effects of the resource and waste intensive organisation of economies include the lack of focus on happiness and well-being, the quality of life, and the spiritual dimension of society. The materialistic way of life that industrial capitalism has fostered may have created a more convenient life for many through the improvement of infrastructure, the availability of water, sanitation and electricity, etc. However, the increasingly fast pace of urban working life, wasteful use of material goods, and a lifestyle characterised by a high level of consumption may actually have a negative effect on our well-being. This is evident in the increasing rates of obesity, psychological disorders, and drug abuse in developed countries.

The high rate of production and consumption can satisfy many peoples' material needs but there is little proof whether a life saturated with goods, services and material gadgets is really more fulfilling. In fact, the GDP of economies only indicates the rate of economic growth; it is not at all concerned with the overall well-being and happiness of citizens. This is because the market is not an ethical construct and without adequate regulation the market itself will not seek to distribute goods and wealth equally. Unregulated capitalism has a way of running rampant, because while the overall access to material wealth may have increased on a global scale, the gap between the *haves* and *have-nots* is widening.

The concept of Economic value often dominates the sustainability debate. On a macro-economic level economic value, often used as a synonym for the (economic) progress of a society, is measured according to the concept of Gross Domestic Product (GDP), which is based on the monetary value of the outputs from given economic activities.This system however, does not fully account for the real value of the "human and natural capital" and a broad range of its services. For some time progressive ecological economists have been working on developing alternative indexes to measure and compare benefits and costs of growth, such as the Index of Sustainable Economic Welfare (ISEW) and the Genuine Progress Indicator (GPI). ISEW compensates for the loss of natural capital and provides an effective measure of welfare, adding some measures of untraded benefits and by correcting for income inequality.

Some countries in Asia and the Pacific have recognised the importance of using Gross National Happiness (GNH) as a means to measure the welfare of society. For the last two decades the Kingdom of Bhutan has followed the guiding principle enunciated by His Majesty King Jigme Siongye Wangchuck, who stated that "*Gross National Happiness is more important than Gross National Product*". The principle describes development as a continuous process towards a balance between material and non-material needs of individuals and society. The country's philosophy of development, while recognising the importance of economic growth as essential to support and nurture the spiritual and social needs of the community, is not an end in itself, but one among many means of achieving sustainable development.

The Economic and Social Cost of "Business as Usual" Growth in Asia and the Pacific

The speed of economic growth in Asia-Pacific developing countries has been surpassing global growth rates for several years. The region's contribution to global GDP has been steadily rising over the last decade but its role as a global production centre has also brought about major environmental pressures. Due to industrialization and increased trade flows, fast-growing Asian and Pacific developing countries are shouldering an increasingly greater share of regional and global environmental production-related burdens. Evolving production patterns and their impacts are both driving, and driven by, changes in consumption patterns. Despite the region's high poverty levels, current consumption pressures, as measured by the ecological footprint, exceed the available bio-productive area (or the productive natural resource endowment) per capita in at least 18 countries.

While this may be a global problem, the Asia-Pacific region in particular is growing beyond its given bio-capacity. It is estimated that the region will be unable to sustain its current economic growth rates over the long-term. The increasing pressure on the environment can be observed using the Ecological Footprint (EF) method. ESCAP's regional environmental report indicates that the environmental pressures as gauged by its ecological footprint are real and mounting. Examining the link between economic growth and environmental sustainability, the report stresses that these environmental pressures are beginning to limit the region's long-term prospects for economic growth.

The key issues for the national economies of Asia-Pacific are related to water and water availability, which will affect billions of people. Changes in the water cycle will cause severe draughts in some parts of the region, while other parts will encounter flooding. Water is already a limiting factor for not only agricultural, but also for industrial production. India's industrial water use, for example, is expected to almost quadruple by 2050, but water shortages at the height of drought have temporarily slowed industrial activity in parts of the country. In China, water shortages have been responsible for an estimated annual loss of some US$28 billion in industrial output in recent years.

The number of people affected by drought in Asia and Pacific between 1995 and 2004 is almost equalled by the number affected by flooding in the same time period. Climate change is predicted to result in even more highly differentiated temporal and spatial variations in the distribution of water resources across the region, some places will flood while others are hit by droughts. This threat points to the need for new investments in infrastructure. Yet, urban centres, the engines of regional growth, continue to be poorly equipped to meet these challenges. An increasingly extreme weather events serve as a sinister reminder of the importance of incorporating climatic vulnerability assessments into infrastructure planning. Fortunately, these goals can be achieved synonymously with action to adapt and mitigate climate change, and are becoming increasingly compatible with overall economic objectives. One of the ways to achieve the double objective of climate action and energy security can be achieved by moving towards sustainable consumption and production.

Global Initiatives on SCP

Commitments to promote sustainable consumption and production (SCP) patterns were first elaborated in Agenda 21 during the 1992 United Nations Conference on Environment and Development (UNCED) held in Rio de Janeiro. In 2002, the World Summit on Sustainable Development

(WSSD) or Earth Summit took place in Johannesburg, South Africa where all countries agreed that achieving SCP was one of the three main priorities to realize sustainable development. As a result of the Earth Summit the Johannesburg Plan of Implementation (JPOI) called for support to be given to regional and national initiatives to accelerate the shift towards SCP. The first meeting to discuss a 10 -Year Framework of Programmes (10YFP) on SCP was in Marrakech, Morocco, hence the name - The Marrakech Process.

The Need for Greening Business in Asia and the Pacific

It is now becoming imperative for governments across the region to institute legislation and polices to encourage the greening of businesses. Resource scarcity, climate change and population growth pressures are compounding existing challenges to economic growth and poverty alleviation across the region. The questions posed by the recent financial crisis highlight the pressures governments face, namely; how can businesses harness eco-efficiency as a driver of economic growth and environmental sustainability and how can the environment and eco-efficiency be presented as a business opportunity, rather than an extra burden and cost? The power of the markets can be harnessed to find lasting solutions to the environmental problems caused by globalisation. Technology and innovation can contribute to de-linking economic development from environmental degradation by increasing eco-efficiencies in production and by increasing resource productivity in the future. Significant reductions in energy and materials intensity, pollution, green house gas emissions and water pollution will demand more efficient ways of converting energy and cleaner manufacturing processes. This will need to be accompanied by major organisational and behavioral changes.

The current economic system is being driven by the strive for economic efficiency in the use of resources, based on a market price that does not reflect the full costs of the processing of inputs (e.g. natural resources) and outputs (e.g. wastes, effluents, and emissions). Thus, there is a need to pursue ecological efficiency by internalising the ecological costs of the use of natural resources into the prices of goods, making them subject to the workings of the market forces. As long as the environmental and social costs remain outside the workings of market transactions, then economic distortions that have pushed the Earth into an ecological deficit will persist. As the ecological deficit continues to deepen, the frequency and intensity of natural disasters have the potential to increase.

Governments must take the lead and encourage the greening of business throughout all levels of the economy, in order to:

(1) create an enabling environment for more green jobs;

(2) adapt to the impacts of climate change;

(3) support new markets for sustainable products;

(4) improve the use of natural resources, and

(3) to reduce environmental degradation caused by business activities.

Greening business will involve multiple stakeholders as well as the business community. To avoid further unsustainable patterns of consumption and production from becoming entrenched through the globalisation process, the help and cooperation of the private sector working in conjunction with governments is of primary importance. Multinational Corporations (MNCs) as well as small and medium enterprises (SMEs) will need to improve the efficiency of their business practices if they wish to remain competitive in the future. Business leaders need to think a little more outside the box. There are a plethora of ways to make money while being sustainable and contributing to development. Concepts such as bottom of the pyramid (BoP) are becoming more widespread. This approach argues that there are opportunities for corporations to source from or sell to disadvantaged people in ways that generate wealth, improve their quality of life while being simultaneously profitable. If policy makers are to find sustainable solutions to the problems caused by globalisation then it is vital to engage businesses.The active cooperation of local communities and civil society - harnessing support through public awareness campaigns - can also foster more inclusive economic and social development based on indigenous knowledge and traditional livelihoods.

Reinvestment into Human and Natural Capital

Natural capital is both ecosystem goods (raw materials) that enterprises transform into value for humanity everyday (trees, fish, agricultural products, water and minerals) coupled with ecosystem services that make the Earth habitable; including cleansing the water and air, pollinating agricultural crops and storing nutrients in soils. Transforming business practices to restore, rather than destroy investment in natural capital is key to long-term environmental sustainability.

Human capital refers to people's skills, education, health and family stability. By supporting policies which encourage investment in human capital governments can start to move away from their existing growth models based primarily on reinvestment in physical capital. From the government perspective reinvesting in human and natural capital is a crucial public policy strategy for ensuring sustained prosperity and well being for members of society.

Social Capital

Social capital describes circumstances in which individuals and organizations can use membership in groups and networks to secure benefits. Connections within and between networks reinforce the belief that these social networks have a value and can be used as a platform for further social progress. In this light, natural capital and social capital are closely related, and policies that build or destroy one often build or destroy the other as well, especially in the long run. Building and preserving social capital, not only allow people to prosper or at least survive, but also allow people to invest in natural capital rather than simply consume it.

The current capitalistic model in Asia and the Pacific region is designed around exports. Countries invested heavily in production, and as foreign reserves began to increase, further capital was invested towards improving production capabilities. Now, as demand is falling, an opportunity has arisen to begin reinvesting more heavily in natural and social capital. It is up to governments to support this reinvestment by correcting price signals to the market. Â Green tax and budget reform, in combination with other complimentary policy mixes, can provide governments with the tools to do so.

The Whole Systems Approach towards Greening Business

The whole systems approach can be defined as a way of viewing all parts of a system or process at once and analysing how they interact and feed into each other. It is an approach to problem solving that views problems as parts of an overall system, rather than focusing on just one area. This holistic view encompasses all aspects of a system or process and can encourage creative and innovative solutions to individual problems. Resource productivity, a component of eco-efficiency, is fundamental to greening business. If the production processes use fewer materials and less energy and water to produce the same amount of output, then in today's context of volatile energy and commodity prices the companies will be more resilient to change and therefore competitive. Eco-efficiency concepts should be applied to national, economy-wide development planning to de-link economic growth from negative environmental impacts and to improve the sustainability of economic growth patterns.

Eco-industrial Development and Circular Economy Systems

The practice of a Circular Economy can potentially cover the whole life cycle of products. Circular economy concepts generally focus on production, such as cleaner production, eco industrial park development and integrated resource-based planning. A Circular Economy can be viewed as an economy which balances economic development with environmental and resource protection. It places emphasis on the most efficient use and recycling of resources, and environmental protection. A Circular Economy works towards low consumption of energy, low emissions of pollutants and high efficiency.

Placing complementary industries in close proximity can produce considerable cost reductions for all participants because they can encourage the use of waste from one industrial operation as raw materials for another. It involves applying Cleaner Production in companies, eco-industrial park development and integrated resource-based planning for development in industry, as well in agriculture and urban areas.

Sustainable Master Planning

Sustainable master planning provides a strategic framework towards the planning, construction, operation and maintenance of sustainable infrastructure systems. Emphasis is placed on sectors with high potential for "green" job creation-employment that contributes to protecting and preserving the environment and identifying how these activities can accelerate the transition to Green Growth.

Construction, at its most basic level, is the process of assembling the structures and facilities that support human settlements and make infrastructure operational. Fundamental to social and economic development, construction shapes the way decisions are made about the production and distribution of goods and services and determines how the essential needs of a population are met. The construction of eco-efficient infrastructure-economically efficient, environmentally sustainable systems that provide citizens with safe and reliable access to shelter, energy, transportation, water, proper sanitation and disposal of wastes- is becoming increasingly critical in Asia and the Pacific.

Eco-efficient construction is based on a whole-systems approach- various types of infrastructure (including transport, energy, water, shelter etc.) and the physical landscape are seen as comprised of interdependent components that interact with the greater natural, social and economic environment. By carefully assessing socio-economic and environmental impacts throughout the various stages of a project's life-cycle, eco-efficient construction practices seek to ensure that infrastructure operates in ways that optimize performance and cost, expanding the delivery of services to those most in need. The mismanaged expansion of many Asian cities has contributed to the environmental degradation of the region, negatively affecting the quality of its air, soil and water, leading to the collapse of biodiversity, and leaving human settlements more vulnerable to the impacts of climate change. More than half of the world's new construction is occurring in Asia, following practices that continue to have an enormous negative impact on the environment. Construction is frequently planned and coordinated with little attention to environmental performance, often resulting in non-durable, energy inefficient designs that are assembled without regard for long-term sustainability or human health. A limited supply of quality, affordable housing constrains disadvantaged groups from securing adequate accommodation, many of which must resort to living in environmentally degraded or deteriorating areas, such as urban slums.

Sustainable master planning thus refers to a decision-making process whereby communities are involved in enhancing the efficiency of infrastructure services, as well as conserving and restoring local ecology, to better address the challenges people face in accessing land and basic needs. When developed alongside supportive vocational training and employment policies, sustainable master planning represents a primary vehicle in moving towards Green Growth.

Introduction to Green Tax and Budget Reform

Green Tax and Budget Reform (GTBR) refers to a wide spectrum of fiscal pricing measures that have the potential to simultaneously increase revenue and foster Green Growth. More specifically, it entails (1) a shifting of the tax burden from traditional areas of taxation, such as income, savings, and capital gains, to environmentally relevant products and activities like fossil fuels and waste; and (2) the redirecting of subsidies from environmentally perverse activities towards activities that promote Green Growth and poverty reduction.The entire reform of the fiscal system is done with the aim of maintaining revenue neutrality: a net-zero increase in the level of taxation on the economy.

GTBR encompasses a broad array of fiscal instruments in areas such as transportation, raw materials, natural resources, waste, and energy.Applying GTBR policies within these areas can create jobs; reduce poverty; and improve resource productivity, international competiveness, and environmental quality. Effectively educating the public and private sectors, as well as a country's citizenry on the benefits of GTBR, has been deemed as crucial for ensuring effective implementation and long-term adoption. In addition to recycling revenue from subsidy reform and green taxation into pro-poor development programmes, the setting of thresholds for taxation is another means for reducing any negative distributive impact on lower income groups.

Green Taxes can be effectively imposed in many areas, for example, transport, energy, products, waste, raw materials, and natural resources.

Evidence shows that they are an effective tool of environmental policy and are more cost-efficient to implement and maintain than traditional "command and control" approaches. Revenue from Green Taxes can be used for financing sustainable infrastructure projects that can increase green jobs, monitoring and adjusting the reformed tax system itself, or for other poverty reduction programmes. Considering that Green Taxes have the potential to be regressive, steps such as setting thresholds for taxes to ensure that the poor are not disproportionately adversely affected should be undertaken from the initial design phase. Educating both citizens and public officials alike on the benefits of GTBR is crucial for garnering political support. Border tax adjustments and short-term tax exemptions are measures that can be taken to reduce the impact on international and sectoral competitiveness. Sequencing of not only various green taxes, but also other complementary policies, such as transportation infrastructure projects or eco-labeling, for instance, must be

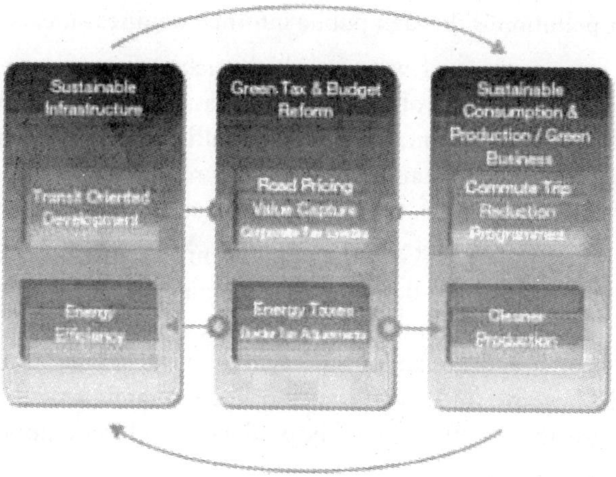

closely coordinated to ensure policy effectiveness.

Each country will require a unique blend of GTBR instruments. For developing countries in particular, GTBR may be most applicable to the transport sector, commercial scale forestry sector, commercial fisheries sector, energy sector, drinking water, and for industrial pollution control. Applying GTBR to these sectors is an effective means for improving environmental quality, reducing poverty, and fostering Green Growth.

Policy Strategies

Until recently, the conventional environmental management approach just focused on improving environmental performance by controlling and regulating pollution and effluents from production processes. Despite the progress achieved, pollution control alone does not provide for lessening the pressures from the current pattern of economic growth. Nor does it promote "*development that meets the needs of the present generation without compromising the ability of future generations to meet their own needs.*" In order to "ensure the environmental sustainability" of the society, it is imperative to also improve the efficiency of the way natural resources are being used.

Regulation is necessary to ensure some improvement in eco-efficiency, essentially with regard to pollution prevention and control. This can be done through extended producer responsibility, recycling targets, landfill and other waste directives, and voluntary agreements. One very effective tool to influence production facilities especially in the private sector to be eco-efficient and reduce their pollution is through public information disclosure.

There are a number of ways in which such policy incentives can be implemented. Thus, in view of the rapidly increasing volume of consumption in Asia and the Pacific region, addressing eco-efficiency of the consumption pattern is imperative for maintaining the environmental sustainability on regional and global levels.

This is where the Green Growth policy incentive comes into play. It seeks to harmonize economic growth for poverty reduction and improved well-being with environmental sustainability, while improving the eco-efficiency of economic growth and enhancing the synergy between environment and economy. To improve the eco-efficiency of the economic growth, there is a need to improve the eco-efficiency of the production and consumption patterns of society.

The public sector's role is to create sustainable consumption choices, which the private sector has not made available to consumers. Linking sustainable consumption to transport proved relevant to the experiences of countries. The important role of cultural values and traditional lifestyles in promoting sustainable consumption choices for a resource saving society are also important.

Government could influence consumption patterns both by raising revenue (taxation) and by spending revenue (budget expenditure). While "green" purchasing has been the focus of recent policy developments, the role of public investment in development of infrastructure for sustainable consumption choices, such as public transportation, including railroads for example, has been little discussed. Taxation is also a powerful tool in improving eco-efficiency of consumption patterns.

The Co-benefits Approach to Climate Change and Development

The co-benefits approach to climate change mitigation action seeks to unite climate action with existing development strategies. For many developing countries across the region climate change efforts can be constrained by existing development priorities or by financial constraints. Thus, the co-benefits approach aspires to achieve tangible economic and social developments, such as poverty alleviation while simultaneously reducing GHG emissions leading to "no regret" actions by countries. It is also considered to be a practical approach for developed countries to cooperate with developing countries on climate change issues, where economic and social development is a priority at the national and local levels 13.

The co-benefits approach is achieved by the introduction of integrated policies and measures into development planning to plan for GHG emission reduction efforts. These co-benefits can be realized in a number of important sectors, including manufacturing, energy, pollution abatement and rural development and have proven particularly successful when engaging policy makers in these areas.

In 2006, the Ministry of the Environment, Japan (MOEJ) and the Overseas Environmental Cooperation Center, Japan (OECC) jointly launched an initiative on the "Co-benefits Approach called the Oriented Efforts to Address Climate Change and CDM. These recent efforts to promote the co-benefits approach in pollution abatement, such as improvements in local air quality have been highlighted by the Japanese government particularly because of the damages to health caused by economic activities in the region. To promote the co-benefits approach more effectively, in addition to the project based approaches of CDM, co-benefits need to be regarded at the earliest stages of

Applying ISA to Green Growth

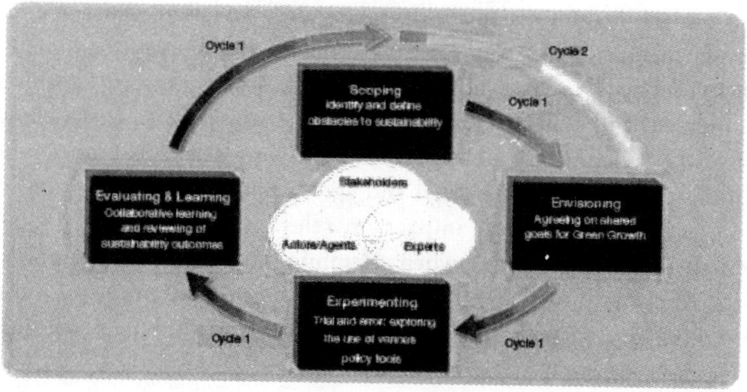

program design and policy formulation in developing countries. In addition, it would be beneficial to climate action if official development assistance (ODA), CDM projects and other financial mechanisms took the co-benefits approach into consideration when instigating future development planning. Dialogues between climate authorities and development agencies should incorporate the co-benefits approach to help build capacity in developing countries across the Asia and Pacific region.

Framework for Implementing Green Growth: Integrated Sustainability Assessments

There exist a wide variety of instruments available for evaluating the overall implications policies have for sustainable development. These include, for example, Environmental Impact Assessment, Regulatory Impact Assessment, Sustainability Impact Assessment, and the EU regime of Impact Assessment. While these tools have been very useful in assessing individual policies, they have yet to provide much assistance in mapping out a sustainable, holistic, development strategy. The Integrated Sustainability Assessment (ISA) works to this end.

According to the Methods and Tools for Integrated Sustainability Assessment (MATISSE) Project, "ISA is a cyclical, participatory process of scoping, envisioning, experimenting, and learning through which a shared interpretation of sustainability for a specific context is developed and applied in an integrated manner in order to explore solutions to persistent problems of unsustainable development. ISA can serve as an indispensible instrument for governments and policy makers seeking to effectively undertake and coordinate complimentary policies in an effort to foster green growth. ISA underscores four major stages that are often continuous and overlapping.

1. Scoping Stage. A key objective of this stage is to attempt to clearly identify, define, and understand any pressing problems that are contributing to unsustainability, for instance, natural resource depletion, issues of chronic unemployment, and poor economic performance. Recognising the root causes of these problems, such as incorrect price signals from perverse subsidies or lax command and control, is also important. At the same time stakeholders must also be identified and engaged, and a consensus based on country-specific problems must be framed and agreed upon. Collecting sound data on the problems and their impact on relevant stakeholders will be an important asset for the future when attempting to garner public support for reform. After the ISA cycle has been completed once, the problems must be reformulated and stakeholders again identified to fit within the new context.

2. Envisioning Stage. Moving into this stage first involves envisioning among stakeholders what green growth and sustainability would resemble in their own country context. Indentifying the vision of and challenges to sustainability and green growth will require the use of various participatory assessments. In line with the Sustainable Livelihoods Approach (SLA), the concerns of vulnerable (including the poor) men and women in particular, should be included. Based on this consensus, the envisioning stage entails designing a long-term, holistic strategy to achieve green growth and sustainability. GTBR and other non-MBI complimentary instruments (e.g. eco-labeling), as well as the proper sequencing of these policies, should be examined. This vision should contain multiple pathways including both a "business as usual" and green growth scenarios. Short-term policy proposals should strike a balance between cost-effectiveness, equity, and political feasibility. However, considerations of cost-effectiveness should only be focused on in the short-term, as it will not be relevant for long-term strategies ranging from 25-50 years. This strategy might be effectively articulated in a Map to Green Growth that could be referenced and disseminated during windows of political opportunity. Wide-reaching public education and awareness campaigns on the persistent problems facing the achievement of sustainability, and the subsequent reasons for and benefits of adopting GTBR, for example, can greatly enhance political support.

3. Experimental Stage. This stage focuses on utilizing ISA tools to analyze the feasibility, consistency, and adequacy of the vision of sustainability, in particular the drivers of various possible trajectories (pathways) of development. Stakeholder input should be a criterion for determining which tools would be the most appropriate. Nonetheless, a combination of both qualitative processes and quantitative tools (e.g. models of systems and subsystems) would be ideal. The quantitative component is especially important for assessing eco-systems, as well as tax and subsidy incidence on the poor.

4. Learning Stage. Formulating "lessons learned" from previous monitoring and evaluation activities is crucial for readjusting and fine-tuning visions for sustainability. These will feed into the first stage (scoping stage) of the next ISA cycle. It is also important to underline whether or not the policies achieved their intended goals and objectives in transitioning to a more sustainable pathway of development. They may have caused unintended consequences that must now also be addressed. Widely presenting information on the results of GTBR— such as the amount of revenue mobilized or improvements to environmental quality— is a method for maintaining long-term support for this process.

References

The United Nations (2001), Indicators of Sustainable Development: Guidelines and Methodologies (New York: United Nations), developed the prototype list of sustainable development indicators. ISBN: 9211045061.

Bartelmus (ed., 2002), Unveiling Wealth – On Money, Quality of Life and Sustainability (Dordrecht, Boston and London: Kluwer), reviews the main indicators and indices related to sustainable development. ISBN: 1402008147.

Bartelmus and Seifert (eds, 2003), Green Accounting (Aldershot and Burlington: Ashgate), is a reader on the history and approaches of green accounting at national and corporate levels. ISBN: 0754622320.

United Nations (1993), Integrated Environmental and Economic Accounting (New York: United Nations), is the original handbook on the concepts and methods of the SEEA. The United Nations also issued a practical manual for SEEA implementation: United Nations (2000), Integrated Environmental and Economic Accounting – An Operational Manual (New York: United Nations). Therevised SEEA 2003 is available on the web as a 'final' draft.

A special issue of Ecological Economics (2007, 61/4) reviews critically the revised SEEA.

Andreoni, J. and A. Levinson (2001), "The Simple Analytics of the Environmental Kuznets Curve", Journal of Public Economics, 80, 269-86.

Annandale D., A. Fry, W. Halal, and P. King (2005), Asian Environment Outlook 2005–Making Profits, Protecting Our Planet: Corporate Responsibility for Environmental Performance in Asia and the Pacific, Asian Development Bank (forthcoming).

Asia-Pacific Forum for Environment and Development (APFED) (2005), Paradigm Shifts Towards Sustainability for Asia and the Pacific – Turning Challenges into Opportunities, The APFED Final Report.

Brock, W. A. and M. S. Taylor (2004a), "The Green Solow Model", NBER Working Paper No. 10557, June.

Brock, W. A. and M. S. Taylor (2004b), "Economic Growth and the Environment: A Review of Theory and Empirics", in S. Durlauf and P. Aghion eds. Handbook of Economic Growth, North Holland.

Copeland, B. R. and M. S. Taylor (2003), Trade and the Environment: Theory and Evidence, Princeton, New Jersey, United States: Princeton University Press.

Esty, D. C., M. A. Levy, T. Srebotnjak, and A. d Sherbinin (2005), 2005

Environmental Sustainability Index: Benchmarking National Environmental Stewardship, New Haven, Connecticut, United States Yale Center for Environmental Law and Policy.

Food and Agriculture Organization of the United Nations (FAO) (2004). Towards a Food-Secure Asia and Pacific: Regional Strategic Framework for Asia and the Pacific (second edition), Bangkok, FAO Regional Office for Asia and the Pacific.

Grossman, G. M. and A. B. Krueger (1991), "Environmental Impacts of a North American Free Trade Agreement", NBER Working Paper No. 3914, Cambridge: National Bureau of Economic Research. Also in P. Garber ed. (1993) The US-Mexico Free Trade Agreement, Cambridge, M.A.: MIT Press.

Grossman, G. M. and A. B. Krueger (1994), "Economic Growth and the Environment", Quarterly Journal of Economics, 110, 353-377.

IUCN/UNEP/WWF (1991) Caring for the Earth - A Strategy for Sustainable Living. Gland, Switzerland.

Jaffe, A., S. Peterson, P. Portney, and R. Stavins (1995), "Environmental Regulation and the Competitiveness of US Manufacturing: What Does the Evidence Tell US", Journal of Economic Literature, XXXIII, 132-163.40.

Lee, H. H., R. K Chung and C. M. Koo (2005), "On the Relationship between Economic Growth and Environmental Sustainability," paper presented at Eminent Environmental Economists Symposium, the 5th Ministerial Conference on Environment and Development for Asia and the Pacific, Seoul, March.

Meadows, D. H., J. Randers, and D. L. Meadows (2004), Limits to Growth: The 30-Year Update, Chelsea Green Publishing Company.

Moore, C., and A. Miller (1994), Green Gold: Japan, Germany, the United States, and the Race for Environmental Technology, Boston, Massachusetts, United States: Beacon Press.

Porter, M. (1991), "America's Green Strategy," Scientific American, 28, 1-28.

Porter, M. and C. van der Linde (1995), "Toward a New Conception of the Environment-Competitiveness Relationship," Journal of Economic Perspectives, 9, 97-118.

Rees, W. E. (1996), "Revisiting Carrying Capacity: Area-Based Indicators of Sustainability," Population and Environment, Vol. 3, No. 3, Vancouver, Canada: Human Sciences Press.

Seldon, T. and D. Song (1994), "Environmental Quality and Development: Is There a Kuznets Curve for Air Pollution Emissions?" Journal of Environmental Economics and Management, 27, 147-162.

Stokey, N. (1998), "Are There Limits to Growth?" International Economic Review, 39(1), 1-31.

Vickery, G. and M. Iarrera (2000), "Mapping the Environmental Goods and Services Industry", STI Review, 25, 121-141.

World Bank (1992), World Development Report 1992: Development and the Environment.

World Business Council on Sustainable Development (WBCSD) (2000), Eco-Efficiency: Creating More Value with Less Impact, WBCSD.

World Commission on Environment and Development (Brundtland Commission), Our Common Future, Oxford, New York: Oxford University Press, 1987.

World Wildlife Fund (WWF) International (2004), Living Planet Report 2004, Gland, Switzerland, 2005 (www.panda.org)

Index

A

A Beautiful Mind (Movie), 284

Adike Pathrike (journal) and media
  creativity, 265
  production of farm writers, 265

Adolescents Family vs friends, 61
  Years, 61

Advertising in social media, 162-63
  successful campaigns, 164

Age appropriateness of programmes, 213

Agriculture Information and Communication Centre (AICC) purpose, 29

Agriculture Information Service (AIS) Bangladesh, 29

American homes and types/number of electronic media, 62

Anna Hazare, 157
  on Facebook, 157

Asia-Pacific region economic growth, 296-97

B

Bangladesh Institute of ICT in Development (BIID) initiative, 27-28, 30
  mission, 28

Bangladesh, 27
  mobile subscribers, 28

Banglalink (mobile phone operator), 31

Behaviour Therapy for OCD, 138

Biased reporting, 259

Bioscope to new media phase research, 50

Blog based books (Blooks), 57

Blogs, 55-56

Booz Allen and Hamilton research
  of new products, 187
  New Prod III Research, 188

Brandenberg test replacing, 224

Brundtland Commission, 294

Bullycide, 65

C

Cancer risk and social networking, 117

Caste System, 81

CBS/ NBC programming strategies, 214

CD-ROM, 19

CDM Projects, 306

Cell phone companies competition, 44

Children's Act (US), 218

Children's Comprehension of TV
  programmes, 207
  learning from TV, 206, 208
  favourite programmes, 209-210, 214

Children's Protection Act 1999, 220

Children's Television Act (CTA), 203-204

Children's TV Act 1990, 208

Cholesterol Management reporting guidelines, 144

Cinema, 272

Circular Economy Practice, concepts, 300

CNN innovation, 183

Co-benefits approach to Climate Change and Development, 305

Collective Intelligence, 49

Communicating advice, 44

Communication, 257
- impact on communication, 231
- media kinds of, 129
- meaning, 230
- importance, 229
- objectives, 229
- role in, 220, 230
- role, 263

Compact Disc, 19

Comprehensibility, 211

Compulsions, 135

Computer, 18
- Misuse, 232

Computer Technology history, 123-24

Conflict Resolution, 260

Conflicts, 76
- forms, 76

Content/ Image processing, 58

Convergence devices information awareness, 47-48
- .. newspapers role in, 48

Convergence, 41-46

Conversion term, 91

Conversion Disorders, 91
- causes, 92
- ..India, 93
- ..Karachi, 93
- promotion activities, 97
- prevalence, 94
- stages of life, 93
- statistics, 92-93
- symptoms, 92, 95
- ..US, 93-94
- Workplace, 95

Corruption causes, 79, 232
- consequences, 80
- effects of, 233
- responsibility, 231
- suggestions for removing, 233

Creative People/ Team Characteristics, 192-93

Cross-Cultural Communication, 74
- aspects, 75

CTA emergence, consequence, 215
- educational requirements, 216
- role, 216-17

Culture, 84 conceptualisation, 84

Cyber Crime, 232

Cyber Relationship Addiction, 105

Cyber Sexual Addiction, 105

Cyberbullying, 113

Cyber culture, 125

D

D-Net Activities Chronological Development, 30

Davidson vs Time Warner, 223

Developing new product, 197

Digital Footprint, 113

Digital Radio Modulation Technology (DRM), 250

Disagreement, 76

Doordarshan and All India Radio, 171

E

e-auction of Channels, 254

e-Krishok initiative Bangladesh, 28-29

E- Mail, 19

Earth Summit, 298

Eating disorder and social networking, 117
- Media role, 83

Eco-efficient construction, 301

Economic efficiency in use of resources, 298

Economic Efficiency Indicators (EEI), 294
Educational and informational TV programmes, 211
...audience, 213
Electronic Media,171
Manipur, 259
Environmental Management Approach (Conventional), 303
ESCAP (UN's Economic and Social Commission for Asia and the Pacific), 294
Regional Environment Report, 297
Excessive Net Searching, 106
Facebook launch, 99
addiction,107
and poor social adjustments, 114
causes, 108
comments/ posts, 66-69
curing ways, 118-19
depression, 112
effect on kids, 110
effect on youths, 112
fatigue, 64
founders, 106
facebook Addiction Disorder (FAD), 107-108
health impact, 116-17
health impact, 116
impact on moral values' 116
interaction, 101
leading to divorce, 115
petitions for preventing non-students, 64
phases, 108
popularity, 155
privacy, 65, 88
privacy blowup, 114
symptoms, 109
world scene, 106

F

Farmers clubs Bangladesh, 29
Fashion Movies, 275
Federal Communications Commission (FCC), 217
Censorship, 220
Regulations, 218-19
on Network Violations, 219
Federal Trade Commission (FTC) Report 2000 - US, 221
Films influence, 273-75
and society, 272
industry, 275
noted names, 273-74
role in life, 271, 273
titling, 273
topics, 272
First Amendment Rights, 220, 226
and students, 220
FM Channels, 245
start, 245
vs AIR clash, 246
Privatisation, 246

G

Gali Gali Mein Chor Hai, 277
Gas lamp technology vs electric bulb, 181
Gender differences in TV programmes watched, 211-12
Gender equality, 177
Genuine Progress Indicator (GPI), 296
Global Village, 82
Globalisation, 73
Grameenphone Community Information Centre, 30
Services, 30
Gramyavani (newspaper)
observations from, 266
banana cultivation article, 267
.. impact, 268
launch approach, 267
programme for Rural Youth, 268
target audience participation, 268

Green Growth Programme, 293
Green Tax and Budget Reform (GTBR), 302-303
Greening Business in Asia and the Pacific, 298
..initiative, 298-99
..Systems Approach, 300
Gross National Happiness, 296

H

Half a Century of TV in the Lives of Our Children, 63
HBO innovation, 183
Health Reporting TV / Movie Role, 151
Radio/ Newspapers, 151
Health Reporting/ Reporters, 139-40
strategies, 141
Hindustan Times village adoption ....impact, 264
HIV/AIDs, 235
Communicating, 235
Media .. role in preventing, 236
..coverage, 239
prevalence in India state-wise, 238
HR Department, 96
and Conversion Disorder, 96
HTML, 18
Human capital, 299
reinvestment in, 299
Hysteria, 91

I

IBM's innovation to
microprocessors, 184
mainframe computer, 184
ICT impact/ awareness, 20
accessing places, 21
reasons for using, 22
use in career, 23
affect on life, 23
and interest in education ..role/ use in Bangladesh, 29, 32
Idea generation (for new product) stages, 188
Ideation, 195
Improving product, 199
Index of Sustainable Economic Welfare, (ISEW), 296
Information Centres (IC)
Bangladesh, 30
Lady in (Mobile Lady), 30
Information Overload, 106
Information, Education and Communication (IEC), 82
Innovation Continuum, 182
Innovation mindset, 191
Innovation, 180
challenges to, 181
meaning, 180
motivations for, 188
power of, 180
..reacting to, 181
reasons for, 184
stifling, 192
Integrated Sustainability Assessment (ISA) Stages, 306-307
Interactivity, 129
industry, 131
meaning, 130
and New Media,129
Intercultural communication
improving, 78
....ways, 78
Intercultural Competence, 74
Internet, 18
addiction, 105
browsing time spent, 21
Investigation Stage of Product, 196

J

Johannesburg Plan of Implementation, 298

K

Katalyst (Bangladesh) role as facilitator, 27

Keyboarding skills-children, 214

Kids impact of facebook on, 110-12
..reduced study time, 114

Killer app, 183

Killer Technologies, 100

L

Launch (Product), 198

Launching new products activities involved, 187

Live Coverage and news credibility, 43

Lulu Booker Prize, 57

M

Magazines and journals, 174
content, 174
portrayal of women, 175

Managing product process, 199

Manipur Demographic
distribution, 257
ethnic tribes, 257
local TV networks, 259
mass media, 258

Mass Media and Health promotion, 96
programmes advantages, 97

Materialistic way of life, 295

Marrakech Process, 298

Media coverage in HIV/ AIDS, 237
censorship, 220
convergence, 47, 49
creator/destructor role, 82
effectiveness in transparency
familiarity with, 47, 49
in 2020, 179
in public administration, 42
negative effects, 83
opposition to, 221
.. role, 241
sector concerns, 240
support, 222-23

Media Dependance teenagers on, 62-64

Media Doctor (Website), 142
criteria, 142

Medical Reports on Statins, 144
coverage exclusivity, 146-47
on cancer drug trials, 144
on recent breakthrough, 143
selling, 145- 47
voice of People role, 149

Methods and Tools for Integrated Sustainability Assessment (MATISSA) Project, 306
MGNREGA-2005, 287

Miller vs California test, 224

Mis-communication, 232

Mischief mongering, 232

Mitra Committee, 248

Mobile, 19 subscribers Bangladesh, 28

Motivation for new product, 189-90
for innovation, 195
. Resources, 190

Munna Bhai MBBS, 276

N

Nagas, 257

Narcissistic tendencies, 114

Narendra Modi on Social Media, 157

Narrative styles, 53

National Security New Media role, 129

Natural capital, 299
reinvestment in, 299

Net Compulsions, 105

New Communication Technology in Media Convergence-Access-Application Study, 38-39

age-wise, 39
findings, 40
sample, 39

New Media, 123
role, 124

New Media/ Communication Technologies, 17

New Product Process, 193-94
creating-steps, 194
Key Roles, 194
Motivation for, 193
Research, 188

New Products strategic roles, 184
success rates, 185
failure- reasons, 186-87

Newspapers, 258
and Electronic Media, 259
conflict Resolution initiatives, 259
portrayal of women in, 173
culture page, 173
Manipur, 258

Nickelodeon / PBS vs Commercial stations childrens learning from, 208-210

Nickelodeon programmes, 208, 214
audience, 214

O

Observer/participant, 57

Obsessions, 135

Obsessive Compulsive Disorder (OCD), 135
causes, 136
famous people,139
signs and symptoms, 136-37

Olivia N vs Nat'l Broad Co, 222

One Time Entry Fee, 249

Over Population, 79

P

Participatory culture, 49

People Say I'm Crazy, 285

Perceived threat, 76

Personal Space, 62

Phad Vachno (art form), 54

Phads, 54

Poverty, 79

Pre-recorded fantasy, 55

Pre-school children TV role, 203

Print Media innovations in, 183

Print Media women in, 175

Privacy blow up-Facebook, 115

Private FM Broadcasting, Phase II, 249
Phase III, 251
policy, 251
..review, 254

Private FM Broadcasting, 246
Expansion policy, 252-53
First Phase, 246
..failure, 247

Product Improvement, 182

Prototyping, 198

Public sphere concept, 127

Publicity in newspapers power of, 264

Q

Quality Medicine Use Media Role, 149

R

Radio Broadcasting Policy Committee, 247

Reception Theory / Studies, 50-51

Recruitment use of social media in, 160-61

Rights, values and needs, 77

RIKEN Brain Science Institute (BSI), 58
on Brain Focus, 58

Risk Avoidance Curve (in innovation), 186

Role Models imitating, 83
Rural Information Centre (RIC) - Bangladesh, 31

S

Sanitation, 81
measures, 82
Schizophrenia Awareness Association (SAA), 284
Schizophrenia, 279
and suicide, 282
and violence and jail, 282-83
awareness activities, 283
causes, 280
diagnosis, 281
famous people with, 285
movies / documentaries, 284
myths, 283-84
prevalence, 282
prognosis, 282
risks of getting, 281
signs/symptoms, 280
types, 279-80
Screening of New Product, 196
Self-regulatory mechanisms - media, 176
Sensory Perception, 58
Serotonin Reuptaka Inhibitors (SRI) in OCD, 137
Sexting, 113
Slumdog Millionaire, 276
SMS, 96
use in TV programmes and TRP, 43
Social capital, 300
Social Change Communication Theory, 240
Social identity, 53 theory, 55
Social Issues, 79
Social Media Power of, 155, 158
..indicators, 155
.. ..survey, 156
.. classification, 156
and suicides, 65
Impact on Business, 158-59
on Recruitment, 160
advertising in, 162
Social Networking on Managing friends, 155
Social Networking Sites, 232
as social parasites, 100
as weapon, 88
as a threat, 88
causes of prefering, 87
growth, 99
power, 89
privacy settings, 88
target, 89
Social Space, 52
Somatoform Disorder, 91
Spatiality, 51
Sripur Poultry farmers (study) use of mobile, 33
Status Update (Social Networking), 62
study, 64
.. subjects, 66, 69
Sub Group on Information and Broadcasting, 250
Sustainable Consumption and Production (SCP), 293
definition, 294
global initiatives, 297
Sustainable Development, 294
Sustainable Master Planning, 301

T

Technology and degree of employment, 48
effectiveness in adverse situation, 43, 45
Teenager Students (US) Media Use, 63
Telecom Regulatory Authority of India (TRAI), 248

Recommendation, 248
Consultation Phase III, 251

Terrorism, 80 impact, 81

The American Prospects (Blog), 57

Thomas Edison invention of bulb, 180
challenges to, 181

Thomson's Target Media new launch, 183

Three - Hour Rule, 205
Guidelines, 205

Todd Gitlin (US Commentator/ Author), 221
on TV Violence, 221-22
TOI vs Hindu News, 288
Articles, 288
Editorial, 289
op-ed, 289
Comparison, 290

Transformational leadership tools of, 190

TV Parental Guidelines, 223

TV Programme Improvement Act - 1990 (US), 218

U

Ubiquitous, 52
technology, 52
computing, 52

Udayavani advertisement impact, 264-65

V

V-Chip system, 222

Video Conferencing, 19

Violence on TV impact on viewers, 217
marketing, 220
regulation (US), 220
proposed solutions, 224

Virtual Community, 53-55, 127

W

Water cycle changes, 297

Web Page, 18

Web Server, 19

Weblog, 56

Welfare Information Lady (WIL) - Designation facilities to, 31

Wikipedia, 123

Winning New Products, 188

Women in media, 69
participation and expression, 170
portrayal, 170-71, 175

Women's rights, 177

World Wide Web, 18, 48

WTBS (Atlanta's Superstation) Challenge to FCC, 219

Y

Youths Facebook Addiction, 114

Youtube, 57
usage, 50

Z

Zapatista Army use of New Media, 128

Zuckerberg, Mark (facebook), 106
..petition to, 64